CW01497444

The Man Who
Tested Parachutes

The Man Who Tested Parachutes

Charles Agate and the Development of Britain's Airborne Forces for D-Day and Arnhem

Andrew Colley

May 2025

Andrew Colley and John Neil

AIR WORLD

First published in Great Britain in 2025 by
Air World Books
An imprint of
Pen & Sword Books Ltd
Yorkshire - Philadelphia

ISBN: 978 1 03611 586 9

Typeset in INDIA by IMPEC eSolutions
Printed and bound in the UK by CPI Group (UK) Ltd, Croydon, CR0 4YY.

Pen & Sword Books Ltd incorporates the imprints of Pen & Sword Archaeology,
Air World Books, Atlas, Aviation, Battleground, Discovery, Family History,
History, Maritime, Military, Naval, Politics, Social History, Transport, True Crime,
Claymore Press, Frontline Books, Praetorian Press, Seaforth Publishing and
White Owl

For a complete list of Pen & Sword titles please contact:

PEN & SWORD BOOKS LTD
47 Church Street, Barnsley, South Yorkshire, S70 2AS, UK.
E-mail: enquiries@pen-and-sword.co.uk
Website: www.pen-and-sword.co.uk

or

PEN AND SWORD BOOKS,
1950 Lawrence Road, Havertown, PA 19083, USA
E-mail: Uspen-and-sword@casematepublishers.com
Website: www.penandswordbooks.com

Contents

List of Plates

1. Charles Agate with a packed parachute. (*Courtesy of Lynette Bramidge*)
2. No. 9 Frenches Road, Redhill. (*John Neil, 2023*)
3. RGS Scholarship Boys 1918. (*Courtesy of Reigate Grammar School Foundation*)
4. RGS Football Team 1920–1. (*Courtesy of Reigate Grammar School Foundation*)
5. The Agate family at Shoreham Beach. (*Courtesy of Lynette Bramidge*)
6. 'Norton', West Drive, Burgh Heath. (*John Neil, 2023*)
7. Jumping from the rear platform of a Whitley Mk II. (*Public domain*)
8. Flying Office Charles Agate, AFC. (*Courtesy of Lynette Bramidge*)
9. Agate outside his caravan in Tatton Park. (*Courtesy of Caravan & Motorhome Club Collection*)
10. WAAF parachute packers at RAF Ringway. (*Public domain*)
11. Charles Agate and Bernard Winfield wearing their AFC medal ribbons. (*Courtesy of ParaData*)
12. General Crawford after jumping into Rostherne Mere. Agate on the right. (*From* Prelude to Glory *by Maurice Newnham*)
13. An American paradog. (*Public domain*)
14. Charles Agate making a test jump from a DC-3 Dakota. (*Courtesy of Lynette Bramidge*)
15. Charles Agate's retirement assembly. (*Courtesy of Lynette Bramidge*)
16. Charles and Marjorie Agate in their garden. (*Courtesy of Lynette Bramidge*)

Acknowledgements

This book would not have been possible without the co-operation, assistance and research of others. We have made frequent reference to the admirable Paradata.org.uk website which documents the history of the British Parachute Regiment and airborne forces, bringing together the experiences of the men and women of our airborne forces with the official records. We are particularly grateful for the personal assistance of Ben Hill, Paradata manager at The Airborne Assault Museum, IWM Duxford.

Lynette and Jim Bramidge and Lynette's son Paul were exceptionally generous with their time, sharing their memories freely, openly and unsentimentally.

We received vital help and information from the staff team at Tatton Park, especially Carolyn Latham, Darren Morris and Duncan Wilks, and from Kate Tobias-Buick and the other archivists at The National Archives at Kew and the Cheshire Record Office.

We also received recollections, insights and invaluable help from Marion Allen, Wendy Barnes, Steven Bogie, Allan Brown, Peter Burgess, Bridget Chappuis, Derek Chavner, Sue Clelland, Heather Cooper, Helen Fedchak, Elinor Florence, Robin Foote, Tony Foote, Will Fry, Marion Goulder, John Grehan, Marc Heighway of the Beaulieu Archive, David Helman, Nicolas Kinloch, Peter Knott (ex-1Para), Martin Mace, Kevin Morrow, Mike Murphy-Pyle, press officer at Manchester International Airport, Jeremy Newell, Penny Newman, Sara Riccabone of the National Motor Museum Trust, Paul Shrimpton, Linda Taylor, Martin Thomas, and Lindy Zubairy.

Prologue – 'Mr Agate'

The narrow wooden stairway leading up to the office was lined with framed photographs in black and white. Photographs of aeroplanes, some in flight, others idling on runways, their crew sitting on the wings. Blurry pictures of white canopies floating down from the sky. The boy paused on the stairs, entranced by these pictures from a war a little more than 20 years before. His nerves calmed.

'Hello? Are you there?'

A man's voice from the top of the stairs. A pitch or so higher than the boy had expected, but kind, somehow, even in those few words.

'Come on up.'

The nerves returned as he climbed to the top of the stairs. The man was standing by the open window, looking up to the sky. Not tall, but he stood straight, and had a shock of white hair. He wasn't wearing a dark suit as the boy had expected, but an open necked white shirt and light, well-pressed trousers. He was holding a piece of paper which he glanced at.

'And you must be . . .?'

But the boy's gaze had already turned away to the walls of the office, covered also with photographs: more aeroplanes, and runways seen from the air, more of those blossoming white canopies, but also balloons: huge white balloons tethered high above acres of green grass. RAF, definitely, he thought.

In a way, this was not unusual, for this was 1966 and the boy was used to meeting men and women who had 'served' as he had learnt to say, in the two great wars which had marked the first half of that century: his grandfather, scarred at the Somme, sitting silently by the fire, smoking and occasionally weeping; the old man shuffling along the High Street wearing his medals on his stained raincoat; another man, younger, who always wore white gloves and whose face was a livid purple, with no eyelashes or brows. Another RAF man.

His friend's father who had lost a leg, but never mentioned why, and the family doctor, revered by all in the village for surviving a Japanese prisoner of war camp. His own mother too, who had meticulously checked aircraft parts for faults at a secret location, and her friend the parachute packer. And later, at the big school, he would meet the teacher who had landed in Normandy on D-Day, another who had dropped into Arnhem, and the Polish maths teacher, his skin yellow, who used to sit silently on the edge of his desk, sucking the arm of his glasses and rocking backwards and forwards, lost in his thoughts. It was said that he had taken part in the last successful cavalry charge in history at the Battle of Schoenfeld in March 1945. By then, warfare had moved on. This smiling man in the office at the top of the stairs had served too.

'Welcome to the school. I'm Mr Agate.'

The boy would soon learn that this man was a hero to the children of this village school, though not a war hero, for he rarely mentioned this, even in the long colourful stories he told in morning assembly, stories which seemed to spring spontaneously from his mind. Bible stories, of course, but also stories of far-off lands, of adventures, of obstacles overcome, of precious things lost and found. Sometimes during these stories, his dentures would slip but he wouldn't be put off or embarrassed. He would just pause, adjust them, smile, and carry on. Unflappable.

For the children it was the games of cricket and penny-a-catch on the field with Mr Agate wielding the bat and handing out coins to anyone who caught the ball or sending the whole school out for hours onto the grass to look for four-leaf clovers or driving round the school field in an open-top Mercedes, throwing out sweets.

Then, when it snowed, which it always seemed to in winter back then, the children arrived at school (which never closed) to find him already out on the playground making long icy slides from top to bottom and then extending the lunch break so that the children could slide with him at breakneck speed down to the bottom before crash-landing in a pile of snow. He was kind too: driving sick children to hospital, picking up a pupil from home every morning after she broke her leg and then carrying her into school, because her parents could not afford the bus fare, and then his tears, so near the surface, when he told the school one morning of the death of a pupil from leukaemia.

Perhaps the other teachers occasionally felt frustrated by some of this, by the long stories in assembly which cut into lesson time, by the days cut short to rush out to the field, by the over-excited children, by the fact that the headmaster used a far corner of the playground to keep battered old cars he would do up and sell at the weekends. But if they were frustrated, they probably kept quiet, because he was, after all, Mr Agate, and they knew perhaps just a bit more about him than he ever told the children. And then, one Christmas Day, a couple of years after that first meeting at the top of the stairs, the boy found out too . . .

A present under the tree. Clearly a book, and a hardback. The boy unwrapped it, but he knew what it was because he had asked for it: *The Guinness Book of Records*. Later, after lunch, after listening to the Queen, after the party hats and the mince pies, after the not-really-an-uncle who came every year had slumped into sleep in the armchair, it was his father who found it in the book and showed it to him: on page 259. In the margin the topic: 'Greatest Number of Parachute Jumps' and beside it, these words:

The British Record is believed to have been set by Flight Lieutenant Charles Agate A.F.C. (born March 1905) of the RAF, who totalled 1,601 descents with packed parachute between 1940 and 1946.

Because Mr Agate was not just one of the many men who returned from the war to take up if they were able their old professions. He had served, he was like so many of them scarred in unseen ways, but he was also someone with a unique place in the history of warfare, a man twice mentioned in despatches and whom Sir Winston Churchill had insisted on meeting at the end of the war so he could thank him personally: he was the man who tested parachutes.

***

Twenty years earlier, in 1946, Charles Agate had made the national news when he made the last of his record-breaking 1,601 jumps over an airfield in Oxfordshire, with his flying suit stuffed with £250 in £1 notes and the instruction: 'If my chute fails . . . you can give it all to the groundcrew.'

Charles Agate was in fact one in a long line of brave, eccentric – some might say crazy – men and women who for centuries had taken incalculable risks both in peace and war to perfect the science, and the art, of falling through the sky under a silken canopy. But Agate had not been a showman in the popular flying circuses of the 1930s, and he was too young to have been a First World War flying ace. In 1939 he had been an ordinary schoolteacher in a reserved profession in a most ordinary part of Surrey, with a wife and young daughter at home. He gave no sign of any interest in flight, let alone parachuting, until he was approaching middle age, and he didn't fly in an aircraft until he was 36 years old and – as he loved to remark – although he took off in that plane, he didn't land in it.

So how did this man slip so easily into the footsteps of the mavericks who went before him? How was he able to jump many hundreds of times more than anyone else in the whole war? What drove him on and what were the real effects of an apparent addiction to danger on him and on his family? This book will try to answer those questions.

This is a story of the unparalleled courage of one man, but also of the skill and pioneering ingenuity of many like him who played such a significant but largely unheralded part in the Second World War. It is also a tale of how Britain's airborne forces developed from humble and chaotic beginnings to be ready for the challenges of D-Day and Arnhem, and as such this book embraces the vagaries of war, the class differences and snobbery, the political short-termism.

Death was ever present for Flight Lieutenant Charles Agate and was all too often very close indeed. Forty-six men died in training at the Parachute Training School at RAF Ringway in Manchester between 1941 and 1946. Agate himself told an interviewer after the war that he had witnessed '22 good men hit the deck'. Many of them he had himself despatched from an aircraft or balloon on the fatal jump. In this book we seek to name and honour those forty-six men, but also to show how, when it was all over, one man overcame what would today undoubtedly be diagnosed as post-traumatic stress disorder (PTSD) to go on to bring joy and learning to the lives of so many young people.

The UK history curriculum teaches modern children a lot about Henry VIII and his wives, Nelson and Churchill, but it is the ordinary person who is compelled by extraordinary circumstances to do extraordinary things that stands at the heart of the story of our nation. Charles Agate was just such a man.

PART ONE

Beginnings

Chapter 1

Dandelions and Silken Canopies

Albert Edward Charles Agate was born on 24 March 1905 in Redhill, about 25 miles south of London. He was the first child of Albert Edward Agate, a 28-year-old railway telegraphist with the South-Eastern Railway (SER) in Tonbridge. Albert Senior was responsible for sending morse code messages along the wires that ran alongside the railway lines. His mother, Annie Eliza Morrow, was born in County Leitrim in Northern Ireland where her father, Grimes Morrow, was the gardener and steward of Killegar House.[1]

Albert and Annie had married in Tunbridge Wells in April 1904 but moved to Redhill when Albert was promoted to become the senior telegraphist at Redhill Station. Because he was fast, accurate and reliable, he was highly valued by his employers and was sufficiently well-paid to be able to buy a modest, newly-built house near the railway line at 9 Frenches Road, Redhill. Most of the houses along this road were rented by employees of the railway and the local water board. They were modern and spacious and must have seemed glorious when the Agates moved there. Albert Senior loved the house and was to live here for the rest of his very long life.

Their first son, Albert Edward Charles Agate, was christened at St Matthews Parish church in Redhill, and although he used the name 'Charles' throughout his careers in both the RAF and in teaching, he was always 'Bert' or 'Bertie' to his family. Charles Agate's upbringing was to define the man: steady, loyal, dependable, and with a keen sense of duty.

He was born at a time of great change. 1905 saw the first public protest by suffragettes in Westminster, increasing violence against Jewish emigres in the East End, and political unrest in Ireland. It also saw the founding of Crystal Palace Football Club which Agate would support throughout his life. Perhaps of more relevance to the man he was to become, it was in 1905 that Ralph Carhart claimed to have made the first 'freefall' jump with a parachute tied to his chest. To release the canopy Carhart had to undo a series of safety pins with freezing fingers whilst plummeting through the skies towards the earth. Somehow, he succeeded and survived. So given that the year 1905 not only saw the birth of the man who tested parachutes and a key moment in the development of the parachute itself, it is perhaps relevant to explore briefly the history of parachuting and meet some of the pioneering men and women among whom Agate would take his place.

***

For centuries man had sought to mimic the dandelion seeds that float gently in the air before falling to the ground. Botanists had observed that the letting of a little bit of air through the hairs above the seed stabilized the vortex in its wake, increasing the drag on the seed. Thinking men and women realized that if these features could be replicated, it had the potential to be used for several purposes.

There is some evidence that rigid, umbrella-like contraptions were used for entertainment in China as early as the twelfth century, allowing people to jump from high towers and float to the ground, but the first clear and recorded design was drawn by Leonardo da Vinci in 1495. It consisted of a pyramid-shaped, linen canopy held open by a square, wooden frame. It was proposed as an escape device to allow people to jump from a burning building, but there is no evidence that it was ever developed or used for this purpose.

The term 'parachute' was first used in 1783 by Louis-Sebastien Lenormand, a French physicist, as a hybrid of the Italian prefix 'para' meaning to avert, resist, and 'chute', the French word for fall. Lenormand jumped from the Montpelier observatory with a rigid 14ft (4.3m) wooden frame. Two years later, J.P. Blanchard, another Frenchman, used silk to make the first parachute that was not held open by a frame. There is some evidence that he used the device to jump from a hot-air balloon. In the event of the balloon being punctured, or catching fire, the pilot attached himself to a line poking out of the parachute housing. When the pilot jumped, the canopy was dragged out of the housing by his weight as he fell. This was the basis of what would become known as the 'static line' method, but it was notoriously unreliable. It was a practice Agate would test and refine hundreds of times between 1941 and 1946 from converted bomber aircraft and 'Bessie', the big balloon which floated over Tatton Park in Cheshire.

Andre Jacques Garnerin made numerous parachute jumps from hot-air balloons. His first jump, in Paris in 1797, was from an altitude of at least 2,000ft (600m) in a basket attached to a wooden pole that extended downward from a canopy made of canvas. The parachute assembly weighed about 100lb (45kg) and oscillated so wildly that Garnerin reportedly 'usually experienced painful vomiting for several hours after a descent'. It wasn't until 1804 that French scientist Joseph Lelandes introduced the apex vent: a circular hole in the centre of the canopy which helped stabilize the parachute. More than 100 years later Charles Agate and his colleagues would still be testing and refining equipment and methods to reduce oscillation.

A safe and effective parachute was, as the historian John Lucas reminds us, very much 'a toy of showman balloonists, idling in the wings of time like an actor waiting for his cue'. That cue came in December 1903, when the American brothers Orville and Wilbur Wright took off from the ground and made the first powered flights in their biplane

Flyer.[2] By October 1905 the brothers could remain aloft for over half an hour at a time, performing circles and other manoeuvres.

Shortly after the Wright brothers' exploits in America, the first trials of a full-size, powered aircraft by a British pilot took place at Brooklands in Surrey in 1908. The pilot was Alliott Verdon-Roe (of Avro fame). Just a few years before there was not a single practicable man-lifting machine in existence, but there were now dozens of machines capable of carrying a man through the air.

Not everyone welcomed this progress. The elderly rector of the parish church in Merstham, close to Agate's home, wrote ruefully in 1911 that 'the conquest of the air seems assured, but only at the expense of many deaths'.

Bertie Agate on the other hand was thrilled by the hot-blooded accounts in *The Sketch* and *The Graphic* of intrepid British balloon and aeroplane pilots who had escaped from their doomed craft by using a parachute. These parachutes were mostly of the Guardian Angel type, developed by Everard Calthrop. He was a British railway engineer and close friend of Charles Rolls (of Rolls-Royce fame), a pioneer aviator, who was the first man to fly to France and back, across the English Channel.

On 12 July 1910 Calthrop accompanied Rolls to the Bournemouth International Aviation Meeting and was present when Rolls died after he lost control of his biplane. This tragedy, and a non-fatal accident involving his son Tev, led Calthrop to design a device to save pilots in similar circumstances. His first parachute, which was patented in 1913, was a complex system, incorporating a silk canopy packed between metal discs stowed in a canvas container attached underneath the aeroplane. The deployment was initiated by the falling weight of the jumper.

Parachute jumps from tethered balloons were now commonplace, warranting no more than odd paragraphs in local newspapers. However, parachute jumps from tall structures were more newsworthy. In 1912, Henry François Reichelt attempted a parachute jump from the Eiffel Tower while testing a wearable parachute of his own design. Reichelt had become obsessed with creating a suit for aviators that would allow them to survive should they be forced to leave their aircraft in mid-air. Initial experiments conducted with dummies dropped from the fifth floor of his apartment building had been successful, but believing that he needed more height to prove his invention, Reichelt petitioned the Paris Police Prefecture for permission to conduct a test from the Eiffel Tower.

He received the necessary permission in 1912 and arrived at the Tower on 4 February with Pathé newsreel cameras in tow. Despite attempts to dissuade him, he made it clear that he intended to jump himself rather than conduct an experiment with dummies. Before jumping, Reichelt shouted, 'à bientôt!' but sadly that was not to be the case. His parachute failed to open, and he plummeted 187ft (57m) to his death. The next day, newspapers were full of illustrated stories about the death of the 'reckless inventor', describing the moment when onlookers knew something was wrong and had watched him drop like a stone. The jump was shown in newsreels to horrified music-hall and cinema audiences across the country. Today, Reichelt's story is usually presented as a target for mockery. He has been described as the 'Flying Tailor' and his story has appeared in books with titles like *The Mammoth Book of Losers* (Shaw, 2014) but that is not how the young Bertie Agate saw it. To him, there was something truly epic about entrusting your own life to an unproven design made by your own hand.

The first jumps from powered aircraft took place that same year. There are two claimants for this record. Grant Morton is reported to have jumped from a Wright Model B over Venice Beach, California. He was a veteran parachutist from balloons and was 54 when he made this jump from an aeroplane. The other contender is Captain Albert Berry.[3] Berry also had extensive experience parachuting from balloons owned by his father, John Berry. He made his first aircraft jump on 1 March 1912, in St. Louis, Missouri, leaping from a trapeze bar hanging from the front of a Benoist biplane. The parachute was contained in a metal canister attached to the underside of the plane, and to a harness that Berry was wearing. At 1,500ft, Berry dropped from the plane and his weight pulled the parachute from the canister. He then dropped a further 500ft before the parachute opened. Hundreds of watchers held their breath as Berry shot toward the earth, the parachute tailing after him. Suddenly the parachute opened, the rapidity of his descent was checked, and amid cheers, he floated to the ground. Asked if he would do it again, he replied: 'Never again! I believe I turned five somersaults on my way down . . . My course downward . . . was like a crazy arrow' (Reichhardt, 2012). True to his word, Berry never made another jump.

It was the Russian actor Gleb Kotelnikov who is credited with inventing the first backpack parachute. He felt compelled to do so after witnessing the death of a pilot during an airshow in St. Petersburg. Kotelnikov's innovation came with the realization that for a parachute to save lives, it had to meet two primary qualifications: it had to be attached to him in some way and it had to open automatically if he lost consciousness. He developed several prototypes that met these qualifications, as well as a parachute helmet, belt, and harness. He dubbed the invention 'RK-1'.

Showmen and women would play a key role in the development of the parachute. The German balloonist Katchen Paulus made nearly 150 jumps from balloons in the first 10 years of the century, but the American, 'Tiny' Broadwick was the first woman to parachute from an aircraft. She was born Georgia Ann Thompson in 1893 and was the last of seven daughters. She was given the nickname 'Tiny' because she was just 4ft 8in tall, but by the age of 13, Tiny Broadwick had already married and borne a daughter. Her husband left her shortly after the birth and she was working in a cotton mill, aged 15, when she saw Charles Broadwick's World Famous Aeronauts parachute from a hot air balloon. Tiny decided there and then to leave her daughter in the care of her parents so that she could join the travelling troupe.

Tiny became Broadwick's adopted daughter and later his common-law wife. Billed as 'The Doll Girl', the Broadwicks travelled across the USA, performing at fairs and carnivals and in 1914, she demonstrated parachutes to the US Army. On her fourth demonstration jump, the static line became entangled in the tail assembly of the aircraft, so for her next jump she cut the static line short and did not attach it to the plane. Instead, she deployed her parachute manually by pulling the shortened, unattached line while falling in what may have been the first planned free-fall jump from an aeroplane. This demonstrated that pilots could safely escape aircraft by using what was later called a 'ripcord'. In the same year, Broadwick jumped into Lake Michigan, becoming the first woman to parachute into a body of water. She was then said to have made over 1,100 jumps in total. It would be more than 30 years before that record was broken, by Charles Agate.

Chapter 2

To School

In 1910, Bertie Agate became a pupil at Frenches Road School, almost opposite his house. It was the kind of school he would dedicate his teaching career to. Frenches Road was a public elementary school, sometimes referred to disparagingly as a 'Council School'. It opened in 1905 to cater for the increase in population around Redhill, much to the concern of the ratepayers of Reigate who agonized about how much it would cost. The local newspaper, the *Surrey Mirror*, reported the parsimony of one Conservative councillor about the extravagance of the new school having a foundation stone. He asked rhetorically: 'Where had the money come from?' (*Surrey Mirror*, 1905).

When the school was opened formally, the *Surrey Mirror* expressed surprise that so many people should 'gather on a bitterly cold day for an event concerned with the somewhat unenthusiastic subject of education'. In direct answer to these critics the mayor of Reigate said to the applause of the crowd assembled 'if there was one thing in which they might be a little extravagant it was in giving their children the very best possible education that they could provide' (*Dorking & Leatherhead Advertiser*, 1905).

It was a sentiment that would be echoed half a century later by the headmaster of a school just a mile away who was dedicated to giving the children the best possible education.

Bertie took to school life enthusiastically. The curriculum was like that in most Surrey public elementary schools with its emphasis on reading, writing and arithmetic, but it was supplemented with practical instruction in cottage gardening, poultry keeping and woodcarving and, much to Bertie's delight, plenty of sport. He sang in the choir and performed a solo at a grand concert in aid of the school.

His enthusiasm for schools and education would define the rest of his life, but he was also influenced by the patriotic fervour of the school and every year he joined in the ceremony in the playground to mark Empire Day. This ritual celebration had been introduced in 1904 by the Empire movement:

> A non-party, non-sectarian, non-aggressive effort to awaken the peoples who constitute the British Empire to the serious duties that lie at their door. Many otherwise excellent subjects of the King fail to realise the magnitude and consequent seriousness of the responsibilities attaching to British citizenship. The watchwords of the movement are 'Responsibility, Duty, sympathy, self-sacrifice.' May these words be engraved on the hearts of all British subjects, but especially of young, who in a few years' time will be responsible for the government of this mighty Empire consisting of over 400 millions of souls[4] (*Weekly Dispatch*, 1910).

The idea was not popular with every ratepayer, with some opposed the notion of imperialist indoctrination and others who objected to the cost of the associated half-day holiday.

Agate was just 9 years old when the Great War began, and by 1915 the national mood of patriotism had reached a peak. Empire Day celebrations had ramped up. Lessons in the morning centred on teaching the children of the superiority and civilizing mission of empire (Brabazon, 1905). The younger boys and girls then performed English country folk dances around a maypole, reflecting Cecil Sharp's determination that English folk song and 'National Songs' should be at the heart of the curriculum. After the entertainment, the headmaster addressed the school and all of the boys then marched to the flagstaff in the playground. At the signal, the flag was hoisted, and all came to the salute, before singing *The Flag of Britain*, two hymns by Rudyard Kipling, *The Children's Song* and *Recessional*, and finally three verses of the National Anthem.

The selection of Kipling songs is interesting. *The Children's Song* is a familiar exhortation to the children to love and serve God and Country. It contains the verses:

> Land of our Birth, we pledge to thee.
> Our love and toil in the years to be.
> Father in Heaven who lovest all,
> Oh, help Thy children when they call.
> That they may build from age to age
> An undefiled heritage.
> Land of our Birth, our faith, our pride,
> For whose dear sake our fathers died.
> Oh, Motherland, we pledge to thee.
> Head, heart and hand through the years to be!

However, *Recessional* is more reflective. It was written for Queen Victoria's Jubilee celebrations in July 1897 and provided a reminder of the transient nature of British Imperial power:

> God of our fathers, known of old,
> Lord of our far-flung battle line,
> Beneath whose awful hand we hold
> Dominion over palm and pine —
> Lord God of Hosts, be with us yet,
> Lest we forget—lest we forget!

These songs were selected to remind the children that their fathers and grandfathers had made, and were still making, sacrifices to defend the

Empire and that, if called to make a similar sacrifice, they must not be found wanting.

Bertie Agate was at an impressionable age and the many boys' comics and magazines that were read eagerly by him and his friends presented the Great War as a fight between civilization and barbarism. Notions of duty and sacrifice for the country filled the heads of these young men.

However, there was also fun to be had right on his doorstep because of the War. When sixty-two of the seventy-five men employed at nearby Trower's brickyard had gone into the armed services, production ceased, and the works were left deserted, creating a very exciting adventure playground. Many of these men from the brickyard would never return.

***

Across the Channel and above the battlefields of Belgium and Northern France aeroplanes were becoming increasingly important, with fearless aviators engaging in direct combat with other airmen. Few of these aviators had the benefit of a parachute.

There has been much debate about why this was so. Although parachutes were provided for observers in balloons as early as 1915, it has been suggested (without quoting provenance) that the Air Ministry and Royal Flying Corps were reluctant to deploy parachutes in fighter aircraft in case it encouraged pilots to abandon their machines prematurely. The source for this claim is, apparently, a report by the Air Board that stated that: 'It is the opinion of the Board that the presence of such an apparatus might impair the fighting spirit of pilots and cause them to abandon machines which might otherwise be capable of returning to base for repair' (Barker, 2002).

This may or may not be genuine, but there is evidence however that the Air Ministry was not confident that parachutes would actually save lives and they refer to several very real and pragmatic reasons why using a parachute was not always the best solution for an aeroplane pilot in trouble. Firstly, jumping out of a single-seat biplane in flight is very difficult. Biplanes of this era did not fly themselves. As soon as the pilot took his hands off the controls the aeroplane would go into a tailspin which was not very conducive to making a smooth exit. Secondly, if a biplane suffers mechanical failure, the pilot has a much better chance of survival if he tries to steer it to a landing site than if he jumps out of it. In Gwilym Lewis's book *Wings Over the Somme* (Lewis G., 1994) there are many descriptions of crash-landings from which the pilots escaped with only minor injuries.

Secondly, and possibly most tellingly, early parachutes like the Guardian Angel were heavy. If a pilot got into trouble in a dogfight his best hope was to get the aircraft to climb. In order to climb the pilot needed to be carrying as little weight as possible. Many pilots believed that, because of this extra weight, a parachute was more likely to kill you than save you.

Calthrop though was convinced of the efficacy of his Guardian Angel invention, and in 1917 sponsored an exhibition at Tower Bridge. In front of an invited audience of reporters, the Hon Lieutenant Bowen and Major Thomas Orde-Lees agreed to demonstrate Calthrop's design. Bowen was the son of the baronet and successful race-horse trainer who had served as a Lieutenant in the Inniskilling Dragoons. Thomas Hans Orde-Lees was the illegitimate child of Thomas Orde Hastings Lees, a former barrister and the Chief Constable of Northampton. Major Orde-Lees had joined the Royal Marines as a lieutenant in 1896 and while still serving in the Army he achieved a degree of fame as the Amateur Champion Trick Bicycle Rider.

At the request of Ernest Shackleton he had been released from his military duties and allowed to join his Imperial Trans-Antarctic Expedition as storekeeper, and after Shackleton's ship *Endurance* became stuck in the pack ice, Orde-Lees spent most of the next year and a half managing the food, cooking, and worrying about sufficient food for survival of the party while they waited in vain for the ice to melt. Upon returning to England, Orde Lees joined the RFC and as a 40-year-old was assigned to observation balloons, where he became fascinated with parachutes and made many jumps to demonstrate their usefulness.

For the exhibition from Tower Bridge in November 1917, Bowen and Orde-Lees jumped from the upper parapet of the bridge only 150ft above the Thames. Orde-Lees made his jump head-first and his parachute opened just before he hit the water. After the demonstration, Orde-Lees was made secretary of the Army Parachute Committee that was established to consider the suitability of deploying parachutes to RFC pilots. He became a regular demonstrator and promoter of Calthrop's system, in the UK and abroad, but the Air Ministry remained unconvinced. They did not though object to RFC pilots purchasing their own Guardian Angels, and some did; no doubt encouraged by the offer by Lloyd's underwriters of a 20 per cent discount on premiums if pilots took one of these parachutes on their planes.

While the Air Ministry hesitated, Major John Carter, an intelligence officer in Italy, came up with a new use for parachutes in June 1918. Carter's proposals under the codename Tinpot (National Army Museum, n.d.) involved dropping agents by parachute behind enemy lines to sabotage Austrian factories involved in war production. Carter and his British and Italian colleagues developed a way of dropping a Captain Bowen at low level through the floor of a converted Savoia-Pomilio SP4 reconnaissance aircraft. Before leaving the ground, the parachute container and supporting rod were pulled up under the forward observer's post where they were held by a rope and steadied by a small forked shaped piece of metal. The parachutist sat on the backseat with his legs hanging down. The seat was held in place by two bolts attached by cables to a handle in the forward observation post. Immediately before the man was to be dropped, the parachute container and supporting rod were lowered to the fullest extent of the rope, the other end of which was made fast to the machine-gun bracket in the forward observer's post. When the pilot was given the sign to drop the machine's nose the bolts supporting the backseat were drawn. The seat under the parachutist then swung down on its hinges and the man fell clear, pulling out the parachute from the container as he went.

Further trials of the equipment were conducted at Grossa and San Pelagio aerodromes on 26 and 28 June 1918. Carter sent a series of photographs of the tests with his report to his superiors demonstrating the dangers of parachuting at low level:

> In some unaccountable way the parachute body was torn on leaving the machine, and the speed of descent was about 23ft per second instead of 15ft per second. Also, the rope attached to the parachute got between Bowen's legs and caused him to turn two somersaults before the parachute opened. Otherwise, the descent was satisfactory, and Bowen landed safely . . .

Members of his team also suggested that black parachute silk be substituted for the white used in the trials to aid concealment as agents descended into enemy territory under cover of darkness.

In August 1918, Carter reported on the first mission involving a fearless man called Alessandro Tandura from the Italian 8th Army Corps. The night for the attempt was pitch dark and arrangements had to be made for lighthouses and signals on the way. Captain William Barker piloted the machine, with Captain William Wedgewood Benn, the father of Tony Benn, acting as observer. At 1,200ft, east of Vittorio, they let the parachute go and it opened out beautifully. Tandura survived for three months behind enemy lines, providing much useful information and organizing sabotage operations. He was twice captured by the Austrians but managed to escape on both occasions.

Rumours that the German air force was using parachutes in aeroplanes had begun to spread in the spring of 1918 and newspaper editorials began to get louder in asking why British airmen were not being provided with this advantage. The capture of a German parachute-equipped aeroplane gave the Allies the chance to examine the Heinecke parachute that had been developed by Schroeder in Berlin. Experiments on several types of parachute then began in England and France. Although in at least one of these tests the parachute snagged on the tail of the aircraft, the Air Ministry was convinced about the potential, and an order was placed for 500 Guardian Angels. At a conference held in Paris in early November 1918 this decision was announced to representatives from France, England, England, Italy and the USA. The conference was also told that a small number of Guardian Angels had already been sent to the front and that more were on their way.

In June 1919, the British Government agreed that parachutes would in future be fitted to all RAF aircraft, but many senior officials remained sceptical. It took a string of fatal aeroplane crashes immediately after the war and the persistent urging of Orde-Lees to turn the tide. In an attempt to demonstrate the 'infallibility' of the Guardian Angel, Orde-Lees made a descent at Nantes in May 1921 involving two parachutes. He dropped 1,000ft with the first, before discarding it and continuing with a second parachute that he was holding. He told the assembled newspaper reporters that using a parachute was 'as simple and safe a process as stepping off a bus or tram'. It was a phrase that 20 years later would be used about Charles Agate's casual approach to the dangers of parachuting.

Chapter 3

Doing the Right Thing

It was in 1918, after a highly competitive exam and at his third and final attempt, that Bert Agate won a scholarship to Reigate Grammar School (RGS) in Surrey. His was one of twenty scholarships awarded that year to boys from 'council schools' who had shown the potential to get to university or, more likely, join a profession. Had he not won this scholarship it is quite likely that he would have left Frenches School at 14 and followed his father into a job on the railways.

The object of these scholarships was to make the schools 'fully accessible to children of all classes and to give all children in the neighbourhood a chance of admission' (*Surrey Mirror*, 1917). Perhaps to enable him to fit in better, it was at this time that he adopted the name 'Charles'.

As a scholarship boy, Charles Agate was exempt from fees, but that did not free his parents from the obligation to meet the incidental costs of secondary education such as books and uniform. His education placed a considerable strain on the Agate family finances. They were very aware that many bright children were unable to take up scholarship places because their parents could not afford the cost. Agate felt this debt to his parents keenly and remained very close to his father all his life.

Charles Agate arrived at RGS just weeks before the end of the Great War and at a time that his parents were still grieving the loss of their 9-year-old daughter Winifred. Death was all around. Some 306 recent or past pupils of RGS had served in the Great War, and of these, 54 were killed – a ratio comparable with other grammar and public schools of the time.[5] This was primarily because of the number who had been junior officers in the Officer Training Corps (OTC). Of the fifty-four RGS Old Boys who died, twenty-three were Lieutenants or

Second Lieutenants who had the responsibility for leading their men over the top. Many of these died as a result in their first engagement with the enemy.

In his first term at the school, a bronze plaque was unveiled on the main staircase dedicated to the memory of the Old Boys of the School who had lost their lives. Agate already knew some of the names: the older brothers or fathers of his friends and neighbours and they were heroic figures to him, summed up by these words from Ecclesiasticus which were engraved at the top of the memorial plaque: 'Sons of this school let this of you be said – that you who live are worthy of your dead. These gave their lives that you who live may reap a richer harvest ere you fall asleep.'

The school's aspirations lay in the English public school system with its values of patriotism, imperialism and 'Muscular Christianity'. Class divisions were never far from the surface. The British public schools which RGS sought to emulate were elitist establishments where those with money ensured that their sons were mixing with the 'right' people, absorbing their values and establishing connections that would serve them well throughout their adult lives. They made sure that each new generation was bonded to the previous ones and smoothed the way to lucrative future careers in politics, the professions, or the civil service. A.N. Wilson has argued in *The Victorians* (Wilson, 2003) that these schools served the purpose of allowing the aristocracy to remain within the governing class while co-opting the growingly powerful bourgeoisie into their ranks.

Scholarship boys from poorer backgrounds did not always have it easy and were only awarded their scholarships on an annual basis, so young Agate had to work exceptionally hard just to keep his place. It was a challenge which he would come up against again later during his wartime service with the RAF. Fortunately for him, his sporting prowess was the ticket to acceptance at RGS and he became a valued member of the school's football and rugby teams. Charles Kingsley, the children's author and leading exponent of 'Muscular Christianity', had, some 40 years before, summed up the importance of sport in schools as follows:

In the playing field boys acquire virtues which no books can give them; not merely daring and endurance, but, better still, temper, self-restraint, fairness, honour, unenvious approbation of another's success, and all that 'give and take' of life which stand a man in such good stead when he goes forth into the world (Kingsley, 1875).

The Pilgrim – the school magazine – reported in very much the same vein on Agate's first and particularly wet, school Sports Day: 'It takes much to damp the ardour of the true sportsman: schoolboys are perhaps the least easily daunted of sportsmen; they'll play through rain, hail and snow, they'll run till they drop.'

Charles Agate spent four very happy years at RGS as he acknowledged in an interview with the BBC's Don Durbridge in 1974. In that time, he also attended several memorial services as the school sought to honour their dead and recognize their sacrifice. In 1919, the *Surrey Mirror* carried the following account of a Memorial Service in St Mary's Church, Reigate: 'Old boys of the Reigate Grammar School gathered at the Reigate Parish Church on Sunday afternoon, and in a service impressive by its simplicity, remembered with proud sympathy and thanksgiving, their comrades who had laid down their lives for their country in the great war. Practically every seat in the sacred building was filled.'

A more permanent School War Memorial was unveiled the following year and the words of Edwin Heesom, the chairman of the governors (and himself an Old Boy), struck a chord with Agate:

When the Great War fell upon our country a wonderful spirit ran through every class, through all the schools, through all the institutions, and through every man into every heart in the country. A wonderful spirit which none of them who lived through it would ever forget; a spirit of sacrifice, a spirit of

hopefulness, and a spirit, above all, of unity, a spirit which one
sought with great regret and great hopefulness in the time
through which they were now living, now that the Great War
had become memory. Of all the institutions in this country
none took its place with greater ardour and a greater desire
to help than those who had been bred in school. In the great
moment when this School was called upon to do its duty it was
not found wanting.

In his final year at the school Agate witnessed the unveiling of an
imposing bronze figure at Shaw's Corner just down the road from
RGS. The figure was of a man carrying a child with one arm, whilst
holding aloft a flaming torch with the other and bearing the inscription:

This bronze represents the triumphant struggle of mankind
against the difficulties that beset him in the path of life.
Shielding and bearing onward the child, the figure holds aloft
the symbol of self-sacrifice to light the way. The flaming cross
is used to indicate the suffering endured by men in the War.
Flames consume the flesh. The spirit is unconquerable.

It was a message which young Charles Agate had heard many times,
but he could not have known that it would not be long before he would
have the opportunity to volunteer to do his duty to his country.

Most of the boys who attended RGS were destined for jobs in the
professions, the military or in family businesses locally. For scholarship
boys with fewer connections the choices were more restricted. Richard
Hoggart's portrait of 'Scholarship Boys' in *The Uses of Literacy*, first
published in 1957, described the psychological tensions and social
predicaments that affected academically-gifted working- and lower-
middle-class boys like Agate in early twentieth-century Britain.
Hoggart argued that: 'Each boy is between two worlds: the worlds of

school and home; and they meet at few points. Encouraged by some and mocked by others, scholarship boys constantly negotiated the conflicting expectations of parents, teachers, peers, and their own ambitions' (Hoggart, 1957).

Despite these social and academic pressures, Charles Agate's career choice was clear. In his 1974 radio interview, the BBC's Don Durbridge had asked him when he first decided that he wanted to become a teacher. Agate replied:

> It was possible to better yourself if you went to college. And my father, who worked on the railway, I think, pushed me to become a teacher. And I must say, if I started my career again, I would still be a teacher because I've had more happiness, and I've had received much more, from children, I think, than from any other type of person that I've ever met.

Teaching offered an attractive career path, but spending cuts meant that state scholarships were no longer issued for teacher training and universities, so in 1924, Agate was offered the opportunity of going on a two-year day student course for prospective teachers at Goldsmiths College in New Cross. Agate's award consisted of a grant of £20 per annum towards his tuition with an additional maintenance grant of £35 per annum. Agate chose to specialize in advanced physical training and science. He told Don Durbridge:

> We weren't undergraduates. Everything in that course was to prepare you to become an actual teacher. They were more interested in you being able to manage a class of children, rather than being able to teach them. Not surprising really when classes could be up to 50 or 55 children. The point was, unless you can manage the children, you can't teach them. You would only get a first-class teaching certificate if your practical teaching was of the highest standard.

Goldsmiths provided a stark contrast to the more conservative and traditional atmosphere of Reigate Grammar. It was one of the first British colleges to pioneer the expressive performance art form of Eurythmics and this became central to the curriculum. Students were encouraged to develop a movement repertoire relating to the sounds and rhythms of speech, to the tones and rhythms of music, and to 'soul experiences', such as joy and sorrow. However, the Goldsmiths' College students themselves were also issued with a handbook in which they were instructed on rules of gender segregation and strict behavioural standards.

Despite these rules, Goldsmiths' students had a reputation for being distinctive, radical and questioning. Photographs of Goldsmiths alumni from Agate's time show men behaving badly: sticking their tongues out, making rude gestures with their hands, and in one case smoking a cigarette and pipe at the same time. The local police and wider community lived in fear of the Goldsmiths' Rag Week. Sometimes matters got out of hand.

He was not impressed by the quality of training that he received there. He felt that the primary objective was not to deliver a high-quality education, but rather to equip young teachers to maintain order in overcrowded and under-funded classrooms in Council Schools. He told Don Durbridge:

> We were sent out in three-week spells. Some of these were pretty tough schools in the New Cross area, down to the river. We were given just a short time with the teacher in the classroom, and then the teacher would leave, and you would be left to manage those children on your own. You pretty soon knew whether you could manage children or whether you couldn't.

Agate could, and it was a skill he would use to good effect all his working life.

After qualifying with a Board of Education 'Certificate for Teachers in Elementary Schools' in 1926, Agate's first teaching posting was as a science and PE teacher at Leatherhead Central School.[6] This was a selective secondary education school with a focus on technical and commercial skills and was positioned between the more academic grammar schools and the ordinary elementary schools. He was clearly ambitious and had great plans for his new school. Shortly after his arrival he was instrumental in the school's purchase – at a cost of £628 – of a site of 2.5 acres next to the main buildings for use as a playing field.

Boys' physical education classes consisted of regular 'drill instruction' which was seen as beneficial as it provided healthy exercise and helped instil discipline. Drills involved them following a series of athletic and calisthenic moves. These were done outdoors in the fresh air when weather permitted. Discipline in Central Schools was strict, with corporal punishment for the most serious offences.[7] This was invariably carried out by the headmaster rather than by ordinary teachers, but Agate never felt the need to send boys to the headmaster for the cane. From the outset, and for the rest of his career, he was a very popular teacher who was able to command good discipline in the class simply by his presence. He continued to live with his family in Frenches Road throughout the 1920s and the early years of his teaching career. He kept himself fit by cycling the 13 miles from Redhill to Leatherhead and back every day.

His sisters shared his ambition and work rate. Norah, born in 1907, studied to become a midwife at Queen Charlotte's Maternity Hospital; Mary, born in 1914, worked in the insurance business, and Ivy, the youngest, was an exceptional scholar and an accomplished pianist and gained a scholarship at the Reigate County School for Girls where she went on to become head girl.[8] Holidays were taken together as a family, typically in caravans along the West Sussex coast. The Agates were pillars of the Frenches Road community and the epitome of lower middle-class respectability,

Meanwhile, across the Atlantic forces were at work which would have a direct impact on Agate's future as the man who tested parachutes.

Chapter 4

The Parachute Makers

The end of the Great War removed the imperative to deliver cheap parachutes, but the interest and competition did not disappear after hostilities ended. In America, the US Army assembled a team including test pilot James Floyd Smith and film stuntman Leslie Irvin to perfect the design of a new type of static-line parachute, based on a patent that Irvin had filed in 1918. Irvin made the first jump with this parachute on 28 April 1919 in Dayton Ohio.

Floyd Smith had been a member of the Flying Sylvesters Air Circus who had toured the USA before the war along with his fearless partner in their daring aerial act, Hilda F. Youngberg. Smith had several patents to his name, including The Smith Aerial Life Pack, which was the first manually-operated parachute and consisted of a single piece of waterproof fabric wrapped over a silk parachute and held together by rubber bands that would be released when the jumper pulled a ripcord.

The military team led by Smith and Irvin eventually came up with the Airplane Parachute Type-A. Modelled closely after the Smith Life Pack, the primary components of the Type-A were a 28ft (8.5m) diameter silk canopy, a soft backpack and harness, a ripcord, and a 2ft (0.6m) diameter pilot chute to help deploy the main chute. Naturally, Irvin was the first man to test this new design and upon doing so on 28 April 1919, he became the first American to jump from an aeroplane and open a parachute manually in mid-air. The Type-A was subsequently approved and produced for the US military by Irvin's recently-formed company.

When Floyd Smith left government service in 1919, he helped found the Pioneer Parachute Co where he served as both vice president and chief engineer. He continued to experiment and test existing parachutes but when the lifeline attached to his Guardian Angel caught on his USD-9[9] aeroplane it caused his parachute to fail, and he fell 600ft to his death. This accident, which was witnessed by many spectators, renewed the public perception that parachutes were for the air circus display teams and not suitable for ordinary aviators.

As part of his efforts to restore confidence, Leslie Irvin created an informal association in 1922 for people who had successfully used a parachute to bail out of a disabled aircraft. The association was given the name 'Caterpillar Club' referring to the silk threads that made the original parachutes. Members received a certificate and a distinctive lapel pin. The club motto was 'Life depends on a silken thread', and by 1931, there were 571 members of the Caterpillar Club whose lives had been saved by the Irvin Air-Chute parachute. Of these, 372 were awarded in the USA and 69 awarded in the UK. The club exists to this day.

The popularity of the Irvin parachute in the UK led to the establishment of an Irving Air Chute Company plant in England in 1925, but in the USA, his main competitor was James M. Russell, who, with almost no experience in aviation design but plenty of enthusiasm, had managed to create a modern parachute which would be adopted by the Army Air Corps. Russell tested his own experimental designs and in 1927 he introduced 'The Lobe', a parachute that eliminated the oscillation that plagued early designs and opened with only a third of the shock of other parachutes. The Lobe was a sensation and led to the founding of the Russell Parachute Company, which aimed its marketing efforts at commercial aviation. His parachute was endorsed by the Prince of Wales, the future King Edward VIII, in advertisements with the line 'The Prince dons a Russell parachute on all his airplane flights'. Like Irvin, Russell opened a factory in England, and sold the Lobe parachutes to the RAF which had tentatively established a parachute section at Northolt in 1925, principally to experiment with the dropping of supplies.

Over in America, film makers developed a passion for re-enacting aerial dogfights from the war years with popular stunts including one where a plane was soaked in petrol and set on fire before the pilot parachuted out. Another crowd-pleaser was stuntman Colonel Emmett L. (Buddy) Plunkett's trick of making a long free-fall drop with a parachute he had torn in advance to make it appear he was plummeting to his death. He would then pull the ripcord on a genuine parachute when he was only a few hundred feet above the ground, landing safely to the admiring cheers of the crowd.

A real estate firm in Tampa, Florida paid Emmett $2,000 to help attract attention to their development sites. A few weeks before the stunt was supposed to take place, he pieced together an old aeroplane. It was in such poor shape he could not even test fly it before the stunt was to be performed. He then attached a gallon can of petrol just forward of the cockpit, with two copper tubes leading from the can down to the bottom of the lower wings. At the end of the tubes were two spark plugs attached to a magneto in the cockpit. On the great day, he climbed into the cockpit, started the engine, and nursed it to 3,000ft over Tampa Bay. He then turned the stopcock, allowing the petrol to flow down the copper tubing. The petrol vaporised as soon as it hit the slipstream. Emmett then made a swift turn of the magneto crank and as the aeroplane exploded into a ball of fire, he dived over the side drifting down under his parachute to be picked up by a waiting boat.

In Britain, former pilots as well as untrained civilians continued to make daredevil demonstration jumps. One of these was 17-year-old Sylvia Boyden. She was a spectator at the parachute display at the first RAF pageant at Richmond Park and decided to have a go herself. Lying about her age and giving her grandmother's name, she made three successful parachute jumps that day, becoming the first woman in England to do so. This brave pioneer was dubbed as the 'Famous English Air-Girl' by the *New York Times* and went on to appear in air displays all over Britain and Europe.

It would take the horrific death of another brave young woman in front of more than 20,000 people at the Royal Showground in Leicester to persuade the Air Ministry to tighten up on safety measures. On 9 September 1926, Captain Arthur Frederick Muir[10] of Surrey Air Service had brought his aeroplane to Leicester to give local people a chance to make a parachute descent, and 25-year-old Dorothy 'Dot' Cain whose parents owned the Empire Hotel in Leicester was delighted when Captain Muir stayed at her parents' hotel. Before the event she told him that she was eager to give parachuting a go. She boarded the aeroplane carrying a bunch of lucky heather and Captain Muir climbed to 1,000ft, at which point Dot clambered out onto the wing and waved to the crowd below, among whom were her husband and other members of her family. She stepped over the side and jumped, but the silk of her Guardian Angel parachute caught on the plane's undercarriage, and she slipped out of her harness. It soon became clear to the 40,000 people gathered on the ground that she was no longer attached to her parachute as she plummeted, somersaulting, to earth. Dot's very public death made headlines around the world and in Britain parachute jumps by amateurs were banned.

The idea of a parachute as personal 'safety insurance' was developed further in 1930 when Russell announced a new product that would be sold to commercial airlines. 'The last word in safe aids to air navigation' would be a parachute mounted above the passenger's head in the plane's cabin. The parachute pack could be pulled down and easily attached to a light fabric vest that all passengers would be wearing. 'Ten seconds after passengers on air transports are warned to leave the ship, in case of emergency in midair, they will be able to float safely earthward.'

In September 1930, Russell demonstrated an enormous parachute that could be used by an entire aeroplane. At 6,500ft the pilot of a small biplane shut off his engines and released a parachute from the aeroplane's tail. The *New York Times* reported: 'The plane performed various gyrations as it descended but landed safely with a cracked wing and minor damage to the landing gear'. The company claimed that it received interest in the Russell parachute from 'more than 150 aircraft companies, insurance agencies and others interested in increasing the safety of flying' but the product never sold. There were still many people who were dubious about its value.

Undeterred, the manufacturers and promoters of the parachute attempted ever-more daring display jumps. In May 1933, the *Birmingham Daily Gazette* reported on a world record free-fall jump by the Dutch parachutist, John Tranum. He jumped from a height of 27,000ft from a Hawker Hart at Netheravon. He fell like a stone for 18,000ft before he pulled the cord and his parachute opened. He then drifted about five miles from the aerodrome and onto the West Wiltshire Downs, narrowly missing a tree in landing. Apart from a natural desire to beat the record, he was out to demonstrate the military value of a pilot avoiding the danger of being 'potted at by a combatant if in descent after leaving his aeroplane during an unsuccessful air battle he resorts to his parachute, he drops so quickly that he cannot be seen at all until his parachute opens comparatively near the ground'.[11]

Slowly but surely the resistance to the notion of the parachute being a lifesaver was being eroded. With both Irvin and Russell manufacturing parachutes under licence in the UK, several fliers urged domestic manufacturers to produce an all-British model. This challenge was taken up by Raymond Quilter. Born in 1902, Quilter had been educated at Eton and Oxford, before joining the Grenadier Guards as a Lieutenant. He enjoyed a life of privilege and frivolity and was close friends with Prince Henry, Duke of Gloucester. He owned his own aeroplane, a De Havilland Moth, and took up daredevil parachuting purely for the fun of it. On one occasion he made the papers following a parachute display at Brooklands where he landed on a small island in the River Wey.

However, despite this frivolous streak, Quilter was no fool and he soon saw a gap in the market for a light and cheap parachute. The established parachute manufacturers had failed to convince the airlines with their products, partly on grounds of cost, but mainly because the parachutes were heavy and added too much weight to the aircraft. In 1932 Quilter got together with James Gregory to construct lighter parachutes to their own design. Gregory was a keen parachutist who had an extensive knowledge of the commercially-available parachutes, having first jumped with a Guardian Angel when he served in the RFC in 1919. After leaving the RFC he had become the workshop manager at Calthrop's factory and more recently he had been working for the Russell Parachute Company.

Quilter approached his father, Sir Cuthbert Quilter, and managed to convince him to invest in their new endeavour to produce a commercially viable parachute for use by the airlines and private fliers alike. Sir Cuthbert agreed, and the first few experimental parachutes were made by Gregory and his wife on a sewing machine at their home. By 1932, they had designed a parachute to Air Ministry specifications, which was cheap enough to be within easy reach of the private flier's pocket. It had a fast-release mechanism, and the parachute pack was padded for comfort. Using his royal contacts, he was able to announce in January 1933 that the Prince of Wales had installed a GQ parachute on his new Vickers Viastra monoplane. The new parachute was priced at £35, but Quilter told the press that he would soon be able to market the parachute at just £20, considerably cheaper than the alternatives. In 1934, as interest in their product grew the GQ Company Ltd was formed and moved to new premises in Guildford, Surrey.

The company had very big ambitions and hoped to compete with Irvin and sell parachutes to the RAF. However, when they came to the tendering process the GQ Company lost out, with orders being placed with the two established suppliers, Russell and Irvin. The civil airlines also remained unconvinced. Although the GQ parachute was lighter than the alternatives it was not *that* much lighter and would still have added too much weight to a fully-laden aircraft.

Gregory and Quilter did not give up and they continued to evolve their designs, developing the static-line system under which the parachute was opened automatically rather than by pulling a ripcord. In 1936 GQ's all-British parachute was demonstrated at air displays across the UK and the company continued to lodge patents both in Britain and in the USA, including a parachute designed specifically for jumping from gliders and an 'airsuit' developed for air gunners in the Boulton Paul Defiant two-seater fighter (which had no space in the cockpit for other types of parachutes).

Parachute design and technology was developing fast. Charles Agate meanwhile was developing his own taste for risk and adventure.

Chapter 5

Motorbikes and Flying Circuses

To celebrate his new status as a salaried teacher, Charles Agate became the proud owner of a Norton Model 20 motorcycle and he cut quite a dash, speeding through South London on a Saturday afternoon to watch speedway or his beloved Crystal Palace FC at their new stadium at Selhurst Park. He was prosecuted twice in this period: once for speeding and once for failing to stop at a junction. These would not be his last brushes with the Law.

Writing to the *Surrey Mirror* in 1970 on Agate's retirement, his old friend Henry Ingrams described how Agate and other motorcycle enthusiasts used to gather at the old stables by Frenches School to polish and repair their motorcycles: 'Agate always had the fastest, if not the cleanest motorcycle, which was one of the main factors which caused the three accidents I remember him having.'

The Norton was the first of many motorcycles Charles owned throughout the 1920s and 1930s, and one of these motorcycles led to a life-changing meeting on the London Road in Purley. He explained what happened in his 1974 interview with the BBC's Don Durbridge:

I was going up to Crystal Palace Speedway on a very nice new motorcycle. This young lady ran out of a hairdresser shop in the middle of Purley High Street. And she crashed straight into my brand-new motorbike and over we rolled. Well, a number of people clustered round and we picked her up and I left the bike on the side of the road and saw her across to the hairdressers that she had just run from. I then asked her for her address. She wasn't badly hurt. Just bruised very slightly. And I continued on my way with a slightly bent handlebar. Later that evening, I called on her and that's how we met.

This young lady was Edith Marjorie Coles, a 19-year-old from Coulsdon. Clearly not put off by her accident, nor by the man on the motorcycle who hit her, Marjorie embraced motorcycling enthusiastically, venturing out on the pillion of the Norton most weekends.

One of their favourite destinations together was Shoreham Beach in Sussex. The town of Shoreham was a comparatively unappealing place with a chemical works, a cholera hospital, and a lonely coastguard station. Shoreham Beach on the other hand was more interesting. A few fishermen's huts were about the only buildings, but the daylight at Shoreham drew many artists and photographers. With miles of sea on the one side and the rolling Sussex downs above, the air was sparkling and luminous, and it was for this very reason that a large glass film studio was built by the director, F. L. Lyndhurst – the grandfather of actor Nicholas Lyndhurst. Actors and actresses had bungalows built there to form a small colony which became known as 'Bungalow Town'. Many of the houses were old railway carriages with the wheels removed, set on concrete foundations.

Charles and Marjorie used to spend romantic weekends camping and making fires on the beach and when Agate's father bought one of the former railway carriages as a holiday home they used to stay there. This was the start of a long association with the area which would last till Charles' death in 1986.

Just a mile or so from Shoreham Beach was Shoreham Aerodrome and on 19 and 20 July 1931, Charles and Marjorie were spectators at what was billed as 'The World's First Air Circus' presented by Captain Charles Douglas Barnard. He was a famous British aviator who had served in the RFC and who had taken part in a number of air races.

He had also made a number of long-distance flights, including trips with the Duchess of Bedford to India and Cape Town in his Fokker which he named *The Spider*. According to the local press: 'The aerial circus presented by Captain C D Barnard not only provided thrills in abundance to a large number of spectators, but what is more to the point, demonstrated beyond question the progress that has been made in aircraft construction as a comfortable, swift and safe method of transport' (*West Sussex Gazette*, 1931).

The most popular of the air circuses of this period was Cobham's Flying Circus, founded by De Havilland pilot, Alan Cobham. The star of the show was Harry Ward,[12] a man who just a few years later would have a defining role in Agate's extraordinary wartime service. There was a well-worn joke amongst circus jumpers: 'If you want to make a lasting impression on the public, all you have to do is make a lasting impression on the ground.' Alan Cobham understood the truth behind this and would push his displays to the limits to astonish, and terrify, the paying public. It was Cobham's idea that one of his flyers should emerge from the crowd disguised as a farmer who was very much the worse for drink. The farmer staggered onto the runway, climbed aboard an aeroplane and made a suitably messy take-off, swerving and dipping into the air. At about 1,000ft, the plane turned upside down and the 'farmer' appeared to fall out of the cockpit and plummet to the ground. It was of course a ruse and the pilot had dropped out a passably accurate dummy of himself, but the audience below were for the most part convinced and horrified. It was reported that one lady went into premature labour.

Harry Ward was, in his own words, a 'little cuss' (Hearn, 1990) and was famed for his ever more daring feats in the air. He invented the character of the 'Yorkshire Birdman', astonishing crowds with his death-defying leaps from rickety biplanes wearing his home-made 'birdman' costume with wings and tail, a precursor of today's hi-tech 'wing suits'. Ward's costume incorporated a release mechanism into his rig to enable him to jettison his wings before he pulled the ripcord, so reducing the risk of snagging his parachute.

Ward made hundreds, possibly thousands, of parachute jumps with the flying circuses. He said he 'didn't bother to count them', which was fortunate for Charles Agate's later claim on the world record.

***

On 17 August 1932, Charles and Marjorie married at St James Church, Riddlesdown, near Purley. With his salary of £180 a year, they were able to buy what he later described as a lovely little detached bungalow at No. 29 West Drive, Burgh Heath, close to Epsom Downs and the racecourse. They called their first home 'Norton' after the motorcycle, and over 40 years later in his BBC radio interview, Charles would wonder 'if the name is still on the outside of that bungalow now and if the present owners would ever realise where the name came from'. Sadly, the bungalow no longer bears that proud name.

It was shortly after moving to their new home in Burgh Heath that an incident occurred which illustrates what a fearless man Charles had become. He was in the kitchen at the back of his new house on New Year's Eve when he heard a woman's scream from the direction of the nearby Epsom Road. An account of what happened next was reported in the *Surrey Mirror*:

> Albert Agate, a schoolteacher of West Drive, Burgh Heath, said that on the night in question he heard an awful scream. He ran into the Epsom-road, where he saw a car coming towards him from Burgh Heath. He sprang onto the running board and confronted the driver. 'His eyes were red', Agate said. 'I have never seen any other person's eyes like it. I have seen a dog's eyes look like his in the half-light. I shouted to him: "Where is the girl that shrieked?"' (*Surrey Mirror*, 1933)

Unable to wrest control of the car from the driver, Agate jumped off the running board and ran to look for a police officer as the car sped off.

The driver was Frederick William Deats,[13] a 46-year-old motor engineer who ran a petrol station and garage that stood on the corner of Brighton Road and Reigate Road. There was a tea-room attached to the garage, which was run by Deats' wife, Ellen. Just two years earlier Deats had been the prime suspect in the murder of 20-year-old Agnes Kesson. She had been employed by Mrs Deats in the tea-rooms and had disappeared on one of their busiest days of the year, Epsom Derby Day. Her body had dumped in woods off Horton Lane, Epsom. Although Deats was never charged, he was widely suspected locally, and he was not a popular man.

The girl who screamed on this occasion was another young woman, 18-year-old Nita Elmer, a domestic servant who worked for Mrs Burrows of Terrier's House, Burgh Heath. She knew Deats vaguely because he used to repair Mrs Burrow's car. Nita had been to see some friends in Reigate, and she had got off the bus at about 11.15pm. She heard a car coming from behind, and heard someone say: 'Good evening, Nita. There's terrible trouble at home. Mrs. Burrows has had a telephone message to say you are to go home soon. She telephoned me to meet you off the bus and take you home. Jump in the car. I'll drive you there.'

Nita got in the car and Deats drove off along the Epsom road, but when they reached the turning leading to Mrs. Burrows' house, Deats accelerated and drove straight on. Nita asked him why he wasn't going to Mrs. Burrows' house, and he replied, 'It's no good going there. There's no one there.'

Nita Elmer told the court that she opened the door of the car and tried to get out, but Deats caught her by the neck with his left hand and brought the car to a standstill. She managed to get away and started to run but fell over. Deats caught her before she could get up and said: 'Get in the car.' He held her by the shoulders and, holding her neck with his right hand, he opened the door of the car with his left. She pulled away again, but he caught hold of her coat. Fortunately for her, the fur collar came off and she ran off screaming.

As a result of Agate's testimony, Deats was taken into custody and charged with assaulting and beating Nita Elmer. He was sentenced to three months in prison with hard labour.

***

In 1935, Charles and Marjorie welcomed into the world their daughter Lynette and nine decades later it was Lynette and her husband Jim who so generously welcomed the authors of this book into their home where she shared so many memories of her father. One of the first questions we asked her was simply: 'What were your mother and father like?' Her answer: 'Mother was fabulous . . . glamorous. He was a terrific father. Unconventional, but I couldn't have had better parents.'

However, like many other marriages, the Agates had their difficult times. In 1938, Agate was working at Stoughton School, near Leatherhead where a young woman called Eileen Queenie Davies worked as a domestic. Eileen fell pregnant and named Charles Agate as the father. In March 1939, she gave birth to a son, Keith. It is not clear if Marjorie was informed of Eileen's claim, but at the time the National Register was taken in September 1939, Agate was living alone in a small cottage on Banstead Downs about a mile away from their bungalow in Epsom. Lynette was just 4 years old at the time. Shortly after Keith's birth, Eileen gave him up for adoption and he disappeared from Agate family history until he would dramatically re-emerge 80 years later.

So, at the outbreak of the Second World War in 1939, Charles Agate was 34 years old and separated from his wife and young daughter. With Marjorie it appeared that the damage had been done. Science teachers were, at that time, exempt from the call-up, but despite that Agate volunteered immediately for military service. He was given a commission in the Royal Air Force Volunteer Reserve (RAF V.R.) which was the main pathway for aircrew entry into the RAF.

Agate was sent to one of the newly created Officer Training Units (OTU) for training. Prior to their expansion, the existing OTUs turned out around 39 pilots every two weeks, but the new OTUs produced around 115 every two weeks – an almost threefold increase.

The rapid growth in the RAF's Fighter Command in 1939–40 had created a high demand for aircrew of all ranks and trades and absorbed all those who were available. It was then the policy of the RAF for the machine-gun fire of bomber formations to be controlled by a specially trained officer in one of the aircraft, known as the gunnery leader. Agate set his sights on that role and in November 1940, he graduated as Pilot Officer Air Gunner 89642.

However, with the end of the Battle of Britain the attrition rate decreased and new aircraft and new offensive roles for Fighter Command created a surplus of air gunners. The RAF no longer had such a high demand for gunnery leads and all new gunnery posts were cancelled, leaving the newly qualified Agate, in his own words, 'high and dry'. He would have loved to become a pilot, but the upper age limit for pilots at that time was 32 – and Agate was 34. He learned with great frustration that he was unlikely to be employed in a front-line role at all. He was looking for action, and the prospect of permanent duties as a ground instructor or radar operator did not appeal to him.

What he didn't know though, in fact what very few people knew, was that more than 200 miles away on the outskirts of Manchester, tentative and top secret plans were being laid which would finally give him an outlet for his bravery and recklessness and that within a few weeks, and almost by accident, he would join a small band of likeminded individuals whose actions would change the face of warfare and lead to the Allies' ultimate victory.

Chapter 6

Trouble Brewing

While the RAF continued to see the parachute as an emergency safety device for exiting a doomed aircraft, other countries had been training airborne troops as an aggressive force. The Soviet Union carried out several experimental military mass jumps as early as August 1930 and established a parachute brigade the following year. In 1936 the Soviet Army carried out a parachute drop of 1,200 men, 150 machine guns and 18 light field guns. General Archibald Wavell, who observed the exercise in his role as the British Army's Russian liaison officer, reported: 'If I had not witnessed the descents, I could not have believed such an operation was possible.' In 1935, Italy used parachutes in Abyssinia for dropping materials and troops, and in Poland, parachuting by the armed forces started under the Air and Chemical Defence League, a paramilitary organization that had 14,000 local branches and some 1.5 million members. The French meanwhile were training women as parachute medics in the *Infirmières Pilotes – Sécouristes de l'Air* (IPSA). More ominously, in Germany, Hermann Göring had formed paratroop units with the intention that they could be used to create confusion at critical moments. On 1 October 1935, the unit was incorporated into the newly-formed *Fallschirmschützen Bataillon* (the paratrooper branch of the German Luftwaffe; the first paratroopers to be committed to large-scale airborne operations).

In the UK, the military historian Basil Liddell Hart argued that an airborne aggressive force was not needed. He went further and said that no troops should be sent to the Continent and that the best option for Britain was a purely defensive air force. He theorised that a strong British air force could defeat her enemies while avoiding the high casualties that would come from dropping a large conscript army into mainland Europe.

These ideas were adopted by Neville Chamberlain, then Chancellor of the Exchequer, who cut defence spending significantly in his early budgets. In time, he became convinced of the need for rearmament in the face of a resurgent Germany and he urged the strengthening of the RAF, but as a purely defensive force as envisaged by Liddell Hart although supported by heavy bomber capability that could reach German cities.

Other members of the Government were still wedded to appeasement and Lord Londonderry, Minister for Air, told Parliament:

> There has been demand in some quarters of late for large increase in Britain's air strength. The Government, however, has wisely declined to let itself be driven by scaremongers into taking panic measures which would add to the general feeling of insecurity all over the world and would afford an excuse for other countries to accelerate the rate of their increase of armaments (*Hampshire Telegraph & Post*, 1936).

The rise of Hitler and the aggression that led to outbreak of the Second World War has been thoroughly described elsewhere, but when Chamberlain announced the existence of a state of war between this country and Germany, Winston Churchill, who was then First Lord of the Admiralty, responded in typical form, echoing the words Charles Agate and many thousands of young men up and down the land had heard at memorial ceremonies after the Great War:

> There is a generation of Britons here now ready to prove itself not unworthy of the days of yore and not unworthy of those great men, the fathers of our land, who laid the foundations of our laws and shaped the greatness of our country. This is

not a question of fighting for Danzig or fighting for Poland. We are fighting to save the whole world from the pestilence of Nazi tyranny and in defence of all that is most sacred to man (*Sunderland Daily Echo & Shipping Gazette*, 1939).

The following day King George VI issued the following message:

The RAF has behind it a tradition no less inspiring than those of the other Services and in campaigns which we have now been compelled to undertake you will have to assume responsibilities far greater than those which your Service had to shoulder in the last War. One of the greatest of them will be the safeguarding of this Island from the menace of the air. I can assure all ranks of the Air Force of my supreme confidence in their skill and courage and their ability to meet whatever calls may be made upon them.

The RAF, formed just 20 years earlier, was still seen as essentially romantic and chivalrous. Flying was restricted to a small band of people, many of whom came from privileged backgrounds. Within the RAF those who had seen aerial combat in the Great War were revered by their fellow officers who had been born too late to fight. Aviation though was now a thoroughly modern business. The question was, how would the RAF rise to these new challenges?

***

One of the most immediate problems was the scarcity of modern aircraft and the lack of manufacturing capacity to rapidly increase production. In December 1939, as part of a morale-boosting publicity campaign, a three-day tour was laid on for journalists to see the production line for the new Amstrong Whitworth Whitley heavy bomber. A test pilot was quoted as saying that the Whitley was a 'plane with no vices at all'.

He went on to say that 'The Whitley is Great Britain's answer to the Heinkels of the German Air Force' (*Liverpool Daily Post*, 1939).

The Whitley was designed to meet the Air Ministry-issued Specification B.3/34, for a heavy night bomber/troop transport to replace the Handley Page Heyford biplane. Flaps were included late in the design stage, but the wing remained unaltered; as a result, the Whitley flew with a pronounced nose-down attitude when at cruising speed, resulting in considerable drag. The Whitley bomber would go on to play a crucial, but not always welcome, role in Agate's life and in the development of Britain's airborne forces, not as a bomber, but as a dispatcher of airborne troops.

The wake-up call for Britain came with the German invasions of the Low Countries in May 1940, led by an assault force of German paratroopers. Using Junkers Ju 52s[14] with sliding doors the Germans first dropped pyrotechnic dummies to create confusion and surprise, then paratroops; the *Falschirmtruppe* Göring had been preparing since the mid-1930s. Although the German airborne troops suffered heavy casualties during the operation, they succeeded in bypassing the defensive positions and advancing into Belgium. In the space of just 24 days, Belgium and Holland were overrun, and the British Expeditionary Force was evacuated from Dunkirk leaving 68,111 of its personnel in France killed, missing or as prisoners of war. Shortly after Dunkirk, Chamberlain went to Buckingham Palace to resign and advise the King to send for Winston Churchill, who became Britain's Prime Minister on 10 May 1940. As Churchill was to write: 'I felt . . . that all my past life had been but a preparation for this hour and for this trial'.

The demand for fighter support to cover the evacuation from Dunkirk had left the War Cabinet with the unenviable task of choosing between home defence and the pleas of the Army and their Allies for air cover in France. However, it soon became clear that the RAF simply did not have the resources to support the army in France and defend the skies of Southern England from the Luftwaffe.

The lack of air support provided by the RAF caused bitter resentment to the soldiers stranded on the beaches of Dunkirk and led to a growing perception within senior ranks in the Army that they had been let down by the RAF. The souring of Army-RAF relations spread to all ranks with members of the Army shouting abuse at men in RAF uniforms at Victoria Station. These tensions and prejudices would persist for some time.

The impact of the German airborne operations in the Low Countries was considerable, but the confusion of war made it difficult for the British to form an accurate picture of precisely what had happened. The uncertainty was increased by German propaganda and misinformation. The British were, however, able to gain sufficient information on German tactics, as well as vital technical information, to gain a clear idea of what would be needed to establish an equivalent British capability. *The Times* newspaper published relatively accurate accounts of German techniques and equipment in early June, and UK public opinion in favour of the development of a British airborne force started to grow louder.

On 3 June 1940, Churchill wrote to his chief military assistant and staff officer, General Hastings 'Pug' Ismay, expressing concern over the possibility of German landings from both the air and sea, and warning against the dangers of adopting the 'completely defensive habit of mind which has ruined the French'. He went on to raise the possibilities of taking the airborne initiative away from the Germans, writing 'if it is so easy for the Germans to invade us, why should it be thought impossible for us to do anything of the same kind to them?'

Churchill expanded on this theme in another minute to Ismay two days later. This called for the appropriate authorities to investigate ways of expediting his suggestions, and recommended that yet-to-arrive Australian troops be divided into:

detachments of 250, equipped with grenades, trench mortars, tommy guns, armoured vehicles and the like, capable of landing on the friendly coasts now held by the enemy. Enterprises must be prepared, with specially trained troops, who can develop a reign of terror down these coasts, first of all on the 'butcher and bolt' policy, but later on, or perhaps as soon as we are organised, we should surprise Calais or Boulogne, kill or capture the Hun garrison and hold the place until all the preparations to reduce it by siege or heavy storm have been made. I look to the Joint Chiefs of the Staff to propose me measures for a vigorous, enterprising and ceaseless offensive against the whole German occupied coastline.

There was little enthusiasm among Army and RAF commanders for this directive. After all, the previously-agreed strategy was focused on preparing for a German invasion of Southern England and a strategic bombing campaign on German cities. The RAF had little interest in developing a new and experimental form of warfare for which there was no obvious purpose. Furthermore, tensions over Dunkirk remained.

That Churchill wanted an airborne force was obvious, but what he wanted it *for* was less clear to everyone. It was pointed out by both Army and RAF senior officers that Churchill's directive was lacking in clarity. The reference to Australian troops was also confusing. Did he have it in mind to turn these into trained guerrilla fighters? By not making himself clear, it was left to others to try to interpret. This task fell to Ismay who was the only effective link between Churchill and the military and civilian leadership.[15]

Following receipt of Churchill's directive of 5 June 1940, the Air Ministry drafted a detailed briefing for a conference to be held on 10 June. The briefing, which was entitled 'Development of Parachute Troops', summarised Churchill's order and stated that a parachute training school should be established as soon as possible. However, the briefing also set out the practical problems: where were the aircraft and crews to come from, where should it be located and what about the parachutes? The briefing noted that it was 'understood that the normal service parachute was unsatisfactory to carry a soldier and his impediments'. This meant that a new type of parachute would need to be developed. The conference concluded that it was not currently possible to drop large numbers of paratroops in one operation because of the lack of suitable transport aircraft. If bombers were used, this would be at the price of reducing the number of aircraft available for their primary role of carrying out bombing raids on German cities. The conference said that aircraft such as the Avro Anson,[16] Airspeed Oxford[17] and De Haviland DH.89[18] could be used as a temporary measure, but it was identified that the Armstrong Whitworth Whitley was the only suitable aircraft as longer-term option. This was on the basis that this was the only RAF aircraft that could carry up to twelve paratroops and 1,000lb (453kg) of equipment. However, Whitleys could not be provided immediately as these aircraft would need to be modified with the addition of a sliding door of the kind used on the German Junkers Ju 52. It was proposed that, in time, twenty-one Whitleys might be deployed to allow 200 parachute jumps each day. No recommendations were made regarding the location of the school.

The conference concluded that the RAF's aircrew parachute was too small, but the training parachute might be suitable, given that it had a larger canopy. However, this would require modification to allow jumping from the recommended height of 500ft (152m). Following the conference, it was agreed that the new school should be provided with six modified Whitleys initially, together with 10,000 training parachutes.

The decision to allocate Whitleys to the school has been criticised by historians, on the grounds that the aircraft was designed as a bomber and not to carry men in the fuselage. Smoking once on board was not permitted, no movement was possible, with ten men huddled in cramped positions on the floor unable to stretch their legs, unable to relieve themselves should they need to and unable to see what was going on outside. It had no windows, and the inside was claustrophobic, oppressive and dark. The sense of imprisonment and the variety of unpleasant smells within the fuselage were not conducive to good spirits.

The blame for the choice of the Whitley has been laid at the doors of the Air Ministry. However, this is a misdirection. It was Churchill's appointee, Max Aitken, 1st Baron Beaverbrook, who had taken the decision that aircraft production should be concentrated on just five aircraft types – the Wellington,[19] Blenheim,[20] Whitley, Hurricane and Spitfire.[21] With hindsight, it is clear that this was a very sensible policy that was instrumental in the outcome of the war. However, it was detrimental to the formation of an airborne aggressive force.

On 16 June 1940 Churchill re-issued a paper that he had first written in 1936 entitled 'Invasion by Air', as part of a demand for the Home Defence authorities to appraise him of preparations to repulse such an event. He then visited Manchester Corporation Civil Airport at Ringway eight miles south of Manchester city centre that had been identified as a potential site for the location of a new parachute training school.

On 17 June the individual RAF Commands were informed that RAF Ringway in Manchester would indeed be the site of the new school with an initial aircraft establishment of six Whitleys and six RAF officers under the command of Squadron Leader Donald Ross Shore and sixty-six other RAF personnel. The new establishment would be named the Central Landing School (CLS) (Air Ministry AIR 29/512, 1940).

Construction of an RAF station at the airport had only just been completed. It consisted of two large hangars, workshops, barrack blocks and ancillary accommodation. Ringway was selected primarily because it was located away from other RAF operational areas. The plans were so obscure at the outset that letters were received addressed to the 'Central Laundry' and the 'Central Sunday School' (Carruthers [ed.] 2012), yet it was to become the base for an extraordinary five-year project to develop Britian's airborne forces for an, as yet unspecified, invasion of mainland Europe.

After the visit to Ringway, Churchill elaborated on his ambitions in a letter to Ismay dated 22 June 1940:

We ought to have a corps of at least 5,000 parachute troops, including a proportion of Australians, New Zealanders and Canadians, together with some trustworthy people from Norway and France. I hear something is being done already to form such a corps but only I believe on a very small scale. Advantage must be taken of the summer to train these forces, who can, none the less, play their part meanwhile as shock troops in home defences. Pray let me have a note from the War Office on the subject.

Although officials continued to meet to plan for the new venture, events overtook them when Hitler ordered Operation Sea Lion, an amphibious assault on Britain, to follow once the Luftwaffe had achieved air superiority over the Channel. The operation began on 16 July with an air and sea blockade that targeted coastal shipping convoys, as well as ports and docks such as Portsmouth.

At this time, RAFs Fighter Command had around 768 aircraft of which only 520 were considered battleworthy. However, as a result of the Air Ministry's response to the Beaverbrook directive to increase fighter and bomber production, this situation was to improve significantly over the next few weeks. By the time the Germans launched their offensive in early August, the number of RAF fighters available had almost doubled to just over 1,000 and Britain's factories had the capacity to turn out over 3,000 fighters over the next 12 months. This capacity exceeded that of the Luftwaffe and allowed the fighter squadrons to maintain the necessary complement to rebuff the German airborne invasion and to mount subsequent aggressive campaigns.

Although Churchill saluted 'the Few', historians such as John Curatola of the Jenny Craig Institute for the Study of War and Democracy have pointed out that the RAF had more and better aircraft and a more sustained supply of new pilots than the Luftwaffe. The proof of the wisdom of the decision to concentrate all of Britain's manufacturing capacity on just five aircraft types was in the outcome. In one of the greatest triumphs in Britain's long military history, the Luftwaffe failed to overwhelm the RAF forcing Hitler to postpone and eventually cancel the planned invasion. This was Germany's first major defeat in the Second World War and a crucial turning point in the conflict.

Chapter 7

The Birth of PTS No. 1

T he Central Landing School (CLS) was established on 21 June 1940, but the designated commander Squadron Leader Shore, who had never parachuted before, broke his leg in his very first jump at RAF Henlow[22] and was unable to continue in his role.

A couple of weeks before, an exercise had been launched to encourage serving Army personnel to volunteer to form the new airborne fighting force that was to become No. 2 Commando.[23] The campaign sought volunteers who were young and fit, preferably able to swim, immune to seasickness, and who had experienced active service. Officers were expected to display 'personality, tactical ability and imagination', whilst other ranks were 'to exhibit a good standard of intelligence, independence of character and a healthy respect for private property'. Non-commissioned volunteers were required 'to be capable of behaving without supervision' and the rules stated bluntly that 'there must be no risk of looting'.

Service with the new force was only expected to last for a few months, and all ranks were to be selected by personal interview, which would make explicit the nature and conditions of their duties. Prospective volunteers were then free to withdraw their application if they wished. A special allowance would be paid to cover food, accommodation, heating, fuel and lighting, at a daily rate of 13s/4d for officers and 6s/8d for other ranks. This was in addition to normal pay and was also payable during leave or sickness.

On 12 June 1940 the recruitment campaign was extended to call for volunteers with the additional physical requirements that: 'Volunteers must not weigh more than 250lb fully clothed and lightly equipped and must be able to pass comfortably through a circular aperture, 3ft in diameter when wearing equipment and a parachute.'

Captain John Rock[24] arrived at Ringway on 27 June and was immediately promoted to Major to give him superiority over the other Army and RAF personnel at the school. The first fifty-three volunteers also arrived at Ringway on the same day and were marched to RAF Ringway from Manchester Piccadilly station. Although they had all volunteered for 'special service of a hazardous nature', none of them had any idea what they had let themselves in for, but one of their new officers, Captain Cleasby-Thompson,[25] told them:

> You are all to be trained as parachutists. You are privileged to be the first men in the British Army to be asked to jump out of aircraft and reach the ground by the aid of parachutes. You should all feel very proud. I must warn you in the most serious manner that you are not to talk to anyone, neither serviceman nor civilian, about this training.

In truth, no-one knew what function they would perform, but it was agreed that their training should be tough and intensive from the very start. It was taken for granted that airborne troops would have to be capable of fighting and surviving against larger and more heavily armed forces until infantry or armoured backup could be provided. Each man was, therefore, required to possess courage, self-discipline and self-reliance. They would also need battle skills to enable them to fight with only the weapons and equipment they could carry. Training exercises would be carried out by day and night and frequently end with long marches back to barracks. The ability to cover long distances at high speed in full battle order became a matter of pride to the newly-formed parachute units – 10 miles in two hours, 20 miles in four hours and, ultimately, 50 miles in 24 hours. With such demanding standards, many volunteers failed to make the grade and were sent back as being unsuitable.

On hearing about the vacancy to command Ringway, Louis Arbon Strange[26] presented himself at the office of his old friend, Group Captain Geoffrey Hilton 'Beery' Bowman, the Deputy Director of Combined Operations (Air) at the Air Ministry in Whitehall. Strange was a Dorsetshire gentleman farmer and Great War air ace with a bad back, who was too old for a regular commission. However, he had earned a DSO, MC, DFC, three Mentions in Despatches and the rank of Lieutenant-Colonel during the Great War. When war broke out, he returned to military service as a 48-year-old pilot officer in the Royal Air Force Volunteer Reserve and had been posted to 24 Squadron, the RAF's transport squadron. His reputation, his social class and his friendship with Bowman were sufficient for him to be duly promoted to Squadron Leader and appointed as a successor to Shore.

Neither Louis Strange nor John Rock had any previous knowledge of parachuting or airborne training, but it was agreed that Strange would be responsible for parachute training while Rock was given responsibility for ground training and equipment. Strange's task was to bring the establishment from paper to reality in just three weeks. As one senior RAF officer was quoted as saying: 'it will be necessary to cover in six months the ground the Germans have covered in six years' (Cartner, 2012, p. 5).

Ringway was a fully functioning RAF station when the school was established but had no ground facilities suitable for housing personnel or parachute packing. Many of the RAF's non-commissioned personnel were, therefore, billeted at Woodside Lane, one mile away. There was also no area suitable for use as a landing zone for regular, large-scale parachute descents. A much larger area for a landing zone was needed and Flight Lieutenant G.W.R. Hodge was sent to examine alternative landing grounds. His first choice was Tatton Park, a large area of parkland, located five miles south-west of Ringway.

Another of the many issues in these early days was the lack of suitable parachutes. Strange tackled this problem by visiting the Parachute Development Flight (PDF) and appropriated their entire stock of Irvin training parachutes. He also tried to address the shortage of personnel by calling for PDF personnel to volunteer to become parachute instructors. Five came forward, but these were fabric workers and parachute packers who knew nothing about parachuting.[27] However, by 4 July 1940, the school had a staff of eleven officers and eighteen men under Squadron Leader Jack Benham (who had been appointed Chief Instructor) and Warrant Officer Bill Brereton[28] from RAF Henlow. In addition to the RAF Parachute Jumping Instructors (PJIs) there were seven Army Physical Training Instructors (PTIs) whose previous professions were listed as: schoolteacher, professional footballer, boxer, ballet dancer, cycling champion, circus acrobat, and a 'Wall of Death' rider.

The first pilots were Flight Lieutenant Boris Romanoff,[29] David McMonnies,[30] C.W.R. Hodges, J.E.M. (Bruce) Williams[31] and Pilot Officers J. Cutler, H. 'Tony' O'Neill and D.B.S. Davie. They arrived at Ringway on 5 July 1940. Flight Lieutenant Earl Bateman Fielden[32] arrived one month later on 5 August 1940 on a posting from 24 Squadron. As a very experienced air circus pilot he was appointed Chief Flying Instructor.

Very early on, doubts emerged about the quality of some of the men recruited as Commando volunteers. On 5 July 1940, Bernard Winfield, the CLE Medical Officer, wrote a lengthy minute expressing his concerns: 'I feel it is my duty to make the strongest possible representations against the present system of training British paratroops. It is having an adverse effect on the spirit of the personnel of this station and is turning out troops inferior in discipline and morale.'

He went on to point out that regiments would not release men that they considered to be good soldiers. He also pointed out that the training regime was unnecessarily and pointlessly gruelling and because the men were drawn from many different regiments and disciplines there was no regimental spirit or pride. He concluded: 'There is an intense desire to work and fight and win the war, but this is instantly quenched because the work done is apparently useless. I have no hesitation in advising in the strongest possible terms that this project be either taken seriously or abandoned altogether.' Winfield's criticisms of his Army colleagues cannot have helped to improve relations between the RAF and Army. In the meantime, Louis Strange pressed on.

On 6 July 1940, Strange visited Tatton Hall, the home of Maurice, 4th Baron Egerton of Tatton, to discuss the plans to use Tatton Park as a landing zone (Cheshire Archives and Local Studies, 1228–1961). Egerton was an enthusiastic airman and friend of the Wright brothers who had cleared a large swathe of the park for use of his own biplane in the inter war years. However, Tatton Park was not ideally suited as a landing ground because there were several wooded areas and two large lakes.

Lord Egerton's primary concern was not about the suitability of his estate, but about aircraft noise disrupting his duck shoots and about receiving compensation for his loss of income from cattle grazing. He had also been approached by the Army about the use of the park as a training ground, but he chose the RAF as he felt the Army would be too 'messy'. Loaning his estate for the duration of the conflict has been presented as a generous contribution to the war effort, but the next five years would be marked by almost constant conflict and complaints about the impact on his home and lands.

Only five of the promised Whitleys had arrived at Ringway.[33] These aircraft were all Mark IIs with the Armstrong Siddeley Tiger engines and had not been modified for parachute jumping with the addition of a side door, as recommended by the Air Ministry. This was because it was found that it was not possible to create a sufficiently large door without compromising the structural integrity of the aircraft.

Instead, on two of the Whitleys the rear gun turret was removed and replaced with a small platform from which pupils could be launched by the simple but hair-raising system of pulling the ripcords on their parachutes as they stood in the aircraft's slipstream. This was referred to as the 'pull-off' method.

It was soon discovered through testing with dummies that this method of exit was useless for the purpose of dropping groups of paratroops reasonably close together and was also particularly hair-raising for the jumper. As a result, the other Whitleys were returned to the Armstrong Whitworth factory to be modified between 30 June and 9 July with the cutting of a circular floor mounting ring and aperture in the floor. This method was tested successfully with sand-bag dummies.

In an interview with Don Durbridge, Agate explained the primary reason why the aperture or 'the hole' as he referred to it, was preferred to the 'pull-off' from the rear gun turret:

> The whole purpose of this type of parachuting is to get as many troops as you can – twenty if you could – down on the ground very close together. When jumping from the back of a Whitley bomber pulling a ripcord was quite useless because by the time the second man got into position, you could be spread a mile apart. So, our engineers recommended that we should cut a hole in the bottom with a wing scoop in the front so that we could jump four aft of the hole and four at the far end of the hole, alternatively. You could then get eight soldiers down pretty close together if they jumped quickly through the hole.

The first training course started on 9 July with air experience flights for three-quarters of the Commando volunteers. The first drops over Tatton Park were made using six dummies. Bad weather ruled out any exercises the next day, but on 13 July the first live descents took place at Tatton Park by RAF parachute personnel using the modified Irvin training parachutes. They were led by Bill Brereton, with the Army instructors and Commando volunteers watching on as spectators.

Two jumps were made from the rear turret of the Whitley, one through the aperture in the floor of the Whitley with 'trainer-type' parachutes and five through the aperture with the Irvin parachutes that had been acquired from the PDF by Strange. This was supposed to be secret, but according to Strange, 'the whole of Manchester turned out to see our first jumps'.

On 14 July, the Army instructors made their first jumps from the rear platform, while six Army personnel made test jumps through the aperture. As one of the Army instructors suffered concussion and another dislocated a shoulder, it was decided immediately after that the pull-off method was too dangerous and all subsequent jumps were made through the hole in the floor.

The day after these demonstration jumps, it was the turn of the trainees, who were taken up in sticks of eight and dropped singly or in pairs on Tatton Park. In the first week or so of the start of the live training exercises, around eighty jumps took place with only minor accident or injury and the progress was deemed to be successful when Air Marshal Sir William Mitchell[34] visited on 16 July.

However, concerns were growing about the safety of the techniques being used and a week later, on 22 July, Louis Strange, Jack Benham, two RAF instructors, five Army officers and six other ranks made jumps through the aperture. Although they all landed safely, a temporary halt was brought to all test jumps to allow modifications to be made to the parachute.

These modifications made to the Irvin parachute involved the attaching of one end of a length of woven tape to the manual ripcord handle on the parachute, the other end being secured with a clip to a strong point within the aircraft. The hope was that this would achieve an automatic opening of the parachute when the line was broken by gravity as the parachutist fell. This became known as the 'static line' or 'Statichute'.

However, presumably because of concerns about the impact of still further delays on the morale of the men of No.2 Commando, training resumed before these modifications could be tested properly.

Tragedy struck on 25 July when men from C Troop boarded Whitley K7230. Among them was 31-year-old Ralph Evans from a small mining village about 16 miles from Cardiff.

Chapter 8

Death Foretold

Ralph Evans was serving with the Royal Service Corps as a Driver when he had volunteered for duties with No. 2 Commando. He was introduced to ground training on 8 July 1940. After some crude ground training exercises the men were split into groups of six for air experience flights, as most had never flown before.

For his first jump on 25 July, Evans was allocated to a stick of eight men from C Troop. L.A.C. Oakes jumped first and made a successful exit, but when Ralph Evans launched himself through the hole a red flare went up from the ground signalling a halt to proceedings. The turbulent airflow beneath the aircraft had tangled the canopy and lines of the parachute and Evans crashed to his death just 50 yards from where Louis Strange was standing.

An inquiry into the death of Ralph Evans was held by the Air Ministry and Royal Aircraft Establishment (RAE) and various shortcomings in the equipment and method were identified. The following day, Flight Lieutenant Harry Myles was sent to Henlow to carry out tests of modified parachutes. He was followed by Louis Strange and Bruce Williams who arrived at Henlow on 27 July.

The inquiry found that the modifications made had failed to address the primary problem of the sequence of the opening of the parachute, which emerged canopy-first from the pack. This was not normally a problem in a free-fall, because the parachutist was already falling with sufficient speed to allow the canopy to inflate properly. With a static line however, the parachute opening sequence occurred while the parachutist was much closer to the aircraft. This resulted in the rigging lines leaving the pack before the canopy was fully inflated. This could be exacerbated if the parachutist's arms and legs became entangled in the rigging lines causing the front and back sets of the rigging lines to become interwoven into two thick ropes. As the development of the canopy was retarded, so the rate of fall was increased, and control was impossible until the body revolved through 360° and the twists were eliminated.

The tests also identified another problem which they referred to as the 'blown periphery' or 'thrown line' when part of the canopy was firstly blown inwards and then outwards through the rigging lines producing a second inverted canopy. It was identified that it was one, or more than one, of these circumstances that had caused the death of Ralph Evans.

The pause in parachute training at Ringway following this accident was embarrassing for the CLE. Proposals were made to the Air Ministry for a revised training programme and a demonstration was laid on involving eight dummies. To the alarm of all concerned, three of the eight parachutes malfunctioned when the bar securing the static lines came adrift, dumping the dummies and unopened parachutes to the ground, and nearly taking the despatcher with them. Following this debacle, the Irvin X-type parachute was removed from service on 29 July 1940 and parachute training at Ringway was stopped entirely. As no suitable alternative existed, parachute training was suspended and the volunteers of No. 2 Commando were sent to the School for Irregular Warfare at Achnacarry.[35]

In desperation, the CLE approached Raymond Quilter of the GQ Parachute Co. and on 30 July a conference was held involving Squadron Leader Ross Shore (now back with the PDF), Flight Lieutenant Bill Brereton and Raymond Quilter which concluded that no more live jumps should be carried out until 500 successful tests involving dummies had been carried out. The conference also decided there should be no more jumps from the rear gun turret using the pull-off method.

A few days later, Quilter produced a modified Irvin parachute fitted with a new type of canopy developed by Quilter's GQ company. The redesigned GQ parachute pack worked in a reverse sequence to the Irvin parachute. When the man jumped, the parachute pack containing the canopy and rigging lines was broken from his back by a series of progressively stronger ties and hung from the aircraft. As he fell, the rigging lines were dragged from this pack and by the time the canopy appeared, the man was the length of the rigging lines, about 20ft below the pack. A final tie, holding the apex of the canopy to the pack, then broke and the parachute was fully extended leaving the pack and static line attached to the aircraft. Quilter said that his factory could supply 500 modified Irvin parachutes with GQ canopies at a rate of 100 a week.

Later that same day, testing of the Irvin parachutes with the Quilter modifications took place with sandbag dummies.[36] The system functioned perfectly, with the parachutes deploying fully at heights as low as 100ft. It was seen immediately that this method of deployment was a considerable improvement as there was less opportunity for the rigging lines to become entangled with the canopy.

The re-start of Commando training was delayed by the lack of availability of the modified parachutes and the decision taken on 30 July 'that testing should continue with dummies'. Frustrated by yet more delays, Louis Strange looked for other options. He had seen the possibilities of using balloons as an alternative to aircraft in his early days in charge at Ringway. He had commented that one balloon could drop as many men in one hour, under training conditions, as three Whitley bombers. Another feature which he noticed was that the absence of slipstream reduced the tendency of the parachute to spin, which would in turn reduce the danger of landing injuries.

Strange visited the RAF Balloon Development Establishment (BDE) at Cardington on 1 August 1940, and examined an airship mooring mast and a 'W'-type observation balloon. Parachutes were despatched to Cardington the next day, and successful tests with sandbags were carried out. An order was then placed for a large passenger cage to be built, but this would take time. A more promising option seemed to be the opportunity to use unpowered gliders.

Group Captain Geoffrey Hilton 'Beery' Bowman, the Deputy Director of Combined Operations (Air), visited Ringway on 2 August to check on progress and to learn about the difficulties that were being encountered with jumps from the Whitleys. When Churchill read Bowman's report and that the current target was to train just 500 parachutists, Churchill was angry. On 6 August 1940, he scrawled on Bowman's report, 'I said 5000', and on 10 August, he requested further clarification from Pug Ismay. When told that the Air Ministry was promising that gliders might provide the increase in capacity, Churchill wrote: 'Of course, if the Glider scheme is better than parachutes, we should pursue it, but is it being seriously taken up? Are we not in danger of being fobbed off with one doubtful and experimental policy and losing the other which has already been proved? Let me have a full report of what has been done about the Gliders.'

Further tests of the Quilter parachutes were then carried out using dummies, but one of these came close to catastrophe when a parachute canopy became snagged on a Whitley's tail wheel, almost causing the aircraft to crash. This was due to excessive slipstream. In search of other options, a single Bristol Bombay[37] bomber arrived at Ringway on 6 August 1940 from 271 Squadron. Tests were then carried out using sandbag dummies from the side door of the aircraft.

On that same day that the Bombay arrived, a conference involving Ross Shore, Bruce Williams and Raymond Quilter recommended that the Quilter-modified parachutes could be used for live training again, provided that, in future, the Whitley's engines should be throttled back to an airspeed of less than 90 miles per hour. However, this recommendation required the endorsement of the Air Ministry.

Frustrated by what he perceived to be unjustified timidity, Louis Strange informed John Rock on 8 August 1940 that he intended to re-commence parachute training the next day. Rock stood firm and told Strange that he would not allow Army personnel to jump from the Whitley without a direct order from either his superior officer, Sir Roger Keyes, or the War Office. According to Strange's own account, he responded that 'it was not customary in the RAF to suspend training just because a man got killed'.

The War Office backed Rock's stand, but defiant as ever, on the very next day Strange led Jack Benham, Bruce Williams and three instructors jumping from a Bombay bomber to demonstrate their confidence in the modified parachutes. Other than as an act of defiance and bravado it is not clear what purpose Strange was hoping to achieve.

On 9 August the first of two Westland Lysander short take-off and landing aircraft arrived at Ringway to be used for the dropping of special agents into occupied Europe without the inconvenience of a parachute jump. On the same day a glider flight was created to continue experiments in dropping parachutists from unpowered aircraft. This was based on the German success with gliders against Belgian positions.

Desperate not to give up on parachuting, Louis Strange pressed the case for using balloons rather than Whitleys. He pointed out that the Germans, Russians and Americans had also perfected the art of using parachute towers for training. Proposals were made for the construction of a steelwork tower at Tatton in early 1941 to lower men from parachutes held open with wire, but after a local engineering firm quoted a cost of £30,000 for a 350ft (106m) tower, the idea was abandoned.

So, with no ready alternative and mounting concerns about the safety and reliability of the Whitley, priority was given to further experiments with gliders. Wing Commander 'Mungo' Buxton duly visited Ringway on 9 August, presumably to clarify matters with Strange. Following the visit, official authorization for a Glider Flight was given by the Air Ministry on 13 August 1940, and it was agreed that two Avro 504[38] biplanes of a type that had once hauled joyride glider flights for Alan Cobham would be delivered to Ringway by test pilots in few days' time.

When Louis Strange learned of this, he was furious, seeing this as a vote of no confidence in the parachute training regime and claiming that he had not been consulted (although Air Ministry records confirm that he was). According to Peter Hearn he had the test pilots arrested (Hearn, 1994).

There is no hint of this incident in the CLE Operational Log but Peter Hearn goes on to suggest that Strange had an understanding with John Rock that when they received contrary instructions from their respective Services, one would place the other under arrest so that the least constructive of the orders could be ignored. If this is true it seems a seriously dysfunctional way for senior officers to behave, even allowing for the unconcealed antipathy between the Army and RAF.

Whatever the truth of this account, the fact is that John Rock was given responsibility for establishing a glider capability and began a search for members of the armed forces who had pre-war experience of flying gliders, or who were interested in learning to do so. One of these was Squadron Leader Robert Kronfeld, an Austrian Jew who had been a very successful glider pilot before the war. The glider was to become a mainstay of the development of airborne forces at Ringway and was supported by the War Ministry who ordered 400 Hotspur gliders in September 1940. Gliders eventually provided transport for nearly a third of the airborne force infantry strength and were used successfully in the invasion of Sicily.[39]

Meanwhile, Louis Strange continued to press his case for the resumption of parachute training from the Whitleys. On 12 August he met with Sir Roger Keyes, Colonel Festing[40] and Air Commodore Capel.[41] However, Keyes refused the request until further modifications could be made to the aperture on the Whitley to reduce the risk of further accidents. In the meantime, seventy-seven descents were made from the Bombay bomber on 12 August with a further twenty-two the following day.

Possibly fearing Churchill's wrath, the War Office lifted the ban on the use of the Whitleys on 14 August 1940 and parachute training continued with thirty-four descents that day from the Bombay. On the same day Flight Lieutenant J.A. O'Neill and Pilot Officer E.J. Cutler flew a Whitley to Henlow so that further modifications could be made to the aperture. On 16 August test jumps were made from the modified Whitley using dummies, but there were now only two serviceable Whitleys and by 20 August it was clear to all that the modifications were not an improvement.

Strange's determination to drive on in the face of these obstacles has been treated with undisguised admiration by several respected historians and it is undoubtedly true that Strange's force of character and determination were remarkable. However, whether a 48-year-old with a disregard for practical realities (and rules) was really the right man for this role is questionable.

The uncomfortable fact was that although their grit and determination is not in doubt, Ringway was nowhere near ready to begin the training of large numbers of paratroops. It had too few aircraft and those that were available were largely unsuitable and unreliable. Their parachutes were largely unproven, and no way had been found for the men to jump with anything more substantial than a rifle. It was plain that a paratroop force that was confined to small groups of men scattered over a wide area with no defences other than Lee Enfield rifles was going to be of very limited military use.

To address the question of how and why the RAF officers at Ringway were allowed to act in this way it is necessary to consider two factors: firstly, the state of national emergency that existed in the summer of 1940 and the desire of all British servicemen – and particularly one as distinguished as Louis Strange – to 'do their bit'.

But secondly, and perhaps less admirably, the culture of the RAF in 1940 not only permitted, but actively fostered such behaviour.

The RAF General Duties (GD) Branch that was responsible for promotion within the RAF was composed almost entirely of pilots. At the junior officer level, they were not responsible for large numbers of men (as they were in the Army and Royal Navy), and consequently the RAF was still run more like a private flying club than a disciplined fighting force. Heavy drinking, high jinks and pranks were commonplace in the Mess among both officers and men. Brave and experienced as they were, it is questionable whether the showmen that were attracted to Ringway were of the right temperament for the roles allocated to them. The group did, however, form a tightly knit band of brothers who were not only very supportive of each other but also united, as one, in their disdain for the Air Ministry and their Army colleagues.

It must have been apparent even to Louis Strange that Churchill's directive was undeliverable and that to continue blindly would almost certainly result in further fatalities; but that is just what they did, and the next death was to occur less than two weeks later. The casualty was Stanley Watts,[42] a trooper who had served previously with the Royal Horse Guards. On 27 August he jumped from Whitley K7220 and was killed when his parachute failed to deploy fully.

Raymond Quilter was again called to look at the cause which he pinpointed to a fault in the way the parachute was secured with the pack. A solution was developed and incorporated into the GQ production line within two days and parachute training started up again: the train was unstoppable.

By 3 September 1940, the school had settled on a ten-week training syllabus, with the first four weeks devoted to weapons training, sabotage and map reading. Trainees then passed to Ringway for what was originally scheduled to be three weeks' parachute training. There was a week of ground training, followed by an aircraft jump from 800ft (243m). Week Two included two more jumps from 500ft (152m). The third week's training included two more aircraft jumps with equipment and weapons containers, first in sticks of four, and then in sticks of eight. Trainees then spent a further three weeks' tactical training at Tatton Park, which included at least one group descent. Thereafter the trainee was considered a fully-fledged parachutist.

However, by this stage, the Air Ministry had seen enough and decided that changes were needed. On 18 September, Group Captain Leslie 'Stiffey' Harvey[43] was placed in overall command, supported by Wing Commander Sir Nigel Norman. Louis Strange retained responsibility for parachute training, but with two seniors RAF officers now above him his wings had to some extent been clipped.

Additional personnel to flesh out the new organization continued to arrive including two new instructors, Harry Ward, and Bill Hire,[44] both of whom were former air circus showman. Bill Hire, who gave his occupation in the 1939 Register as 'professional parachutist and organizer of whist drives and dances', arrived on 31 October 1940. Harry Ward, who was well-known under the stage name 'the Yorkshire Birdman'. arrived on 27 November 1940.

A slightly more traditional appointee whose impact on the programme would be particularly significant was Squadron Leader Maurice Newnham DFC. Newnham, a gentleman farmer from Sussex, was appointed to a new role as Administrative Officer.

The new structure was as follows:

Central Landing Establishment (CLE)
Group Captain Leslie Harvey
Commander Sir Nigel Norman
Squadron Leader Maurice Newnham

Parachute Training Squadron
Squadron Leader Louis Strange
Squadron Leader Jack Benham

Flight Lieutenant Earl Fielden
Flight Lieutenant Boris Romanoff
Flying Officer David McMonnies
Pilot Officer Harry Ward
Pilot Office Bill Hire
Pilot Officer J. Cutler
Pilot Officer Tony O'Neill

Parachute Development Unit
Wing Commander M. Buxton
Flight Lieutenant Bruce Williams
Flying Officer D.B.S. Davie
Glider Training Squadron
Flying Officer H.E. Hervey
Flying Officer P.B.N. Davis
Flying Officer A.B. Wilkinson

However, the re-organization did nothing to reduce the number of accidents. Several recruits were injured when their parachutes fouled on the wheel housing of the Whitley. To address this problem the aircraft had to be taken out of service again, so spats could be fitted to the tail wheels.

Louis Strange managed to obtain two surplus Whitley fuselages from the Armstrong Whitworth works at Coventry on 11 September 1940, which allowed more realistic ground training, but this could not possibly make up for the lack of aircraft for live descents. There was an additional concern regarding aircraft serviceability. Out of the six Whitleys allocated to Ringway there were rarely more than five in serviceable condition at any one time, and obtaining spare parts for the engines was becoming increasingly difficult as time went on.

The third death in training from a Whitley occurred on 19 November, when 25-year-old Corporal Hugh John Carter of No. 2 Commando was killed. Carter came from a well-connected family in

Monmouthshire where his uncle served as High Sherrif. He was killed when the snap-hook on the static-line connecting his parachute to the aircraft caught on the raised border around the Whitley's aperture. Carter had no chance. The accident was witnessed by the former actress and nurse Cicely Paget-Bowman,[45] one of the many remarkable women who served as ambulance driver at Tatton Park. She gave this account of what happened that day:

> It was a routine drop of a stick of men from one of the Whitleys. The last man came out and I thought, 'Oh, they've dropped the overcoats', because they did sometimes drop them separately. Suddenly I saw two hands coming out to feel for the rigging, but it wasn't there — the parachute had failed to open. Everyone, absolutely everyone, was shocked; what had gone wrong was that the bar to which the parachutes were attached had broken. And all they had to do was to put an ordinary dog leash clip on that bar from then on. It was dreadful. Although the troops were pretty shaken, they were so young and keen that they managed to throw it off.

Following the accident, the Parachute Development Unit (PDU) began an investigation and by 27 November 1940 a locking safety pin for the snap-hook had been designed, tested and released for general use.

By 27 November, the cages necessary to enable men to be dropped from tethered balloons were ready and Harry Ward was despatched to Cardington to test the prototype. He was favourably impressed: 'it was a lovely sensation! Real fair-ground stuff. No slipstream to cause malfunctions. Less chance of twisted [rigging] lines. Less likelihood of bloody noses. Better observation of pupils' performance. Definitely, a winner' (Hearn, 1990).

However, Maurice Newnham gave a rather different report: 'The cage was really a pretty dreadful affair and Harry Ward and Captain

Elliot, described the experience as very alarming. This may have been partly due to the novelty of the whole thing, but in each case the parachute did not fully open until after four seconds or about 200ft from the ground. They added that the delayed opening produces an additional thrill' (Newnham, 1946).

Jumping from an aeroplane was a busy and noisy experience and there was always lots to distract the trainees from the thought of the impending jump. From a balloon, it was a case of clinging desperately to handles to avoid falling through the gaping hole, listening to the grind of the winch and the silence when the noise suddenly stopped. This produced a feeling of exposure and apprehension unlike anything experienced in an aircraft. The balloon was never popular, and it was given the nickname 'Bessie the foul and loathsome sausage', but as Maurice Newnham commented later: 'cramped and rickety though the cage beneath the balloon was, Bessie would prove to be a very useful training tool and would soon be joined by others like her'.

Settling into his new role, Group Captain Harvey attempted to bring some strategic thinking into the Ringway operation and in a document produced on 31 October 1940 he set out thoughts about the possible functions for a paratroop force:

1. Immobilization of large numbers of enemy troops 'in dispositions unfavourable to their strategy'.
2. Form the spearhead for offensive action with a range of 500 miles from a suitable airfield.
3. Operate as a self-contained force for small, localised action capable of being supplied by air.
4. Utilised for 'planting' of saboteurs, agents and other irregular troops in enemy territories.

Harvey believed that 500 fully-trained parachute troops could be available by March 1941, and that 1,000 lightly equipped glider-borne troops could be ready by September 1941. He further predicted that an airborne force exceeding 3,000 could be made available 'by concentrated effort' by May 1942. This was still some way short of Churchill's original objective.

There was another problem, the morale of the Ringway staff was being affected by the fact that the men whom they had trained had not yet been deployed on any military operation. In order to validate their efforts – and the injuries and loss of life incurred – the officers at Ringway were in desperate need of a successful airborne operation to demonstrate that this new force merited the investment that had been made in it.

The answer appeared to come with a proposal for an audacious airborne operation in Southern Italy. It was an operation which would also come to the attention of Air Gunner 89642 Agate, still kicking his heels, waiting for a posting.

Chapter 9

The First Airborne Assault

The target for an airborne operation in south-east Italy had first been suggested by Professor Colin Hardie of Magdalen College Oxford eight months earlier in a letter to the Special Operations Executive (SOE) declaring: 'The water supply of the whole area of Southeast Italy . . . is derived from one aqueduct, the Aqueduct Pugliese. If that aqueduct, snaking through Italy's Apennine Mountains, could be severed, two to three million people and two vital naval bases, Taranto and Brindisi, would be starved of water.' It was just the sort of daring plan that Churchill had been looking for. By December 1940, the scheme had acquired official status and the designation 'Water Project: Southern Italy, code-named Project T – for Tragino'.

In January 1941, eight of the more experienced Whitley crews – four from 51 Squadron and four from 78 Squadron – were sent to Ringway to practice paratroop dropping. A request was made for Army volunteers to join the raiding force, and every member of No.2 Commando stepped forward. Thirty-eight of these were then selected and given the designation: X Troop. General Sir John Dill,[46] Chief of the Imperial General Staff (CIGS), then visited Ringway to inspect the volunteers.

The mission was designed to showcase the ability of the RAF to deliver men and equipment accurately. It was then re-branded as Operation Colossus and was to be the very first British airborne raid. Anthony Deane-Drummond who was one of the officers selected for X Troop wrote: 'Our excitement can be imagined, and we all congratulated ourselves on our good fortune in having been chosen for the job from the whole Commando.'

However, on 22 January the high morale of X Troop would be hit by another death. Bombardier William Alfred Dennis[47] from Hornchurch landed in the ice-covered Rostherne Mere and despite being a strong swimmer, he was unable to extricate himself from his parachute lines and drowned. He was just 21.

This time though there would be no pause in the preparations and no enquiry. An Italian civilian, Fortunato Picchi, a 45-year-old who worked as head waiter at the Savoy Hotel, was chosen to accompany the party as interpreter. He had only become a British citizen in 1941 and had been interned as an enemy alien in the Great War, but he had impressed Military Intelligence by his anti-fascist views and his willingness to join the British war effort. He knew full well that if he was captured he would be deemed a traitor and would face certain death.

By 1 February the raiding party had completed their training and they then departed for Mildenhall where they were informed that they were to fly directly to Malta and from there, be dropped into Southern Italy. Wing Commander Nigel Norman went on ahead of the party in a Short Sunderland,[48] but joined Whitley T4235 piloted by Bruce Williams, for the raid.

At 21:42 on 10 February 1941, Deane-Drummond and his stick of troops flew in Whitley (T4165)[49] piloted by Squadron Leader Wally Lashbook. They were dropped just 100 yards from the aqueduct, but Lance-Corporal Harry Boulter had landed badly, crashing into a large boulder and breaking his ankle. Once on the ground, they found themselves alone. Deane-Drummond directed his men to search and secure the nearby farm buildings. The men then strained their eyes for any sign of the other parachutists until they saw Major 'Tag' Pritchard. He explained that his Whitley P5015[50] – the aircraft piloted by Wing Commander Tait – had dropped its party a mile downstream.

Another Whitley (T4215) was still missing and crucially, it was carrying Captain Gerald Daly, of the Royal Engineers, with the sappers who were the demolitions experts. The pilot of their Whitley was running late and had not realized that his men had jumped in the wrong place. It was 40 minutes before they were able to join up with Deane-Drummond and Tag Pritchard.

When all available men had mustered, Deane-Drummond's men formed one of the three covering parties for the demolition team. He acquired some explosives and received permission to move on the viaduct. Pritchard paused to take stock. He had only twenty-six men and one was injured, far short of the thirty-two required. Worse still, only a third of the charge of 2,240lb of explosives was dropped. They also discovered that the piers were made of reinforced concrete, not brick as they had been told. Their only hope was to concentrate all their charges on one pier.

The demolition party laid the explosives and took shelter nearby. After the dust had settled it appeared that half the aqueduct was down, the target pier having completely disintegrated, while a second lay at an angle. X Troop were then divided into three parties to make their way independently to the coast where a submarine, HMS *Triumph*, would be waiting to collect them.

Deane-Drummond and Major Pritchard soon discovered that the ambitious plan of marching 50 miles across mountainous terrain in wintry conditions had been made much worse by the thick mud. On reaching the snowline they encountered several ravines and had to make wide detours, and so by dawn the two officers were discouraged to discover that they had only advanced three miles. They set off again at dusk but found the going no easier. Realizing that they were never going to reach the submarine, Pritchard ordered the men on to the seemingly deserted road below, but they were spotted and before long a group of carabinieri and mountain troops approached their position. The paratroops prepared themselves for a defence, but with the advancing

Italians came a number of curious civilians. Pritchard agonized over the situation, but eventually ordered his men to lay down their arms. Deane-Drummond wrote later: 'I have never felt so ashamed before or since, that we should have surrendered to a lot of practically unarmed Italian peasants.'

Shackled together with a long chain, the party was made to march to Teora, accompanied by the shouts of angry civilians, threatening to lynch them, but the carabinieri formed a protective cordon before locking them up. They were later taken to Calitri railway station, and then to the prison at Naples where they were interrogated first by the Italians and later by the Germans. Fortunato Picchi was taken away from the other POWs, tried, found guilty of treason, and shot on 6 April.

An RAF reconnaissance aircraft that took photos gave the misleading impression the aqueduct was still intact, and Operation Colossus was duly reported to London as being a failure, and those in command concluding that the raiders must have been captured before they could reach the target. As a result, the submarine was recalled from her mission to rescue the raiders.

On the evening of 12 February 1941, the Italian authorities gloated over the failure of the raid and the capture of the men, forcing the Ministry of Information to confirm the bare details of Operation Colossus. The British forces, under the Prime Minister's unrealistic urgings, had overreached themselves. When news of Operation Colossus was reported in the British press *The Times* presented the troops as martyrs to the British war effort: 'The landing of British parachutists in a lonely part of south Italy, has caused great surprise at the daring of the whole enterprise and at the high spirit of sacrifice on the part of those engaged; for as far as one can guess escape is virtually impossible.'

However, back at Ringway, the men and women were not defeated. They argued that Colossus was a strategic success because it demonstrated to the Germans and Italians that the British had an airborne capability. Lessons were also learned which helped shape future airborne operations. It demonstrated the range and flexibility of airborne troops and proved that they could pose a powerful threat.

In terms of technical experience, it was found that the containers used to drop equipment for the troops, which were manufactured from a soft-skinned material which sagged during flight, blocked the bomb bay doors from opening. In future, containers were constructed from metal. Consideration was also given to the cause of the delay between the parachutist landing and locating weapons. As a result, research and development into improving the carrying capacity of parachutes became a primary focus for Ringway throughout the rest of the war.

Maurice Newnham reflected in 1947 that 'the brief excitement of the Italian Raid soon passed away' (p. 34). He was left wondering: 'What did the "high ups" think of the first airborne experiment? Were they impressed by the potential it offered? Would our own confidence be shared' (p. 30).

For several more months Newnham and his staff would have to 'work and wait and wonder' (p. 30). However, when a 35-year-old RAF Pilot Officer and former Surrey P.E. teacher heard of the daring parachute operation he knew that this was precisely the kind of adventure he had been looking for.

PART TWO

Agate at Ringway and Tatton Park

Chapter 10

Agate Arrives at Ringway

Operation Colossus did little to allay the concerns of the Air Ministry that the airborne forces experiment at Ringway was no more than a distraction from more pressing priorities. An airborne force is an invading force and in 1940 Britain was in no place to invade anywhere. Maurice Newnham wrote later that the Tragino raid had left No. 2 Commando 'weaker by fifty keen and gallant men' (Newnham, 1946).

Newnham was also concerned about the number of fatalities and serious injuries that were being experienced by the trainees. As he put it later, the parachute was about 'as capricious a vehicle as could be imagined' (Newnham, 1946, p. 100) and 'no clear instructions seem to have been given as to what should be done after a parachute had opened' (ibid, p. 14).

The truth was that the school had not developed any scientific techniques for jumping or landing, and success or failure still depended on the skill, fitness or sheer acrobatic ability of the trainees. On top of all that, the death of Bombardier William Dennis in the ice-covered lake at Tatton had demonstrated that winter was a bad time to train parachutists. It was clear that more testing was required, but the men of Ringway pressed on.

On 1 February 1941, Flight Lieutenant John Baptist Keast arrived at Ringway with seven crew in Whitley T4264. They stayed for the next three days, to receive training in the dropping of paratroops. Keast and his crew had been tasked by Sir Charles Portal, the Chief of the Air Staff, to assassinate the pilots and aircrews of the Luftwaffe's KG 100 who were using radio beams to hit targets in Coventry under the cover of cloud. The plan was for a small team of Free French agents to be dropped near the Luftwaffe base at Meucon, in southern Brittany. The Luftwaffe medium and heavy bomber wing (KG100) pilots had been reported as using a bus to carry them to their billets in the nearby town of Vannes. The plan was to ambush the bus and kill the aircrew inside.

Although he must have sanctioned the raid, Air Marshal Portal was unhappy about the use of his aircraft and crews:

> I think that the dropping of men dressed in civilian clothes for the purpose of attempting to kill members of the opposing forces is not an operation with which the Royal Air Force should be associated. I think you will agree that there is a vast difference, in ethics, between the time-honoured operation of dropping of a spy from the air and this entirely new scheme for dropping what one can only call assassins.

Portal also made his opinions clear in a meeting with Colonel Colin Gubbins that soldiers in uniform were allowed to kill enemy forces in uniform, but soldiers in civilian clothes were not. Gubbins pointed out that there was no room in the containers for uniforms to enable the agents to change into uniform, and in any case the agents might refuse to go on these terms. They knew that their Free French uniforms would guarantee their execution if they were captured. As Frenchmen in civilian clothes, they might at least stand a chance of melting into the background.

The raid went ahead but having parachuted into France the raiders discovered that the pilots no longer travelled between Vannes and Meucon by bus but had taken to travelling by cars. The ambush had to be aborted.

On 3 March 1941, General Charles de Gaulle, Commander-in-Chief of the Free French forces, visited Ringway and inspected the training regime that the French troops were undergoing there. Here was an opportunity to impress. After a demonstration of every aspect of the ground training, de Gaulle's party were taken to Tatton Park where four sub-sections were dropped. This was the first time that a mass drop had been attempted in front of important spectators, but the demonstration passed off successfully.

As Newnham and Strange lobbied for more personnel, another request was issued for RAF volunteer instructors. Charles Agate saw the memo asking, as he remembered it later, for: 'Somebody to do some experimental parachuting.' This was an opportunity he was not going to miss.

With so much on his mind, however, Newnham was not overjoyed to hear an unexpected knock on his office door early one morning in March 1941. He described this moment in *Prelude to Glory*:

Charles Agate walked into my office at the Headquarters of the Central Landing Establishment. I had received no notification that he was coming and, as it is a Service custom to be terse with people who just arrive without notice, I asked him what he wanted without showing much enthusiasm. He replied that he had been sent to Ringway to learn parachuting, adding that he had read about the raid in Italy and the idea appealed to him. His cheerful grin commended him to me, so I asked him to tell me more about himself and what he expected to do. It appeared that he was a Surrey school teacher who had volunteered for duty as air-gunner (Newnham, 1946).

Newnham phoned Louis Strange at the Parachute School explaining the position and adding that Agate would be coming across to see him.

It wasn't just Agate's cheerful grin which persuaded Newnham not to kick him out of the door that day. He acknowledges in *Prelude to Glory* that 'RAF instructional staff had been largely selected from men who were connected to the teaching profession in peacetime' (Newnham, 1946, p. 147) and he actively sought to attract teachers like Agate to the school. Newnham always maintained that British PJIs were better than the Americans, whom he describes as being selected more for their 'personality and physique' (Newnham, 1946, p. 255) than their ability to teach young recruits.

Agate walked confidently over to the office of Louis Strange who was still smarting from his perceived reduction in status following the arrival of 'Stiffy' Harvey and Nigel Norman. Agate took up the story in his BBC radio interview in 1974: 'Squadron Leader Strange asked me a few questions and then passed me over to Harry Ward with the instruction that I was to be taught parachuting.'

So it was that within less than an hour, that cheerful grin had got Agate from Group Captain Maurice Newnham to Squadron Leader Louis Strange, and thence into the hands of the 'Yorkshire Birdman' himself, Harry Ward. Things moved fast from that point onwards: 'Ward gave me a quizzical glance and said, "you're in luck – we're doing some dropping this morning". I was wearing my best uniform, but nevertheless was sent off to have a parachute fitted.'

Ward fitted the newcomer with an X-type parachute and went with him to board a Whitley. On board were two Poles, and an English soldier. Agate's first jump would be by what Ward called 'the deep end method' as he would later explain: 'There's only one way to find out if a man is going to make a parachutist, and that is to take him up to 2000ft and push him out' (Hearn, 1990, p. 72).

Agate described what happened next:

I had my best blue on and just an ordinary pair of shoes. They had removed the rear gun turret of the Whitley bomber and put a little platform there with a rail. It was the very first time that I had been in an aeroplane. Harry Ward just turned to me and he said, 'You're the only one in the RAF, so you better go first.'

I had to struggle through the fuselage of the aircraft, stand on the platform, holding the rail. Remember, you've got the two big engines with their slipstream blowing your eyelashes into your eye and making you cry. You couldn't help it. You stood outside the rail and just held the ripcord.

I was really frightened, and it was only because the fear of being thought a coward was slightly greater than the fear of jumping that I forced my trembling body through that awful hole at the rear of the aircraft. Fortunately, there was practically no wind, and a cheerful sun inspired a little confidence. Then, when Harry Ward looked through, we were over the smooth piece of ground at Tatton Park. He just put his thumb up and I pulled the ripcord. There was this sudden jerk. I was ripped off the aeroplane and saw it disappearing behind me.

Even allowing for the well-established unconventional behaviour of Louis Strange and Harry Ward, this was an odd way to welcome a new RAF officer volunteer to Ringway. The school had already abandoned the pull-off method from the rear gun turret of a Whitley because of the dangers involved, so why did Ward insist that Agate's very first jump should be made using this treacherous method without any prior training?

It is also questionable why he was not given the opportunity to change out of his RAF 'blues' and into the normal protective boiler suit, helmet and boots that were provided to other trainees. It was a reckless and not to say sadistic initiation meted out by Harry Ward to the new recruit. Whether this was due to a malevolent streak, a desire to put this good-looking, well-educated but naïve schoolteacher in his place, or a more innocent and genuine belief in baptisms of fire, we will never know.

However, the fact that Agate emerged smiling from this ordeal is testament to his bravery and determination to make a go of this new opportunity. As he recalled:

After a perfectly frightful moment of unadulterated fear, I realised that the parachute had opened and that I was floating smoothly down to earth. As I approached the ground, I suppose my physical training experience came to my aid and made me prepare for the impact.

Do you know that from my first parachute jump to my last parachute jump I never believed I was coming down. You look at the ground and you always think the ground is coming up to you in waves. Well, I had a lovely soft landing and I suddenly thought to myself, well, this is more than strange because the very first aeroplane I've got in, I have not landed in. And that was my introduction to parachuting. That was my first jump.

And from that point, he never looked back. Charles Agate was hooked, and he was in his element. For an idea of just how easily he took to jumping out of balloons and planes, we have the words of Maurice Newnham: 'When it was necessary for him to get from the airfield to the dropping ground, he thought it as natural to slip on a parachute and get in an aircraft as a city man does to pick up his umbrella and get on a tube train.'

Chapter 11

Agate Becomes a Parachute Training Instructor (PTI)

One of the first problems facing Agate following his arrival at RAF Ringway was that he had nowhere to live. Accommodation on the aerodrome was extremely limited and most of the commissioned officers lived off-site in shared rooms in Knutsford, or in the villages around Ringway. His daughter Lynette described her father as 'a bit of a loner', and this might explain why he rejected the offer of a place in shared accommodation and why he did not follow the example of Harry Ward who lived in a cottage belonging to the actor and radio presenter Wilfred Pickles.

Instead, Agate brought the family's 1934 Eccles caravan up from Surrey and installed it underneath some trees at Tatton Park. It was in this caravan that he, Marjorie and Lynette had enjoyed holidays before the war. For company, he acquired an Alsatian dog who he named 'Pat'.

For Lord Egerton to agree to this must have taken all of Agate's charm as one of Egerton's many 'rules' was that there should absolutely be no dogs on the estate. Somehow, Agate got away with it, and letters between Agate and Egerton kept in the Cheshire Archives show that they built up a healthy respect for each other, provided of course that Agate never forgot to address Egerton as 'My Lord'.

For nearly five years, it was to his caravan that Agate would retire at the end of a long day. Agate was never a great socialiser and was not a regular attendee at the film shows, lectures and live entertainments at the base. He was, however, particularly drawn to some of the remarkable members of the clergy of different denominations on site at the time. These included the Roman Catholic, Reverend Bernard Egan[51] who became the first chaplain to obtain his wings, and the Methodist Chaplain Robert Talbot-Watkins who became one of the first padres to parachute. Talbot-Watkins subsequently led a stick of parachutists to bolster morale after four of their colleagues were killed in training. Agate also looked up to Father Joseph O'Mahoney, a local Roman Catholic priest in the Manchester area, who he later described as 'a saint', before carefully adding the rider, 'even though I'm Church of England myself'.

Another man that Agate admired and spent his leisure time with was Flying Officer Bernard Winfield,[52] who Agate always referred to affectionately as 'The Doc'. Winfield held the post of Medical Officer at Ringway, but his influence stretched beyond that role. It was Winfield who had so forthrightly expressed his concerns about the quality of the No. 2 Commando troops in the previous summer.

His older brother Roland Henry Winfield was Medical Officer with Bomber Command. The experimental work of the Winfield brothers into the effects of drugs on aircrew and parachutists, would have a profound and long-term effect on Charles Agate himself.

In his book, the respected historian W. D. Buckingham commented about the social tensions at Ringway and 'empire building, patronage and the shabby treatment of dedicated and courageous men who did not fit into their superiors' vision for the CLE' (Buckingham, 2001, p. 208). Harry Ward himself commented after the war that he and Bill Hire felt 'socially unacceptable to Newnham', and Agate, with his lower middle-class upbringing in Redhill may have felt something similar. The fact is that men like Norman, Newnham, Strange and Quilter came from landowning families who would never previously have mixed with some of the men with whom they served. It is striking in *Prelude to Glory* how often Newnham refers to him simply as 'Agate' whilst routinely according rank and first name to those he considered to be his social equal, even when they held the same rank as Agate.

Despite these possible differences, by the spring of 1941, Charles Agate had completed a short training programme, perfected to his own satisfaction this new skill and had begun to earn the full respect of Newnham and his colleagues for his cheerful demeanour, bravery and willingness to volunteer for anything.

Less than four weeks after Agate arrived at Ringway, a motorcade led by police motorcycles arrived at Ringway on the morning of 26 April 1941. The motorcycles were followed by six cars which drove slowly between soldiers and airmen who formed a ceremonial guard of honour. Prime Minister Winston Churchill and his wife Clementine were paying a visit to RAF Ringway. He was accompanied by Ismay and Air Marshal Sir Arthur Barratt, commander of RAF Army Co-operation Command and Averell Harriman,[53] an American businessman who would later serve as President Franklin D. Roosevelt's a special envoy to Europe. The purpose of the visit was to see how things had been progressing since Churchill's memo calling for the creation of a body of 5,000 paratroops.

It was a windy day and Strange and Newnham recalled Group Captain Harvey murmuring: 'It's no good worrying. There's nothing we can do about it. The wind won't stop blowing – even for Winston.' For the staff at RAF Ringway, it was an important moment – the military situation was grave – and vital decisions were about to be made which might well affect the future of the school. The value of the months of work at Ringway was to be put to the test and the lack of personnel, aircraft and equipment could not be easily disguised.

There were only five Whitley bombers available for the demonstration. Newnham and his colleagues were well aware that if the demonstration was not successful the whole idea might be abandoned. All the stops would need to be pulled out for the Prime Minister's visit, and Charles Agate, still a relative novice, would of course be taking part.

Around 400 paratroops were drawn up for inspection by the Prime Minister, including a considerable number of Free French trainees.

Demonstrations of ground training and special airborne equipment were arranged in the CLE's two hangars. Six camouflaged Kirby Kite sport gliders and the first production eight-seat Hotspur were trucked in from the Glider Training School.

The crowning effort was to be a mock assault on Ringway's control tower, with a mass drop by forty-four paratroops using all five of the CLE's serviceable Whitley's. Louis Strange indulged in some stage management. He concealed a further hundred troops amongst trees on the parachute dropping zone with orders that they should emerge simultaneously to make the attackers appear more numerous. He also made a private arrangement with the chief flying instructor, and now Flight Lieutenant Earl Fielden, to carry on even if the wind remained above the official safety limit until Strange signalled otherwise.

Away in a far corner of the airfield Charles Agate, with only a handful of jumps in his logbook, was waiting with his forty or so colleagues in the Whitley bombers, but the windspeed was so strong that Strange had no option but to delay their take-off. This meant that the men were obliged to spend a long period in dark, cramped positions of the fuselage of the Whitleys. When the wind dropped a little, Wing Commander Nigel Norman asked the Prime Minister's permission to carry on. Churchill nodded and Norman turned to his microphone: 'Hallo, formation leader-this is Wing Commander Norman calling. Are you ready to take off? Over to you'.

There was a moment's pause and then the reply came back loud enough for all, including the Prime Minister, to hear: 'No, I'm not ready to take off—five of the blighters have fainted.'

The soldiers who had fainted were removed and the five old Whitley bombers came roaring across the aerodrome and lumbered slowly into the air. While the aircraft were making formation and flying their course preparing for the run-in, Louis Strange used the time to set out his views and his confidence in the Ringway operation. This was just the opportunity he had been wanting and he made the most of it.

The demonstration concluded without mishap and in an interview with journalist John Walsh in 1970, Agate recalled how Churchill then made his way over to the officers' mess to chat to him and some of the other instructors. Newnham subsequently described Churchill's visit to the mess as key to the favourable impression Churchill took away from his visit to Ringway: 'The personality and character of the men of RAF Ringway brooked no discouragement or failure, and it may well have been from that the Prime Minister's own opinion and confidence gained strength as much from the personal contacts he made during his visit as from any other cause' (Newnham, 1946). Churchill was subjected to a good deal of 'sales talk' from the CLE staff in between demonstrations, and Air Marshal Arthur 'Ugly' Barratt '. . . showed some apprehension as to what amount of line-shooting was going off. It is unfortunate that the Prime Minister in his visit to the CLE apparently only received the possibly one-sided view of the local enthusiasts' (Air Ministry AIR 2/7470, 1941).

Despite Churchill's warm engagement with Louis Strange and the instructors, he was less than impressed by what else he saw. He had gone to Ringway expecting to see something approaching a fully functioning airborne force. Instead, after almost a year, he was presented with a partially trained force which numbered less than a tenth of his original requirement, and a glider force consisting of six civilian sport machines and a single purpose-designed one which could carry six men. It was patently obvious that beneath the brave show, the training establishment was struggling to maintain even the present level of development.

On 28 April 1940 Churchill passed another demand to Ismay:

Let me have this day the minute which I wrote in the summer of last year directing that 5,000 Parachute Troops were to be prepared, together with all the minutes of the departments concerned which led to my afterwards agreeing to reduce the number to 500. I shall expect to receive the office files by midnight. Let me have all the present proposals for increasing the Parachute and Glider force together with a timetable of expected results.

Four weeks later he wrote:

This is a sad story, and I feel myself greatly to blame for allowing myself to be overborne by the resistance which was offered. One can see how wrongly based these resistances were when we read paragraph 6 of the Air Staff paper in light of what is happening in Crete and may be soon happening in Cyprus and in Syria. See also my minute on gliders. This is exactly what has happened. The gliders have been produced on the smallest possible scale, and so we have practically now neither parachutists nor the gliders except these 500. Thus, we are always behind-hand the enemy. We ought to have 5,000 parachutists and an Air-borne division on the German model, with any improvements which might suggest themselves from experience. These will all be necessary in the Mediterranean fighting of 1942, or earlier if possible. A whole year has been lost, and I now invite the Chiefs of Staff, so far as is possible, to repair the misfortune.

This time, however, there could be no excuse for mistaking Churchill's ire and impatience. In the weeks and months following Churchill's visit, the Air Ministry and the War Office began moving towards a consensus about what needed to be done, but before then, there were a few things to be ironed out, and one of those problems was the Whitley bomber.

The PTS still had only a maximum of six aircraft and often no more than two or three of these were available for training. However, the RAF had few Whitleys to spare as Bomber Command geared up for its planned bombing operations on German cities. On I June 1941, the school took delivery of an old Whitley Mark III (K8991) which was due to be broken up so that the fuselage could be used for ground training. However, on inspection at Ringway the aircraft was found to be airworthy. As a result, Group Captain Harvey requested permission to exchange it for one of the CLE's original aircraft, which had recently been damaged in a crash. In the process he highlighted the irony '. . . that a ground training machine is in far better condition than the ones used on flying training'. It was a measure of how desperate the situation was.

The Whitley was awkward and uncomfortable for the troops. The door was too small to allow men to pass through it quickly when wearing parachutes and equipment. The cramped interior of the fuselage which the men had to crawl through on their hands and knees was dark, draughty, and smelly. The exit hole was nearly 3ft deep, and it was absolutely vital for the parachutists to maintain a perfectly upright and rigid position to avoid bashing their faces on the opposite side.

This was the dreaded 'Whitley Kiss', otherwise known as 'ringing the bell', when the jumper smashed his face on the edge of the hole, sometimes with serious consequences, as Charles Agate explained in 1974 to the BBC's Don Durbridge:

> You had a big parachute on your back, and you've got to pitch yourself through the middle of the hole. If your parachute caught the back of the hole, you would smash your face and nose against the other side. The hole can also turn you into a nasty upside-down position, which could be dangerous, because it could catch the rigging lines.

It was clear that still more modifications were required to be made to the Whitley, particularly to enable these aircraft to drop large items of equipment that could not fit through the 3ft aperture. All of these changes would have to be tested in 'live' conditions. It would fall to Agate and his colleagues to carry out those tests.

Chapter 12

Testing Times

By April 1941, the British airborne infrastructure was in a paradoxical position. Despite all the enthusiasm and hard work of the personnel, little progress had been made. The CLE remained dependent on a handful of unsuitable and unreliable aircraft, which placed severe limitations upon the work. This problem was exacerbated by issues with the reliability of the X-type parachutes used and the lack of suitable qualified parachute instructors. Something clearly had to change . . .

Since the arrival of Harvey and Newnham, the lines of communication linking the CLE to the rest of the RAF were finally functioning properly and having changed the command structure was Nigel Norman now in a position to make more radical changes. Harvey and Norman did not approve of Louis Strange's unorthodox methods, and Harvey arranged for Strange to be posted to the Merchant Shipping Fighter Unit (MFSU) at RAF Speke on 12 May 1941. The unit had only been formed in the previous week and its role was to provide pilots, crew and support personnel and aircraft to thirty-five merchant ships that had been fitted with a catapult on the bow, capable of launching a converted Hawker Hurricane.

Strange does not appear to have argued the matter, possibly because he was expecting it, as the following quote from his biography suggests: 'He [Wing Commander Nigel Norman] used to say to me "You'd better look out Louis . . . you will go at it bald headed. It attracts too much attention, and you'll find someone taking a pot at you one of these fine days"'.

Strange's immediate successor was Squadron Leader Jack Benham who officially assumed command of the PTS on 5 June 1941. However, Bentham only lasted two weeks before he was transferred to India to help set up a parachute school there.[54]

This was not the only change that Harvey had in mind. He made no secret that he considered that all the pilots at Ringway had been there too long and had become too comfortable and complacent. There was nothing wrong with their flying skills and the RAF could make better use of them in more demanding roles. He commented in a letter to No.70 Group on 15 July 1941: 'The whole Squadron still suffers from the bad effects. Replacing them would do the CLE the power of good and give over five pilots to the war effort who were young enough to be re-trained.'

He referred to Earl Fielden, the former Flying Circus pilot as 'an old gentleman incapable of giving an order', and he decided that he should be moved on, along with Boris Romanoff, David MacMonnies,[55] Bill Hire, Bruce Williams and Harry Ward. Romanoff, Williams and McMonnies were posted to operational squadrons, but Harry Ward was posted further out of harm's way to Iraq, before he managed to secure a position as Air Liaison Officer to HQ 1st Airborne Division at Netheravon. Bill Hire was also posted to Netheravon. The purge had been completed and Harvey's mission to 'create a sober and sensible school took a huge leap forward'.

The primary 'executioner' in this clear-out was Maurice Newnham who was promoted to Squadron Leader and head of the CLE. Newnham had not made a parachute jump prior to his original posting, but he soon put that right. His initiation was not unsimilar to Agate's a couple of months earlier. He was given 'five minutes verbal coaching by Bill Hire, who lent me his plimsoles' (Newnham, 1946, p. 46) and out he went.

Newnham was perhaps a curious appointment. He had no practical experience for the job and had been posted to Ringway originally as the

Administrative Officer. However, Harvey clearly saw him as a safe pair of hands capable of restoring the order and discipline that had become just too lax.

From then on Newnham set out to 'debunk the myths about parachuting', and he understood that Charles Agate was one of the men who could help him do just that. Newnham realized that Agate was brave, charismatic and likeable. He knew that Ringway had found a gem. Agate would go on to work closely with Newnham, and despite one or two fallings out, they retained mutual respect for the rest of the war.

Agate took part in what Newnham himself later referred to as a 'campaign of propaganda' (Newnham, 1946, p. 35) – where 'performing guinea pigs' (ibid, p. 37) aimed to raise support for the school through demonstrations in front of the likes of Alan Brooke, Montgomery and even the Kings of England and Norway. Most of those events were also designed to show that the British Army had been re-formed after Dunkirk; the paratroop aspects were primarily to add colour and spectacle. It may also have helped Newnham's propaganda campaign that people remarked that Charles Agate looked a bit like David Niven, and this may have been why around this time he grew a thin pencil moustache to make himself look even more like the great actor. Charles Agate was finally part of a flying circus!

Meanwhile the search for alternative aircraft continued. Nigel Norman had inspected the Stirling[56] at Shorts' factory and then the Avro Manchester,[57] Avro Lancaster[58] and the Handley Page Halifax.[59] His findings were not encouraging. The Stirling was considered the 'least promising', and the Manchester and Lancaster were deemed to have prohibitively high stalling speeds for dropping parachutists.

However, some hope was retained regarding the Halifax. It had six large wing cells, which were ideal for carrying containers, and the four-engines allowed the pilot to minimize the slipstream by throttling back the inboard engines. The manufacturer had offered to provide a wooden mock-up fuselage for troop trials and short of other options, this offer was accepted.

Considerable modifications (including the re-positioning of gun turrets, bomb racks and ammunition stowage) were then made so that it could be evaluated further. In his early weeks at Ringway, Agate, and his fellow instructor Sergeant 'Jock' Husband carried out experimental live descents from both the Halifax and the Manchester, though they reported that the aperture for exiting the aircraft on the Manchester was even smaller and more challenging than that of the Whitley. Three of the six instructors turned somersaults in the vicious slipstream and a halt was called to these experiments.

The Air Ministry granted permission for Ringway to investigate the suitability of the Vickers Wellington as a backup parachute transport and a single example was allotted to the CLE for tests. A detailed report on the suitability of the Wellington concluded that it might be suitable for parachuting with modifications similar to those on the Whitley. It was noted that the roomier and lighter fuselage might be better for troop morale. On 23 September 1941, dummies were dropped from the Wellington, and trial jump tests were undertaken later by Agate and the other instructors. They reported back that the Wellington was satisfactory, but the unfortunate fact was that the aircraft was also one of the mainstays of Bomber Command and Churchill had been promoting the bomber offensive against Germany with even more enthusiasm than he exhibited for airborne forces. It was inevitable that the needs of Bomber Command would be given priority.

Harvey was resigned to having to make do with the Whitley, but he demanded more aircraft with twelve Mark II or nine Mark V Whitleys considered the absolute minimum. His forthright approach had the desired effect. On 8 October, the RAF Army Co-operation Command agreed to increase Ringway's complement of Whitleys to twelve Mark V machines by October 1941. This was not quite the end of the matter, for Ringway subsequently discovered that some of the new Whitleys had not been modified for parachuting, and the factory-fitted modifications for parachuting had been removed on others. This required eight hours' remedial work per machine.

The Armstrong Whitworth Albemarle[60] and Lockheed Hudson[61] were also examined with a view to assessing their suitability for paratroop dropping. A Hudson III was delivered to Ringway on 22 October 1941 and was modified for static-line parachuting training. By 8 December trials with single sticks of four men had proved satisfactory, but not for Agate. He landed half in the mud and half on the hard concrete of the Ringway runway. He was badly bruised, but fortunately no limbs broken (*Manchester Evening News*, 1945).

Despite the apparent potential of the Halifax and the Albemarle, no new aircraft were forthcoming, and it was made clear that it was to be the Whitleys or nothing. Meanwhile, the Air Ministry and War Office demanded improvements in technique and equipment to reduce the number of injuries and deaths, and this was a challenge that Charles Agate embraced with characteristic enthusiasm.

In the early summer of 1941, he made over 150 jumps to test modifications to parachutes, jumping and landing techniques. He jumped with sandbags strapped to his legs to simulate a hard landing. He also jumped with a wide variety of different types of equipment, including the use of 'sleeves' to carry weapons. He was asked to jump with heavy kit bags. In doing so he pioneered the technique of lowering the kit bag just before hitting the ground. His experiments with tying his 'luggage' to his own parachute were not so successful, though he survived to tell the tale.

He tested the changes made to the snap-hook linking the static-line to the parachute pack, following the death of Hugh Carter. He was also tasked with testing the effects of oscillation and what was known as 'critical opening speed'. It was on one of these tests that he jumped from just 100ft, a height from which the possibilities of serious injury or death were exceptionally high. He landed on a protruding tree stump, fell backwards, and banged his head. Then, whilst in the special ward for Ringway casualties at Davyhulme Military Hospital, Urmston he developed jaundice. It was a very frustrating time for him, but it wasn't going to stop him.

Many of his test jumps were photographed by a young Frank Muir who after the war became a highly successful writer and comedian on television and radio. The photographs were taken from many angles and hundreds of reports were written on all aspects of each new item tested. The issue of where the camera should be mounted took some time to be resolved. In his autobiography, Frank Muir described how on one occasion he was selected for an experiment involving the filming of jumps from the unused bomb bay of the Whitley. Two planks were roped to the bay and Muir was laid face down on them and strapped in place, pointing forwards, looking downwards, camera held firmly in his shaking hand. The plane took off well enough; noisy and draughty, but tolerable. And then when the doors of the bomb bay slowly opened beneath him, he found himself hanging from ropes. The whole terrifying experience proved to be a waste of time. When they landed it was realized that the aperture in the floor of the aircraft through which the parachutists jumped was aft of the bomb bay, so they all jumped out behind him and there was nobody for him to film.

Another experiment involved the photographer lying on the floor in a prone position where the rear turret once stood. The plan was for the photographer's colleague to sit on his ankles to prevent him falling out of the plane so that the photographer could lean downwards at right-angles, with the camera pointing forwards into the slipstream and film the troops as they emerged from the jumping aperture ahead of him. As Muir noted wryly: 'There was so much wrong with this plan that I can hardly believe we eventually won the war' (Muir, 1997).

To reduce the number of landing injuries, experiments began to be carried out to assess whether it was practical to drop parachutists into open water. Following the death of William Alfred Dennis, the assumption had been that a heavily-laden parachutist landing in deep water would drown from the canopy collapsing on top of him. Given the number of lakes and ponds in Tatton Park it was deemed essential that the parachutist should be able to free himself from the parachute before entering the water. A special type of harness release was developed to make this possible. With this new harness, all that was required was to turn and strike a disc for the harness to fall completely away. Agate jumped regularly into the lake even in the most freezing conditions to test this, though there was often a bonus at the end. After landing, Lord Egerton would pick him up by rowing boat for his lunch and drinks, presumably prepared by his butler.

No less dangerous was his involvement with experiments dropping the new canisters that had been developed at the CLE. The CLE canister was a cylindrical container used to airdrop supplies to troops on the ground. Initially, the canisters were made of wood and metal and weighed around 101lb (46kg) empty and 351lb (159kg) when filled. Many of the canisters smashed when hitting the ground and so the second iteration were all metal and slightly heavier. One end of the canister carried a parachute pack. The parachute was deployed by a static line, which opened a pilot parachute, which in turn opened the main canopy. The other end of the canister was fitted with a pan-like structure that cushioned the impact of landing. The canisters were carried in the bomb-racks of bomber aircraft. The canisters were used for food, ammunition, weapons or other equipment. The Mark 1 canister could carry 12 rifles and 1,000 rounds of ammunition. A cylindrical fuel can was also developed to fit the CLE canister.[62] When fully loaded the cannisters descended much faster than a man and if a canister parachute failed to function, they came down like meteorites, scattering the contents around the splintered casing. If the contents were mortar bombs this could be very dangerous for the parachutists on the ground.

Charles Agate took part in experiments involving techniques to ensure that the man who jumped immediately before or immediately after a container would not get his own parachute tangled up with one of the canister's parachutes. On one occasion a canister passed right through one of the tester's parachute rigging, missing the man himself by only a few inches. Inevitably though, serious injuries and fatalities would still occur, and the first of many witnessed by Agate happened on 19 June 1941.

A small contingent of Polish personnel had arrived at Ringway in October 1940. These men were part of the 6,000 Polish troops who had escaped with General Stanisław Sosabowski after the fall of France. In February 1941 a further group of twenty Polish soldiers were sent to Ringway for parachute training. These men were named the Cichociemni (or the Silent Killers) who were parachuted into occupied Poland on 15/16 February 1941. More Polish troops were to follow, but many of these men were in poor condition, and it was agreed that a new physical training camp should be set up at Largo House in Fife, prior to them being sent to Ringway in groups of fifty every two weeks. The training regime involved two weeks of physical training followed by parachute jumping from a parachute tower at a nearby golf course. Those who did not come up to scratch at Largo were required to stay there until they were.[63]

On 19 June, one of these troops, Polish Second Lieutenant Jan Ernest Twardawa[64] was undergoing training for clandestine operations in Poland when the connection between his parachute and the strongpoint in the Whitley became detached and he fell to his death. The formal accident enquiry cleared the despatcher of blame, but criticised PTS procedures. Following Twardawa's death, proposals for change were made. The number of trainees per sortie was reduced to eight, and all sticks of trainees were to be accompanied by two RAF instructors, one at the front of the aircraft and one at the rear. The forward RAF instructor would be responsible for attaching static lines to their respective strongpoints and locking the safety pins. This was to be double-checked by each trainee, and completion of the drill would then be relayed to the pilot before clearance to take-off would be issued. Crucially, it was decided that Polish parachutists should always be accompanied by a Polish instructor, to translate where necessary. Additional written instructions would also be provided in the trainee's native language to avoid potentially fatal misunderstandings. Three months passed before the next fatality when another member of the Polish contingent, Lieutenant Zelewski was killed on 29 September after somersaulting on exiting a Whitley bomber over Tatton.

On 31 August 1941 the decision had been taken to form the 1st Parachute Brigade under Brigadier Richard Gale. This was located at Hardwick Hall near Chesterfield and became the new home for physical training and selection for airborne forces. The Hall was a beautiful Elizabethan mansion on the Chatsworth Estate. A camp, with assault courses, trapeze swing and parachute jump tower were constructed south-west of the Hall. A tethered barrage balloon was installed at Hardwick on 1 November 1941 to provide refresher training for qualified parachutists and supplement descents made from the jumping tower.

After pre-jump training was completed, the recruits that passed out were required to march at speed the 50 miles to join the parachute course at RAF Ringway. They marched back to Ringway from the Tatton Park drop zone each time they completed a training descent.

Although Agate would continue carrying out daring tests of techniques and equipment for the rest of his time at Ringway, his attention now turned to training these troops for the long-postponed 'second front'.[65] By December 1941, it was common knowledge that Churchill and de Gaulle were pressing the Americans to launch an invasion of France to relieve pressure on the Soviet Union in the East and to liberate France. Although the Americans were not yet in agreement, Agate and his colleagues anticipated that this invasion would happen at some stage and that they would play a key role in the preparations.

Responsibilities were re-allocated to support what was planned to be a huge increase in training and Charles Agate was given overall responsibility for the landing ground at Tatton Park, including the lakes, and the balloon station, which was, as described in the booklet *Tatton Park at War*: 'A hub of activity and was maintained by a staff of 40 under the watchful eye of Flight Lt Charles Agate who spent over four years living at the site.'

His new role gave him almost limitless opportunities for parachuting, including the first drop of the day, every day, to test wind speed and direction. He jumped so frequently that he soon became Ringway's 'top scorer'. He explained to Don Durbridge: 'The most I ever did in a day was 16, and the most I ever did in a calendar month was 75. So, I was literally living and sleeping parachuting.' His obsession was looked on with a mixture of admiration and incredulity, as Maurice Newnham remarked: 'His nonchalance and complete confidence were of tremendous value in debunking the perils of parachuting' (Newnham, 1946).

The balloon station where 'Bessie the loathsome yellow sausage' and in time other balloons were to be kept and overseen by Agate, was situated just a few hundred yards along the drive from the main Rostherne entrance to Tatton Park Estate. It is said that this was so that the trainees would not have much time to think about their impending fate after being brought from their accommodation by a fleet of Manchester Corporation double-decker buses. Agate, of course, would always be there to welcome them.

The training course would initially consist of six jumps per trainee, two from a balloon, two individual aircraft jumps, and two stick jumps. If possible, it was planned for at least one of these to take place at night as large-scale night jump training was something of an unknown quantity. No. I Advanced Course was completed on 10 January 1942, at which time Ringway reported only two injuries from a total of 196 balloon descents in total darkness. There were no refusals, and whilst the experience was described as 'eerie', Ringway recommended that henceforth night jumping be included in the standard training syllabus.

An intake rate of 200 trainees every 14 days was scheduled, utilizing the twelve Whitleys for parachuting and as a result two entire battalions were able to complete basic parachute training in a period of eight weeks virtually without a hitch. The British Army finally possessed something approaching the force of 5,000 parachutists that Churchill had called for almost exactly 18 months previously. What was needed now was another successful airborne operation.

In February 1942, almost exactly a year after Operation Colossus, a raid was carried out on the German Würzburg-type radar station at Bruneval, north of Le Havre in France. Würzburg radar systems were used to direct German night-fighters to specific targets and as a result by the end of 1941, Bomber Command losses were running at an unsustainable rate. The raiders were to be dropped a few miles East of the installation at Bruneval. The operation had to be launched when there was sufficient moonlight for the bombers and a rising tide to enable the force to escape. This narrowed it down to a window of four days, 24 to 27 February 1942.

The first wave of paratroops was dropped over a mile short of the correct drop-zone, and their wireless sets failed to function. In addition, the alarm was raised almost immediately as the paratroopers' descent was seen by German observers. However, the raiders managed to dismantle the radar apparatus and then moved it under fire to the beach. The extraction force of assault landing craft successfully lifted all the raiders and the radar apparatus on the morning of 28 February 1942.

The value of the raid proved to be considerable. The mere fact that a parachute force could enter and leave German occupied territory was a useful morale boost, as it came after a series of British defeats. More importantly, however, the capture of the Würzburg components allowed the formulation of countermeasures to aid Bomber Command in its night bombing offensive against Germany. Specifically, it led to the introduction of 'Window', small metal foil strips that showed up on a Würzburg screen as an individual aircraft. Jettisoning bundles of Window also blinded the German night-fighter control system, a technique first used with great effect on a raid against Hamburg on the night of 24/25 July 1943. The raid on Bruneval probably saved a great many lives in RAF Bomber Command.

The ramping-up of training though meant that 1942 was to prove to be the deadliest year for trainee deaths at Tatton Park, with sixteen fatalities. Agate's new role in charge of the balloon station meant he would be present at a number of these fatal incidents and the first of these was that of a Danish national who had been recruited into the SOE. Second Lieutenant Hans Edgardt Thirkildsen died on 29 January 1942. He exited the balloon satisfactorily, but the rigging lines of his parachute became tangled, and his parachute was not able to open fully.

Just two weeks later on the training course that ran from 10 to 24 February 1942 there were two further fatalities that shook the confidence of the Ringway men. A total of 239 men from the 1st and 4th Battalions were on the course, and between them they completed 1,096 aircraft descents and 471 balloon descents. However, visibility was consistently poor and the ground very hard owing to frosts. Lance Corporal James Duckett, a married man from Blackburn, had previously completed two balloon descents under Agate's supervision without incident, but on 16 February he sustained fatal injuries when he turned a somersault when exiting from a Whitley. Just two days later on 18 February and on the same course, Major Gerald McDonough's[66] parachute failed to open when his rigging lines caught on the D-ring attached to the deployment bag into which his parachute was packed. He had previously completed two balloon descents without incident before his fatal accident. He was 32.

In *Prelude to Glory*, Maurice Newnham described Charles Agate's extraordinary response to these two deaths: 'Immediately after the fatal accidents, Pilot Officer Agate volunteered to go up in the balloon to 1000ft to give a demonstration jump in front of a large number of troops. He made a perfect landing and was commended for his bravery' (Newnham, 1946). The following day, the Commanding Officer, and all the instructors including Agate, made further demonstration descents from 600ft to restore morale and to instil confidence in the course participants.

Agate's very next jump though would bring his closest brush with death. Exiting the balloon, his parachute suffered twisted lines and did not open until he was just 80ft (24m), from the ground. He hit the cold, frozen turf very hard, but almost certainly because of his training in physical education, he escaped serious injury. Worse still, Maurice Newnham who took part in the same 'confidence-building' exercise broke his leg with several compacted fractures and Pilot Officer Richards suffered concussion. In the Ringway Operations Log Newnham recorded that the incidents left the watching students 'highly amused' and Newnham acknowledged – with considerable humility – that the morale and spirit of cheerfulness of the trainees also 'served as an encouragement to the instructors who had had a particularly difficult time'.

Despite the bravado of the instructors, it was clear that still further modifications were required to the parachute. Training was suspended between 1 and 6 March 1942 to allow for these modifications to be made. As a result of Agate's recent near miss, Flight Sergeant Maxwell volunteered to test the modified parachute from a Liberator at RAF Polebrook[67] in Northamptonshire.

Training resumed at Ringway, but there was another death on the first day when Sergeant Giron, a Spanish SOE agent, died when making a balloon descent on 7 March. Corporal Thomas Richards from Manchester was the next casualty. He died on 22 March on his first jump from an aircraft.

Newnham agonized about the failure to resolve the problems with the parachutes, and it was decided that training should be suspended again, so that a committee of experts could be convened to commence further experiments. Two hundred parachute canopies were dyed yellow to enable the cine-cameras to pick out evidence of the reasons for the 'twisted' lines. To assist the committee, it was agreed that two 'sticks' of ten instructors, including Agate, would be filmed from multiple angles as they made their descents.

Training of troops then resumed but so did the deaths, Lieutenant Kenneth Alexander, aged 21 from Slough, died on his second jump from a Whitley on the 28 April; Private William Sands, aged 20 from Edinburgh, died on 4 June on his final qualifying jump and Thomas Newton, aged 21 from Nottingham, died on 29 June. The name of another member of the Special Forces who was killed on 15 July is simply recorded as 'S'. Unlike the others whose deaths were recorded as 'tangle' or 'somersault', 'S' was killed by the 'effects of landing'. More bad news hit Ringway on 6 July when Whitley K9013 crashed on a test flight killing all three members of the crew: Warrant Officer R. C. Sims, Sergeant A. C. Fisk and Aircraftman Frank Copland (Air Ministry, 1942).

Despite all this, morale at Ringway remained solid. Newnham put it like this: 'The training staff were inflexibly determined that they were essential to win the war . . . No hours of work were too long, no risks too great, no effort too strenuous' (Newnham, 1946).

And possibly one of the greatest, and unheralded, efforts of all came from the parachute packers of the Women's Auxiliary Air Force – the WAAF. Their intricate and lifesaving work would also present Agate with information that he forever wished that he had never known.

Chapter 13

The Parachute Packers of RAF Ringway

'A man's life depends on every parachute you pack', read the sign above the vast hall at Ringway where members of the Women's Auxiliary Air Force (WAAF) worked 24 hours a day, 7 days a week. Agate had also scrawled it on the back of a photograph discovered after his death. The indispensable work of these women was clearly not lost on Agate. On the same photograph, he had also written: 'Your life in their hands'.

There is no denying the truth of these words. The work of the 'chute girls' was meticulous, with each parachute taking 25 minutes to inspect, pack and inspect again. Then there was the drying, the repairing and the close monitoring of every single chute, which could only be used for twenty-five jumps and could not remain for more than two months in its bag before it had to be removed, re-checked, hung up to avoid damp and mould, and then packed again. The life of every one of the thousands of men and women who trained at Ringway depended on the work of the WAAF in the packing hall.

Writing in *Parachutist* in 1945, 'Pegasus' acknowledged that 'the parachutist's life is in the hands of a number of people, but perhaps none more so than the packer' (p. 64), with Maurice Newnham, writing two years later, highlighting the high regard the packers were held in by the trainees at Ringway: 'With the possible exception of their own instructor, the WAAF packers held pride of place in the affections of the pupils' (Newnham, 1946, p. 272).

One of the parachuting padres confiding to Maurice Newnham after his first jump: 'For thirty-two years my whole trust had been placed in God but for that for five seconds until my parachute opened my confidence was transferred to a WAAF parachute packer.' Another trainee, writing on the Paradata website, puts it like this: 'You drop vertically for a hundred feet until the chute opens with a loud bang, and you pray the paratroop prayer on the way down: "God bless the WAAF who packed it".'

Yet in the lead-up to the war in Europe, even those more enlightened establishment figures who understood the key role women could play in the coming conflict struggled for their voices to be heard. It is a story of barriers and old-fashioned values summarised in the Air Ministry's own account of the formation of the WAAF, published in 1953.

The Great War had seen the creation of the Women's Auxiliary Army Corps and the Women's Royal Navy Service and in April 1918 the Women's Royal Air Force came into existence on the same day as the Royal Air Force. But then, arguably in an echo of Britain's loss of focus and failure to develop the use of airborne forces, in the years after the Great War, the women's service was disbanded in April 1920.

By May 1936, with another conflict looking more and more likely, the issue of women's potential contribution to a future war had been relegated to the Women's Reserve Sub-Committee of the Manpower Sub-Committee of the Committee of Imperial Defence. A subcommittee of a subcommittee. The idea of a professional women's force slipped off the agenda for another two years.

By 1938 though there were plans for a Women's Supplementary Reserve and Auxiliary Territorial Service which included a women's section and from January 1939 this became more and more closely aligned to the RAF itself until on 28 June 1939 the Women's Auxiliary Air Force was founded. An initial drive to recruit suitable WAAF officers was hampered by the Air Ministry's determination to appoint women who had 'free time and an adequate social background' (MoD Air Historical Branch, 1953) but many of these original officers turned out to be completely unsuited to the role because they had 'no experience of handling other women except for their servants' (ibid).

Its first commanding officer however was the eminently capable businesswoman Jane Trefeusis-Forbes, though in line with the thinking of the time that this should be a voluntary service, Mrs Trefeusis-Forbes was not initially offered a salary and for the first months of its existence recruits reported for duty with a no more than 'touching faith in their government and no idea whatever of their possible or probable pay' (p. 54). After significant lobbying however, she was granted a salary of £800 per year and Mrs van Baerle was appointed her second in command. Further lobbying led to the original khaki uniform being replaced with the now familiar blue and an even closer alliance with the RAF. The WAAF would from now on be a salaried service, though until June 1944 the Treasury insisted that the wage for all ranks would be two-thirds of male pay.

On 29 August 1939 enrolment began in earnest and a two-week programme of basic training was put in place which consisted of 14 hours of lectures, films, discussions on 'organization and administration', 15 hours practical study in 'anti gas and station defence', 12 hours drill, and 6 hours of physical training. By May 1943 the WAAF boasted 182,000 women in its ranks, or over 16 per cent of the total strength of the RAF at home and overseas. In the six years of the war, over a quarter of a million women served in some capacity. A quarter of the total work force at Ringway were women. The working conditions were notionally in line with their male counterparts: 8 hours per day, 48 hours per week, meals every 4 hours, one day off per week, though as the workload at Ringway increased through 1943 and 1944 with the approach of D-Day and Arnhem this was largely ignored. The women would do what they needed to do make sure the airborne forces were suitably and safely equipped, however long it took. The women's welfare at Ringway was overseen by Warrant Officer Joe Sunderland.

The number of different roles or 'trades' within the WAAF increased from just six in 1939 to nearly eighty by end of the war and Ringway was typical of airfields all over the country with balloon operators, drivers, medical operatives, motor operators, photographers, mess orderlies, cooks, admin staff and, from 1941 . . . parachute packers. Many of them were from nearby Manchester, and one of the Ringway packers, Mary Wood, remembered darkly: 'I could see my hometown ablaze at night.'

The Parachute Packers Prayer is a poem often attributed to the writer, cricketing journalist and schoolmaster G. D. Martineau (1897–1976), but others claim that it was written anonymously by one of the WAAF packers. Either way, and with only a handful of veterans still alive in 2024, it gives poetic expression to the life of a packer so accurately and poignantly that it is hard now believe it was written by anyone other than one of the chute girls themselves:

> When they posted me here to the section,
> I was free as the pitiless air,
> Unashamed of confessed imperfection,
> Having no sort of burden to bear.
> I was not an incurable slacker.
> Neat, not fussy – I fancied of old,
> But today I'm a Parachute Packer,
> And my heart takes a turn with each fold.

We even learn, in poetic form, of the practicalities of the task itself and the understanding each packer must have of the science of the parachute:

> So, I lay the fine silk on the table.
> And I lift each pale panel in turn.
> They have said that my folding is able.

But it took me a long time to learn.
For the cords must come free for smooth flowing
And the webbing attachment be stout,
For the brute of a breeze will be blowing
If the aircrew have to bale out.

And we hear something of the emotional impact and the enormous stress of a job on which someone's life depends, a responsibility given extra emphasis by the fact that the packers were taken to the Drop Zone in the event of a parachute failure to demonstrate the consequences of a poorly packed parachute:

When I think how I snugly resided
In the lap of this land we could lose,
I believe if I left one cord twisted,
I would place my own neck in a noose.

It was a huge responsibility, and one which was carried out with great care and pride, and with every parachute they packed, a bond was formed with the unknown trainee who would entrust their very life to it, *The Parachute Packers Prayer* again:

Give my heroes kind wind and fair weather,
Let no parachute sidle or slump,
For today we go warring together
And my soul will be there at the jump.

A WAAF parachute packer interviewed in 1942 explained that 'every parachute is a person to me' and unlike many of the other WAAF trades at the time, the packer worked relatively closely to the airmen and women themselves, though they were discouraged from talking when at work in case they forgot to make a vital fold or tie. The trainees got the chance to chat to the packers when they left their valuables with them before a training jump or before departing on a mission over Europe, and it was said that most parachutists preferred to have their parachutes packed by women on the grounds that a woman was likely to take more care and interest in the safety of the man who is going to use it.

Some of the women put their names and addresses in the document wallet of the parachute and corresponded with the trainees during and in some cases long after the war. Romantic relationship between flyers and the WAAF at Ringway and Tatton were a familiar component of air base life, and they feature in the journals and memoirs of aircrew and WAAF personnel and in fictional reconstructions on page and screen. Some men even tried to get sent for a second jumping course just for the pleasure of passing several more days in the company of a WAAF. Winifred Smith from Norfolk, a graduate of the Southern College of Art in Portsmouth and a parachute packer at Ringway, even designed and made a wedding dress for a friend out of spare parachute silk. In some cases, though, the glamour often associated with the RAF in the popular imagination left some WAAF recruits bitterly disappointed when they encountered RAF men in person for the first time (Francis, 2008).

The girls faced terrible tragedy as well of course. Mary McKay, quoted in Escott (1995), recalls: 'We never dared to make definite dates. Often, I heard girls crying at night. I cried myself' (p. 72). For some, their chances of a romantic relationship were thwarted by superstition. At nearly every airbase there was a 'chop girl', a member of the WAAF who, it was believed, brought bad luck, because all her previous flyer boyfriends had been killed in action.

By the end of the war many of the packers had individually packed more than ten thousand parachutes, 'and to each one of them a man had entrusted his life' (Newnham, 1946, p. 317). That trust though was not placed in some anonymous packer – one amongst the nearly 3,000 who undertook this job during the war – a fact revealed in this verse from *The Parachute Packer's Prayer*:

> 'Cos the flyer must float unencumbered,
> Come to earth to complete the design,
> See, the 'chute has been carefully numbered,
> And the name in the logbook is mine.

At some point towards the end of the war, or perhaps in the difficult years he experienced afterwards, Charles Agate wrote on the back of one of the photographs he had kept: 'Only one lost to bad packing.'

William Morter was born on 16 August 1912, in Forest Hill, South London. His father Christopher and his mother Isabel were both 32 when he was born, and he had seven brothers and two sisters. His father died in 1938, and when war broke out William was working as a general labourer in Penge, also in South-east London. He was not married. William Morter Made his first jump at Ringway on Saturday 20 March 1943 from a static balloon under the watchful eye of Charles Agate. The Air Ministry record of fatal accidents at Ringway is succinct: 'Packing error of top tie.' William Morter's parachute had 'roman candled', and he plummeted to the ground at Tatton Park.

The death of William Morter would have a devastating and lifelong impact on Agate. Years later his daughter Lynette revealed that this tragic incident was particularly difficult for her father because not only was it he who dispatched Morter from the balloon on that dreadful day, but he knew very well the name of the woman who had packed the parachute. He would never reveal this name to colleagues, his superiors or even to his wife Marjorie because he recognized the devastating emotional impact this would have on more than one family. As he told journalist John Walsh in 1970: 'I was sworn to secrecy for the rest of my life, and I would not reveal her identity now for a million pounds.' It was a secret he carried to his grave.

Despite William Morter's dreadful fate 'only one lost to bad packing' is an extraordinary statistic, and testament to the skill and dedication of the women who packed tens of thousands of parachutes at Ringway between 1940 and 1946. And yet, as Harry Ward himself acknowledged in his autobiography: 'the only people who really appreciated the worth of those girls were the troops who used the chutes they packed' (Hearn, 1990, p. 180). The men of each training course would make a collection for the packers at the end of each course, and Winifred Smith recalled: 'When an airman used his chute, ten shillings was forwarded to the WAAF packer to say: Thank you. I got down safely.'

There was, however, hardly any official recognition other than little silver wings awarded to a packer after the first eight successful live jumps using parachutes packed by her. These were allowed to be worn above her left pocket, but only when on duty. Harry Ward recommended some of the parachute girls for honours and awards at the end of the war, but they never got them. Today, there is a simple stone memorial to them at Manchester Airport.

Chapter 14

Training the Troops

By the summer of 1942 training at Ringway was ramping up and Maurice Newnham had finally gathered a 'devoted band of RAF instructors who had learnt much about parachuting by the hard method of practical experience' (Newnham, 1946, p. 133).

Newnham was fulsome in his praise of his favoured profession: schoolteachers. Teachers, he knew, understood the psychological factors involved in dealing with the teaching of a subject such as parachuting.

Like all good teachers 'the first duty of a British parachute instructor is to get to know his pupils' (Newnham, 1946, p. 258). He encouraged his instructors to develop their pupils' confidence through as much personal instruction as possible and recognized the 'deep comradely affections which existed between the RAF instructors and the soldiers' (ibid, p. 299). Colonel Ernest 'Eric' Down, commander of the 1st Parachute Battalion went as far as to call the PJIs 'nursemaids in blue', and although that is perhaps an exaggeration, Agate was certainly someone who found it 'much less worrying to jump themselves than to watch their pupils doing so' (ibid, p. 276).

Brigade personnel, still notionally volunteers, were to be cycled through the PTS in fortnightly batches of 200. It was also from the summer of 1942 that governments in exile sent more and more French, Belgian, Dutch, Czech and Norwegian patriots as well as eventually French colonial troops from North Africa. The Polish forces, in particular, had considerable previous experience in parachuting and the Ringway men were able to learn from their expertise. Flight Lieutenant Julian Gebolys, a senior Polish instructor, taught the Ringway men the art of arresting the speed, drift, and oscillation of a parachute by manipulating the shoulder lift webs. Control was exercised over drifting in any direction and so the parachutist was prepared for forward, sideways, and backward landings. It became known as the 'Polish Method' and Gebolys was soon part of the PJI team.

The training course settled into a pattern, starting with a film *Jumps Ahead*, which had been made by the instructors, and followed by two weeks' ground training before the first two jumps by balloon. Ground or 'synthetic' training methods had been first developed by Bruce Williams, and then improved considerably by John Kilkenny. Like Agate, he was a talented sportsman who had played football for The Corinthians and had gained two amateur English caps. Kilkenny attended as many action movies at the local cinemas as he could so he would concentrate intensely on any scenes featuring stuntmen and observe how they managed their falls. His methods evolved into what even to this day is known as 'Kilkenny's Circus'.

Ground training apparatus was built into the airfield hangars or erected nearby and were designed to develop parachuting techniques. The men practised landing drills by standing on mats and rolling over from the attention position followed by jumping from benches and sliding down chutes. Instruction in combined flight and landing drills was given to pupils jumping in fixed harnesses on to mats from various swing and platform appliances and constructions of up to about 15ft in height. The first test of nerve came when the pupil stood on 'The Fan', which was situated 25ft up a hangar wall.

Trainees were required to sit on a duckboard with a belt around the waist and fixed to a cable wound around a small drum with a four-bladed fan on the other end, located some 60ft up in the roof of the hangar. They were then told to launch themselves off the duckboard to land on the mats below. The air resistance on the fan slowed the speed of the trainee's descent. Those who were too slow were pushed off by the instructor. If the instructor was feeling mischievous, he would change the pitch of the fan to make the descent much faster.

Volunteers were to be between the ages of 20 and 32, although the upper limit could be relaxed for officers and NCOs but with the strict proviso that they met all other physical standards. All were to be passed Al fit, were to weigh a maximum of 196lbs naked, to have 6/12 vision in each eye, and to have acuity equivalent to at least Army Hearing Standard Two. Volunteers were also to have a minimum of eight sound or replacement teeth including two molars, in the upper jaw, which were to be in 'good relation' to those in the lower. The training regime was punishing and designed to weed out all but the very best soldiers, though as the challenges of D-Day and Arnhem approached it would take all the skills of Agate the teacher to tame some of the more unruly recruits.

The first two jumps were made from a cage suspended beneath 'Bessie' or one of her siblings. Strange's original vision had been realized and it was now accepted that parachuting from a static balloon was much more suitable for initial instructional purposes than jumping from an aircraft. There was little noise, and this enabled clear instructions to be called out over a loudspeaker to trainees while they were in the air. The balloon could be flown in misty weather and at night and it was almost always possible to know where a pupil would land.

Jumping from a balloon had its dangers too of course and, based on detailed advice from Bernard Winfield, but heavily informed by Agate, Leslie Harvey issued strict new orders to reduce the risks associated with it. Many of these rules set out to make the environment safer, such as banning smoking in the vicinity of the balloon, a ban on dropping in a wind exceeding 15mph and the setting of a maximum height from which live dropping was permitted at 500ft. There was also the precaution that powered aircraft dropping parachutists at Tatton Park would not operate when the balloon was being flown and there would be constant checks of telephone communication to ensure this.

Harvey's list of orders also gives us an insight into Charles Agate's duties and responsibilities both as NCO in charge of the balloon crew and as the instructor:

- The N.C.O. i/c Balloon Crew will contact Operations Room for permission to fly the Balloon and to carry out training.
- The N.C.O. i/c Balloon Crew can at any time decide against flying the Balloon if in his opinion local conditions are not suitable.
- No one, other than a member of the Balloon Crew will touch the Handling Guys until ordered to do so by the N.C.O. i/c Balloon Crew.
- No one, other than members of the Balloon Crew may touch or mount the winch without permission of the N.C.O. i/c Balloon Crew.
- Before an ascent is made, the N.C.O. i/c Balloon Crew will satisfy himself that everything is in order.
- It is the responsibility of the RAF Parachute Instructor to make further inspections of the flying wires and attachments, and no one shall be permitted to enter the car until the Instructor i/c Crew has given the order to do so.
- The maximum number of persons permitted to ascend in the Balloon at one time is five, one Instructor and four pupils. No pupil may enter the car without an instructor.
- No Instructor may ascend in the Balloon Car without wearing an observer type parachute or para-suit.
- Before ascending the instructor will enter the Balloon Car followed by four pupils and will attach statics of each pupil's parachute to the snap hooks on the overhead cross-bar of the Balloon Car and position the safety pins.
- Pupils will be numbered and will take up their positions before leaving the ground and will not be permitted to move about or stand up once the ascent is commenced.
- Parachute Instructor present is satisfied that the Balloon is so positioned as to avoid a parachutist drifting into an obstacle.

Right: Charles Agate with a packed parachute.

Below: 9 Frenches Road, Redhill.

RGS Scholarship Boys, 1918.

RGS Football, 1920-21. Agate seated front right.

The Agate family at Shoreham Beach.

Norton, West Drive Burgh Heath.

Jumping from the rear platform of a Whitley Mk II.

Flying Officer Charles Agate AFC.

Agate outside his caravan in Tatton Park.

WAAF parachute packers at RAF Ringway.

Charles Agate and Bernard Winfield wearing their AFC medal ribbons.

General Crawford after jumping into Rostherne Mere. Agate on the right.

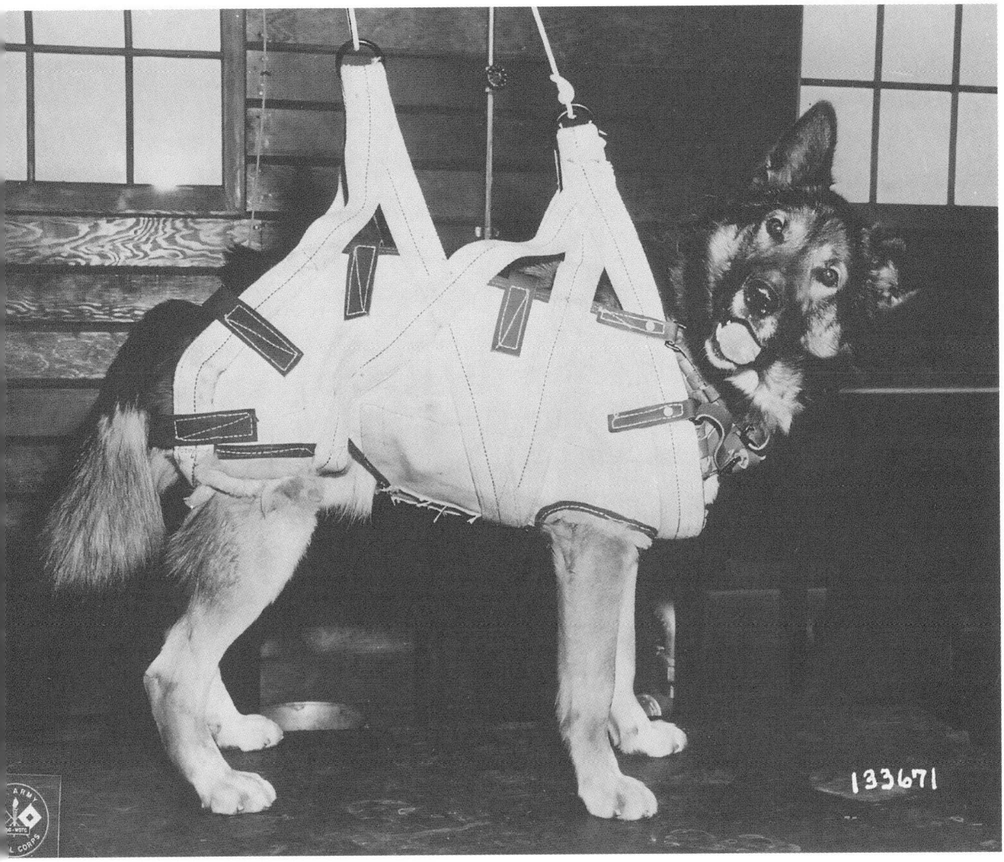

An American Paradog.

Charles Agate making a test jump from a DC3 Dakota.

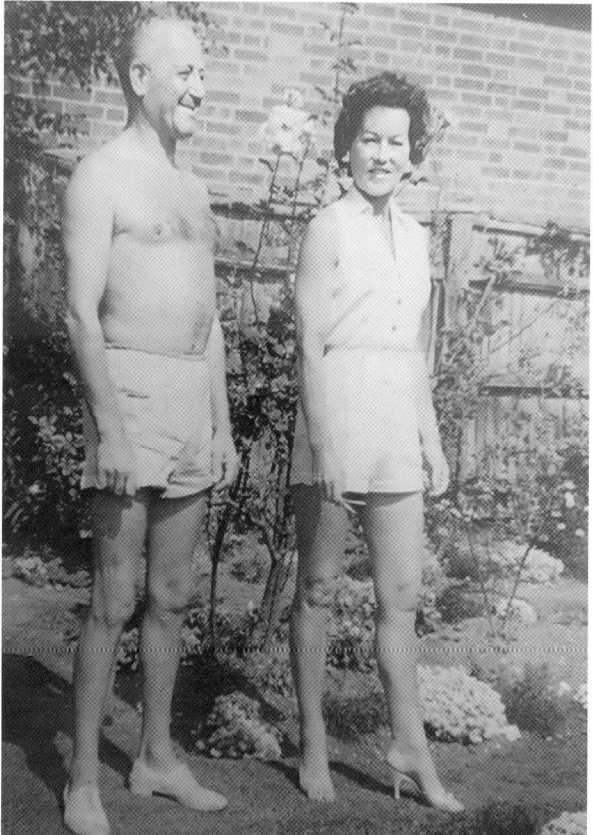

Above: Charles Agate's retirement assembly.

Left: Charles & Marjorie Agate in their garden.

Prior to every balloon jump, tests were carried out using dummies. No live drops took place until a minimum of two dummies had been dropped from 500ft to check direction of drift. To the alarm of many of the recruits, the dummies made a sickening thump when they hit the ground.

Agate then became focussed on getting the trainees to jump:

- When the Instructor and pupils are positioned, he will give the order to the N.C.O. i/c/ Crew, 'READY FOR ASCENT' and the latter will pay out the winch.
- The N.C.O. i/c Balloon Crew will telephone the instructor when 500ft has been reached and will stop winch giving the signal '500 FEET, WINCH STOPPED' to the Instructor, who will signal back, 'MESSAGE RECEIVED, ABOUT TO COMMENCE DROPPING'.
- When ready to commence dropping the instructor will give the order 'ACTION STATIONS', followed by the order, 'NO 1, NO 2, NO 3, NO 4' and the pupils will drop in the order stated and only when their numbers are called out.
- When all the pupils have dropped the instructor will telephone the N.C.O. i/c Crew to 'CLOSE HAUL BALLOON'.

This was what Charles Agate did day in and day out for over 4 years, as he told the BBC's Don Durbridge in 1974:

Once I did nearly 14 hours continuous ballooning. And by ballooning, I mean filling the cage up with four or five pupils, taking them up to about 800ft, putting them out one after the other, and sometimes a little nervous in doing that. Because of course, it is unusual to put yourself into space. And these were just young soldiers who volunteered. And then you come down again, load up again.

A balloon is like a kite, you're all over the sky, in every direction, like a small boat on a rough sea. And having done this for 14 hours, I remember I really couldn't walk when I got out of the balloon cage. I had to hold on for a while because I'd lost my sense of balance. But I eventually got over to my caravan, which was on the landing ground, but I couldn't sleep all night. Literally. It was rock, rock, rock, rock, the sensation I'd been having in a balloon.

Night jumps – whether from planes or balloons – were terrifying and Maurice Newnham gave this chilling description of a fatality from a jump at night at Agate's balloon station. The first thing he hears in the terrible darkness is the voice of the instructor: 'Number four – GO! we heard, but our sensitive ears caught no following sound of rippling silk, but, instead, a sickening thud a few feet away from where we stood'. Like Agate just a few months before it was the Padre this time who offered to do a jump to reassure the pupils.

All soldiers in training were free to refuse to jump if they felt that they could not do it, and these men faced no greater punishment than being returned to their former units. After all, 'the cold-blooded act of throwing themselves out of an aircraft took more courage and determination than many of them possessed' (Newnham, 1946, p. 21). After a man had been awarded his wings, a refusal became a court-martial offence, because it is extremely risky for other trainees to jump past a man who decides at the last moment not to jump, and even if this difficulty can be overcome the delay would mean that the men would be spread over a great distance.

There was though one thing which could be done with a man who had reached the hole-in-the-floor and finds that his confidence has deserted him: give him a hearty push in the back with a boot. Agate confided in his daughter Lynette that on more than one occasion he did have to push a man out, including a reluctant Frenchman who shouted back *'Merci Monsieur!'* There are other unverified reports of Instructors pushing reluctant trainees out, or in one case, taking a trainee's hands ostensibly to help him up but letting him go instead. For the Germans that wasn't necessary. They employed *Absetzer*, whose sole job was to push men out.

Once qualified, the trainee had a very special place in the development of Britain's Airborne Forces. However, injuries and even fatalities were still commonplace. There were two deaths on the same day, 31 October – All Hallows Eve – with Agate in charge of the balloon site. Gunner Frederick Langmaid of Shotton, Newcastle on Tyne, died when his lines became tangled after jumping from the balloon. He had served with the Searchlight Regiment before volunteering for Airborne Forces just a few weeks earlier. Then, just an hour later, Lance Corporal George Staley from Stoke on Trent lost his life in precisely the same way. He had served with the 13th Battalion Royal Welsh Fusiliers, before also volunteering for Airborne Forces. He was 20 years old. As he had done in February following the deaths of James Duckett and Albert McDonagh, Agate took his balloon up 1,000ft, twice the permitted height, and made a jump to reassure the troops that parachuting was perhaps not so dangerous after all.

The following course, No. 36, in November 1942 also saw two fatalities, the first from a balloon. Private Colin Mason McWilliam had enlisted into the North Staffordshire Regiment before volunteering for the Airborne Forces. He died on 8 November 1942 jumping from the balloon when his lines became tangled. He too was 20 years old. On 3 December, Private Siemasko of the Polish Forces died from a tangle on exiting a Whitley.

The potentially fatal 'tangle' was listed – sometimes as 'twist' – on fifteen of the forty-six fatal accidents at Tatton Park during the war. Newnham became more and more frustrated that this and other design issues were not being resolved and wrote later that many of the fatalities were still due to 'faults in the design of the parachute which have not yet been remedied' (Newnham, 1946, p. 163). It would haunt him till the end of the war and beyond. There was however one life-saving device which Newnham was firmly against.

American troops were provided with a reserve parachute, and the Russians had used them from 1931. Even though after each fatality it was suggested that a reserve parachute was needed, it remained Newnham's 'firm conviction that one parachute that worked properly was what was required', and this became the official British line: a secondary parachute was not needed because the X-type parachute was so reliable. This must have sounded very hollow to the brave men who had seen their friends' chutes roman candle, and 'Pegasus' writing in *Parachutist* at the end of the war was unequivocal: 'The finest confidence booster is an emergency chute. The Americans called us "crazy guys" for not using them and for allowing men to die on practice jumps' (Pegasus, 1944, p. 32).

With the Air Ministry now committed to parachute training and recognizing the limitations of the static balloon, it succeeded in locating additional Whitleys and Albemarles, as well as a limited number of Stirling and Halifax bombers for parachute training. But even with these additions the capacity at Ringway was still insufficient, and Britain remained very short of transport aircraft across the service. A desperate Churchill made an appeal to President Roosevelt, asking for early shipment of previously ordered transport aircraft, but the Americans were also building up their transport commands at this time, the request was refused. However, Roosevelt reassured Churchill that four transport groups would be dispatched as soon as the USA had achieved its objective. Six months later, in November 1942, a total of 416 American aircraft and crews were made available to the RAF to assist the British with their transport and airborne operations. Ringway was finally able to contemplate having the ability to train two battalions in a period of eight weeks.

1943 began in style for Charles Agate alongside his friend Bernard Winfield. Agate was made an acting Flight Lieutenant and both he and

Winfield were awarded the Air Force Cross (AFC) for 'an act or acts of exemplary gallantry while flying, though not in active operations against the enemy'.

They travelled down to London together to receive their Honours from King George VI. Marjorie and the 7-year-old Lynette travelled up from Epsom for the occasion though they had to stay in an ante room while Charles and Bernard went to collect their medals. The King was in poor health at the time and the men were instructed not to shake his hand but just to touch his shoulder.

Agate received a letter from the headmaster of his old school congratulating him on the award, and his reply reveals how much he was enjoying his war service:

I thank you for your letter offering congratulations on my A.F.C.

For service reasons I cannot give very much detail about my interesting job of work but can give you a few facts. I was the first parachuting instructor who had not been a parachutist before the war to be trained in the modern low altitude parachuting used for paratroops. I have made many experimental descents from various types of aircraft and have been injured once only. The thrill of a descent has not worn off and modern low altitude jumping is now quite safe.

I am at a Parachute Training School where all preliminary training for parachuting is carried out by RAF Instructors, and the Army appear very well pleased with results. We work in close co-operation with the Army because, while the paratrooper is airborne, either by plane or parachute, he is under the care of the RAF, but once he 'touches down' and his real work begins, he is again a soldier. All our pupils, either British or Allied are fine fellows and volunteers for a job which only begins with parachuting.

Back at Ringway it was business as usual for acting Flight Lieutenant Agate, though there would be six more deaths in the first three months of the New Year, the first four from the Whitley: on 4 January, Kazimierez Gokal died following a somersault on exit and just two days later Private Czesław Sadkowski, a radio telephone operator, became entangled with another jumper and fell to his death. Two weeks later Corporal William Edwin Friskney also suffered a fatal somersault and on 10 February Lance Corporal William Drummond Heron's rigging lines fouled on the bomber's fuselage. On 24 February 1943, during a night training exercise two Whitleys collided on the runway at Ringway. The aircraft piloted by Flight Lieutenant Robin Hooper, DFC, which was carrying fourteen men, caught fire. Fortunately, all the men escaped without injury.

In March 1943 one of the Tatton Park balloons broke free of its moorings taking Sergeant Grant and Sergeant Blake with it. Grant managed to get the balloon to deflate before both men bailed out at 2,000ft, thereby qualifying themselves for membership of the Caterpillar Club. The balloon itself came down safely at the boundary of Tatton Park. Eight months later three balloons broke free and one caught fire taking all three out of service.

The heroic and multi-skilled women of the WAAF were of course by no means the only women who passed through RAF Ringway. As the war progressed Agate's attention would turn to the training of men and women of the Special Operations Executive (SOE) as they prepared to drop into the occupied territories and begin to pave the way for invasion in 1944. Agate would also make sorties as despatcher over occupied territory.

Chapter 15

Training the SOE

Winston Churchill was determined to keep the spirit of resistance alive in occupied countries. In July 1940, he gave the Labour politician and Minister of Economic Warfare Hugh Dalton the responsibility of forming a new underground organization – the Special Operations Executive (SOE). According to the historian and politician Michael Foot, Dalton was a 'forceful rather than a loveable man, with a booming voice, acute intellect and thrusting personality, many found him overwhelming' (Foot, 1984).

On 22 June the War Cabinet approved Churchill's proposal to establish the SOE. Its purpose was sabotage, subversion, brief cross-Channel raids, and the creation of a secret force of agents behind the lines. Churchill's instruction for this new organization was set out in three words: 'Set Europe Ablaze!'

Colonel Colin Gubbins[68] was given the responsibility for organizing the training for recruits in unarmed combat, firearms, sabotage and wireless techniques, but only two of these agents had been sent to Ringway for parachute training until 24 October when a contingent of eleven men arrived. It was decided that special arrangements were required if secrecy was to be maintained. Firstly, it was ordered that every agent would wear normal British Army battledress. A small house in the vicinity was requisitioned where the agents could be accommodated and fed away from the other troops. All training would take place at the far side of the aerodrome with just one or two instructors who would be sworn to secrecy. Charles Agate was one of the trusted men. It was further agreed in November 1941 that one specific aircraft, a Whitley Mk V (Z6797), and Pilot Officer Sawdon should be allocated to the special agents.

Warrant Officer Joe Sunderland was tasked with recommending changes to equipment and processes to cater for this new challenge. In a lengthy memo dated 13 October 1941 he made a series of proposals and he had this to say about the role of the dispatcher:

> It is an idea that anyone can push the bodies out, but this is entirely wrong. Because a man has packed several parachutes it does not follow that he can carry out the special and complicated work of the dispatcher and until it is realized that only the best material should be employed really easy and efficient operations will not be possible (Air Ministry AIR 2/7470, 1941).

From these modest beginnings came an open-ended commitment to provide basic parachute training for the men and women of the SOE. As more countries had come under Nazi control, so underground resistance movements were formed. Around 1,300 SOE agents were trained at Ringway to enable them to be dropped back into occupied territory to disrupt the Nazis and support resistance groups.

The training of SOE agents took time, and much of it took place in the wilds of Scotland, but their presence was urgently needed in mainland Europe, and France in particular, so by the time they arrived at Ringway, there was very little time to give them the full training normally accorded to paratroops. Agate and the other PJIs had to devise a training programme based initially, and inexplicably, around just four jumps for women and five for men, though sometimes fewer. It was a startling fact that if the weather was not favourable – and Agate himself made the first jump of every day to find out – a small number made no practice jumps at all before their mission.

Not all the SOE agents were trained fighters, many were ordinary men and women who had the ability to speak the language of an occupied country. Some of these would-be agents were injured on landing because they tended to be less physically fit than the trainee paratroopers.

Special devices and gadgets had to be designed and tested. This was especially the case for those agents who were trained to drop into the more mountainous areas of France or Scandinavia, sometimes carrying with them a pair of skis as well as radio sets, explosives, and other equipment. The risk of injury was considerable and yet a broken limb might well result in discovery and execution.

Two squadrons (Nos 138 and 161) were formed to support covert SOE operations in Europe during the Second World War, flying a mixture of aircraft that included Hudsons, Halifaxes, Whitleys and Lysanders. The larger aircraft were used for parachute drops of agents or supplies whereas the Lysander was used for short take-off and landing. Agate admitted to pushing SOE agents out because their equipment was simply too heavy for them to move out of the hatch. The more fortunate SOE agents missed the thrill of parachuting from a Whitley by being flown in the Lysander, which with its excellent short take-off and landing capabilities, was able to touch down in enemy-held territory.

On 28 September 1942 two Soviet nationals arrived at Glasgow aboard HMS *Bulldog*. They were Nikitina and Emilya Novikova. They were given food coupons and taken to a flat in Maida Vale. There they were given papers in the name Kersti Boska, an unmarried stenographer from Haapsalu, code name 'Tonic' and Anna Unter, an unmarried governess from Virz-Yarvi, code-named 'Soda Water'. Both women were originally from occupied Estonia (Immigration & Nationality Department, Home Office, 1942).

Having ensured that they were kept away from all other SOE agents they were then sent to Alderton Hall Farm in Loughton. On 27 October they were taken to Ringway for parachute training where they were boarded at Dunham House near Altrincham. The Commandant at Dunham House, Major Edwards, provided the following report of their training:

Anna Unter tried hard in all her ground training and had a happy disposition. In her balloon descent she showed slight signs of nervousness, but made a good egress and had soft landing. Kersti Peska however, was a very nervous type of person who was so frightened in the ground training and also in the balloon descent that she did well to jump at all.

The members of this party had all jumped previously from Dakota aircraft they were required to jump through the hole of a Whitley, but Kersti Peska found this very hard and it was feared that she might refuse. Capt. Thornton, Flight Lieutenants Winfield and Agate guided their packs as they jumped. Without their consideration and tactful handling, I do not think she would have jumped (O'Connor, 2011).

It was a source of great frustration and resentment for many of these heroic women and their families that they were not awarded their parachute wings at the end of their training on the grounds that as women they had not completed enough training jumps. Many of them, in contravention of orders, sewed parachute wings to their battledress after returning to Britain.

In his autobiography, Frank Muir described how Roland Gant, who was his editor at Heinemann and who spoke perfect French, was employed in the SOE. One night he had to rendezvous with a British radio operator due to be dropped from a Lysander plane at 1,000ft onto a secret dropping point in Normandy. The Lysander was on time, and all was going well until the agent jumped. Then, to Roland's horror, he saw in the moonlight that the parachute was not opening. The dark figure hanging beneath the white silk streak gathered speed and finally hit the earth with a sickening thud. As Roland ran towards the parachute, the parachutist suddenly rose up and called out: 'That you, Roland? Fuck this for a game of soldiers!' By a million to one chance the agent had landed in a soft peat bog. He had broken bones, but he had survived (Muir, 1997).

Churchill considered the activities of the SOE to be legitimate, but the Germans took a different view. Agents of foreign governments who supported resistance fighters were 'bandits' and 'terrorists', who had no legal rights.

It has been argued that the methods of warfare encouraged and promoted by SOE were emulated by terrorist organizations and as the British military historian John Keegan wrote:

> We must recognize that our response to the scourge of terrorism is compromised by what we did through SOE. The justification . . . That we had no other means of striking back at the enemy . . . is exactly the argument used by the Red Brigades, the Baader-Meinhoff gang, the PFLP, the IRA and every other half-articulate terrorist organization on Earth. Futile to argue that we were a democracy and Hitler a tyrant. Means besmirch ends. SOE besmirched Britain. The 'SOE was inefficient as an organization, unnecessarily dangerous to work for, ineffective in its pursuit of its aims, and counter-productive in the results achieved' (Keegan, 2002).

Agate acted as dispatcher on seventeen of these highly dangerous operations and had the responsibility for ensuring that the agent was reassured on the flight over, dispatched safely, and landed as close as possible to the designated target. For many, he was the last friendly face they would see.

A fellow schoolmaster who passed through Agate's hands at Tatton in training for the SOE was Harry Ree, whose diaries were edited by his son Jonathan. Ree and Agate had much in common, and Ree's son says this of his father, but his words could just as well be applied to Charles Agate: 'His nonchalant charm bore witness to an enormous inarticulate grief' (Rees, 2020, p. xix).

Chapter 16

Behaving Badly

Training agents to jump secretly into occupied territory would mean that they should be able to parachute into water if necessary, and in 1942 the War Office made this a training priority. At a mile long and reputed to be over 100ft deep, Rostherne Mere in Tatton Park was ideally situated, though the trainees were not so keen and made up a song 'Mind the Lake', to the tune of 'Bless them All'.

As the officer in charge of the landing area at Tatton, Agate's responsibilities extended to Rostherne Mere as well as to the smaller Melchett Mere and to undertaking regular practice jumps in special watertight suits, carrying inflatable dinghies, flotation for luggage and even skis. Agate was also in charge of a motorboat and a rowing boat which would go out and pick up the cold, wet and bedraggled parachutists.

On one notable occasion, Agate incurred the wrath of his commanding officer, but also showed the ability to talk his way out of trouble which would mark his time as a headmaster and in his occasional run ins with the law.

All the instructors were in peak physical condition and were therefore not representative of many of the individuals who were required to learn to parachute in advance of their SOE missions. Agate was supremely fit, drank little alcohol and, unlike most of the men at Ringway, did not smoke. He agreed, therefore, that further parachuting tests would be required by others who were not in such good condition. This meant finding volunteers who were less physically fit, possibly older and definitely carrying more weight. First among these volunteers was the Commanding Officer of the Parachute School, Maurice Newnham himself. Being a well-built – not to say portly figure – weighing more than 14 stone (89kg) who had only recently returned from a serious leg injury this required considerable bravery on his part, but to add to his apprehension it was further agreed that his jump would need to take place into water and at night.

During the ten minutes or so that the Whitley carrying Newnham was circling into position far above the lake, he felt cold and miserable. When the red warning light flashed on, he swung his legs into the hole. The green light followed a moment or two later and out he went. Newnham had made several previous descents onto land and was familiar with the sensation of jumping and he was therefore able to concentrate immediately upon the task of getting out of his harness without falling out of the parachute altogether. As he could see the water getting nearer and nearer, he could see, too, Charles Agate in the motorboat making for the place where it was thought that he would enter the water.

Clear of the harness, Newnham held grimly to the lift-web until he judged that he was about 10ft from the water and then let go. He hit the water with a mighty splash and the deep breath he had taken exploded out of him with the sudden shock of the immersion. He swallowed what he thought was gallons of water, but, at length, his Mae West brought him to the surface.

He floated in the freezing water wondering why Agate was not coming to save him. 'I couldn't see the boat and assumed that I must be facing away from it. It was all very dark and eerie. Then a call came across the water, and I could just discern the outline of the boat some distance away. Agate's normally cheerful voice seemed to be tinged with some concern.'

Agate shouted to Newnham to say that the motor had broken down, adding: 'Can you swim over here, or you will have to wait till I get the rowing boat?'

Newnham was not amused:

Agate knew full well that I was no swimmer. A sharp stab
of panic shot across my mind. What a dammed silly way to
die. I lay on my back keeping quite still with the small waves
occasionally lapping over my face and accentuating the
impression that I was slowly sinking. My body was chilled to
the marrow. After what seemed like an incredibly long time,
I heard the faint splash of oars and Agate calling out directions
to the rower so that he could find me.

Once safely aboard the rowing boat, Newnham saw that the motorboat
was still out on the lake and Agate was forced to admit that instead
of going straight to rescue his commanding officer, he had decided to
pick up the discarded parachute first. In the darkness he had got the
parachute tangled round the propellor. The boat had not broken down
at all. It had been incapacitated by the man in charge of it. Newnham
was furious: 'I pointed out, rather acidly, to Agate that I might have been
drowned. But he reassured me by saying that he had been standing by
ready to plunge to my rescue if he thought I was in serious difficulties.'

Newnham snarled: 'Indeed? As you can't swim either, that would
have been a great deal of help! And as for giving you a lift to the shore
now, I couldn't possibly care less if you stay out here all night and get
pneumonia!'

It was a rare falling out between the son of a railwayman from
Redhill and the Kensington-born Great War flying ace. Agate and
Newnham respected each other, and Agate always talked fondly about
his Commanding Officer.

From time to time Agate was able to return to his home at West
Drive in Burgh Heath when he had leave, and Lynette still recalls with
great pleasure that when he did, he would always bring extra rations
of sweets that he had been able to get from the shop at the airbase.

Because he was not a smoker, he had plenty of spare tokens for treats and gifts for his wife and daughter.

Marjorie and Lynette occasionally made the long and difficult journey from Burgh Heath by train to visit Charles, but when they did, they did not stay with him, as visitors were not allowed overnight at Tatton Park. They usually stayed in another more spacious caravan outside Knutsford. However, Charles' efforts at a reconciliation were severely tested on one of these visits later. Lynette was just eight or nine years old but she recalled the incident clearly in an interview in 2022:

> Daddy was looking after me for the day. Without telling my mother we went out to the airfield, and he took me up in a Dakota. When the plane got to a certain height, he made a sort of toy parachute tied to a small piece of wood, opened the hatch, and threw it out. Well then, without any warning, he just waved, said 'bye-bye' and jumped out himself! The pilot flew me back to the airfield. Mummy was FURIOUS with him!

Maurice, the 4th Baron Egerton of Tatton, was less forgiving even than Marjorie about poor behaviour in and around his beloved estate, but only once did he have cause to reprimand Agate. On a day off Agate was enjoying some relaxed boating on Melchett Mere, but he was reprimanded by Egerton in one of his many letters of complaint. His boats were 'not to be used for recreational purposes' (Cheshire Archives and Local Studies, 1228-1961).

Agate generally tried to stay on the right side of Lord Egerton. The same could not though be said of his friend Bernard Winfield who on 30 September 1943 was forced to write a grovelling letter of apology for the 'arbitrary way I have behaved in the Park in the past'. He goes on: 'It showed a singular lack of courtesy in view of the kindness with which you have treated all PTS personnel in the Park. I hope you will forgive my bad manners and lack of judgement and let me know if there is any more suitable way I can make amends' (Cheshire Archives and Local Studies, 1228-1961). There is no record in the archives of what exactly Winfield had done, nor of any suitable punishment handed out by Lord Egerton.

In fact, the hundreds of letters from Egerton to PTS personnel during the war do not show him to be a kind and forgiving man at all. He had loaned the use of his lands for the war effort, but was not prepared to accept any of the privations that might have caused him. His most common complaint was about the presence of dogs. However, he also frequently vented his wrath in writing to anyone from Maurice Newnham to the War Office itself about troops using the wrong gate to enter the park, equipment left lying around, the stealing of vegetables, soldiers being rude to his gatekeeper and men using ditches as latrines. His most vitriolic complaints though were reserved for the Americans who he described as 'hooligans' and for the officers in charge at Tatton who he described as 'constantly changing'.

He called Newnham 'perfectly useless'. In an extraordinary letter dated 21 March 1941, complaining, perhaps not unreasonably, about the amount of explosives kept at Tatton Park, he appears to lose all sense of perspective: 'This is just like you arrogant army people! You go off and do something on the sly because you are just too self-satisfied, and pig headed to consult with anyone!!!!'

Agate seemed to be one of the few people who could appease the Lord of Tatton. He was after all effectively living in an old caravan in his very large garden with a dog, and Egerton had to accept to a certain extent that, as he put it in another letter, 'the balloon types have to be here all the time'. Agate's powers of diplomacy were put to the test when on 27 May 1943 a Whitley bomber crash-landed in the park and ran into some of Lord Egerton's trees. None of the crew or the parachutists on board were seriously injured, but that was clearly of no concern to Egerton, who wrote: 'It was only due to the presence of some conifers that the machine did not carry on into the house or turn a somersault into the sunken garden.'

It fell to Charles Agate to pen a reply and his words show all the tact required of a future headmaster as well as a touch of irony that Egerton had apparently not noticed a large aircraft crashing in his garden: 'I have the honour to report that I neglected to inform you of the crash landing of a Whitley aircraft in the grounds of Tatton Hall.' There is then an oblique swipe at the Lord for not asking after any casualties: 'You will be very pleased to know that although the aircraft was loaded to capacity, nobody was injured.' He signs off with due deference: 'I have the honour to be, my lord, your obedient servant, A.E. Agate, Flt Lt.'

The behaviour of some troops at Tatton Park did leave a lot to be desired. Some battalions gained a reputation quite early on for sending their naughty boys and misfits off to parachute training, and Newnham moaned that, 'Good soldiers were discouraged from applying to Ringway. So those who did come had little regimental spirit and very low discipline' (Newnham, 1946, p. 53).

One of the primary causes was that both the trainees and the Ringway staff had a great deal of spare time. Parachute training was weather-dependent, and it is apparent from the Ringway Operational Log that wind, rain, frost and snow frequently led to all training being cancelled. Although the Commando troops were required to keep themselves fit with physical training exercises and route marches, these men (and women) still had long periods with nothing to do. The Ringway authorities sought to fill this time by putting on ENSA shows including top-rank celebrities like Evelyn Laye and Arthur Riscoe, showing up-to-date films, putting on 'improving' lectures and, most popular of all dances at which male and female personnel were permitted to mingle.

Outside the base, there were a very large number of pubs around Tatton Park and Knutsford: The White Hart, The Saracens Head, and The Roebuck to name a few, and the trainees and staff used these whenever they could to unwind, abiding by the strict rules of social apartheid whereby soldiers were not allowed to visit pubs frequented by RAF officers. The most popular with the officers was The Frozen Mop in nearby Mobberley. Frank Muir used to perform sketches in the bar, Leslie Irvin, the parachute designer, regularly did his party trick of standing on his head against a piano playing 'I want to be happy' while drinking a glass of beer and the senior Polish instructor, Lieutenant Julian Gebolys, sang rousing Polish marching songs.

The Frozen Mop was designated off limits to the trainees, but the landlord found that this ban was impacting his profits, so he came up with a plan. He told the junior ranks that he would place a mop with head facing upwards outside the door as a warning signal whenever there were officers in the pub. The scheme worked perfectly until one day when it snowed, and parachute jumping was impossible. As a result, the pub was full of officers. The landlord diligently placed the mop head upwards outside the door. Unfortunately, the mop became covered with snow and obscured from view. The unsuspecting soldiers who rolled into the pub were all put on a charge for ignoring an order.

Venereal disease was a constant concern and on 10 January 1943, a review was undertaken of the arrangements to prevent its spread. It was decided that each of the army camps on the station should be provided with facilities for prophylaxis. The report went on:

> Bad reports had been received recently concerning two hotels in the district which are much frequented by both RAF and Army personnel from this station. These hotels are visited by many undesirable characters who, it was thought, may be the source of many cases of venereal disease. Although only a few cases among RAF personnel could be attributed to this source during the past year, it is thought that a considerable number of Army

personnel may have reported sick with symptoms of venereal disease after the completion of their training when arriving back at their parent unit (Air Ministry AIR 29/250, 1944).

There were undoubtedly problems with a small number of young recruits. They were away from home, risking their lives, and often had time on their hands. Fortunately, though, there was already at Tatton a teacher who had trained in some of the toughest schools in South London and worked in the unforgiving technical colleges with young men who certainly didn't want to be there. Charles Agate came up with a plan to tame these unruly young men and it was a strikingly modern one not unlike the current Forest Schools' Initiative.

In February 1943 he wrote to Lord Egerton suggesting a programme of gardening activities for the troops so as to 'improve the appearance of the site by growing shrubs and plants'. Agate himself would supervise. The project lasted till at least June 1944, or in other words just before the departure of the troops for the Normandy beaches, and Agate wrote to Egerton expressing his 'Gratitude for your generous response to our request for aid with our gardening activities'. Agate signed off in just a slightly less deferential way than over year before: 'I have the honour to be, sir, your obedient servant, Flt Lt. A.E. Agate, AFC.'

Agate's impact on the troops went so much further than just teaching them to parachute.

Chapter 17

Pigeons, Paradogs, and Ruperts

Recruits, of course, came in all shapes and sizes and there were even some celebrities. Evelyn Waugh trained at Tatton in autumn 1943 but broke his leg on his first jump, retired to Devon to recuperate and write *Brideshead Revisited* and never returned. The actors Richard Todd and Anthony Quayle also undertook balloon training under the watchful eye of Charles Agate. But it wasn't only humans, famous or not, who had to be rigorously tested and trained.

As the imperative to prepare for an invasion of occupied Europe became ever more pressing, new ideas and innovative parachuting kit, some more unusual than others, were devised by the Airborne Forces Experimental Establishment (AFEE) at Ringway. One of the more successful of these was the folding bicycle.

It is hard to even imagine gripping the 10kg contraption with wooden pedals and preparing to leap out of a plane into a war zone in the night, but that's exactly what the paratroopers did. Two wingnuts, one at the top of the frame and one at the bottom, could be loosened to fold the bicycle in half, swinging the front wheel around to the right so it ends up next to the rear wheel. Brackets attached to the frame allowed the paratroopers to strap their rifles to the bikes. They held the folded bikes out in front of them, with the wheels attached to the parachute suspension line, as they jumped out and floated to the ground.

Over 60,000 Airborne Folding Paratrooper Bicycles were made by the Birmingham Small Arms company between 1942 and 1945. The bike was used by both British and Canadian troops in major conflicts throughout the Second World War, including on D-Day and at the

Battle of Arnhem in 1944. They were intended to give paratroopers a way to cover larger distances after landing as quietly as possible. They were usually abandoned when no longer needed, but they remained a useful supplementary vehicle throughout the war and were common sights in France and Norway after the war. The few remaining examples are either in museums or owned by collectors.

Amid the complicated mess that is modern warfare, it can be almost comforting to think of these brave men leaping out of airplanes with nothing but their folding bicycles and their courage, though as preparations for the as yet unnamed and secret missions in 1944 went on, new types of paratroop were also being trained to perform tasks in the field. Tasks such as carrying messages: the parachuting pigeons were not so much trained to jump, as carried in boxes on the front of the soldier and then released with messages once they had landed.

Locating mines and explosives, keeping watch, and warning about approaching enemy troops was the remit of the 'paradog', though training one required a little more thought than the pigeons. Their slim bodies proved to be advantageous because, during their test jumps, they could use the parachutes that had been designed to carry the folding bicycles. To make it easier to get the dogs to jump out of the aircraft, they weren't given anything to drink or eat beforehand, and then their handler jumped before them carrying a large chunk of meat. After the dog touched down, the handler immediately ran to her, released her, and gave her the meat. Jump, land, eat that was the simple theory and the dogs would eventually start enjoying it, sometimes even leaping out of the aircraft without any coaxing, though it is not thought that Charles Agate volunteered his own beloved Alsatian Pat to train as a paradog.

One innovation which would have a huge impact on subsequent operations was in fact not new at all. Military planners in 1943 and 1944 saw that in order to give an Allied invasion fleet the best chance at victory on the beaches of Northern France, the German forces would need to be distracted and directed away from the invasion site. The time was right for Alan Cobham's drunken farmer to stagger out of the refreshment tent, leave the flying circuses behind and take his place in the development of British airborne forces.

Operation Titanic was a plan to drop hundreds of dummy paratroopers many miles away from the actual landing zones to lure German firepower. These dummy paratroopers came to be known as 'Ruperts'. They were made from burlap and shaped like soldiers – but only 3ft tall, on the basis that from 100ft below it was almost impossible for a German anti-aircraft gun operator to see that these paratroopers were unusually short. Drawstrings at the top of the head, wrists, and ankles allowed the dummy to be filled with straw or sand and they were dressed in paratrooper uniforms, including boots and helmets. In addition to the parachutes strapped to their burlap backs, each 'Rupert' carried recordings of gunfire and exploding mortar rounds, to add to the authenticity of the simulated air attack. When the 'Ruperts' landed, they would self-destruct, leaving just a charred white parachute behind.

As the summer of 1944 approached, Agate was well on his way towards his 1,000th jump. He had jumped every morning to check the weather, carried out over 150 test jumps with untried equipment, jumped with bags, boats and other baggage strapped to his legs, jumped from Whitleys, Dakotas, Wellingtons, Albemarles, Manchesters, Lancasters, Stirlings, Halifaxes and static balloons, jumped from dangerously low altitudes and into freezing water, trained thousands of troops and jumped with them, and on more than one occasion he had jumped to reassure them after one of their colleagues had died.

He was already used to flying with the SOE agents on secret missions as a dispatcher, but soon he would be called upon to board the very first flights over Normandy and three months later over the Low Countries in Operation Market Garden. His war was far from over, but in the run-up to those decisive operations there was still plenty of testing, training, and jumping for him to do.

Chapter 18

Preparing for D-Day and Arnhem

T he Douglas DC-3 Dakota had long been coveted by the men of Ringway who had heard of its roomy, well-lit fuselage and side door which made it seem like a much more appealing aircraft than the Whitley, which they branded the 'Flying Coffin'.

An initial delivery of Dakotas was sent to Ringway in September 1943, but they could not be used for parachute training because the rigging lines of the X-type parachute frequently snagged on the tail wings. On one occasion a man was killed when an officer who jumped three places in front of him remained suspended from the tail long enough for the man three places behind him to bump into him. Their parachutes tangled together, and they both fell as one.

Agate was involved in the extensive tests to find the most suitable configuration and length of static line needed to clear the tail of the Dakota. These tests took time and so the old unreliable Whitleys were required to soldier on and cope with a huge increase in training drops.

There were eight more deaths jumping from a Whitley up to D-Day in June 1944 and casualties continued to undermine morale at Ringway. On 25 May, Corporal A. Nelson, a RAF PTI, died as a result of tangled lines. On 6 July, Polish Second Lieutenant Jozef Dryll died from the same cause and the following day a fellow Polish trainee, Private Romanouski, drowned when he landed in a pond at Tatton Park.

On 22 July, Private Douglas Haig Charlesworth of nearby Cheetham Hill, Manchester, was killed on the last day of No. 72 course when his parachute failed to open properly, with the words 'faulty design of inner bag' written in the logbook of fatal accidents. He was 24.

On 10 August Private Duffy died as a result of 'thrown lines', though no further details are given and on 25 August Lance Corporal Janocha was killed when he was struck by a passing aircraft. The end of the summer was marked on 31 August when Private Gordon Creech, a bricklayer from Williton-on-Exmoor in Devon, died as a result of a somersault on exiting the Whitley. He was 22.

Given this comparatively high number of deaths, the resistance to reserve parachutes is difficult to understand. In September 1943 a conference was held between British and American officers to compare parachuting equipment and techniques. John Kilkenny reported back that he was very impressed by US casualty figures and the fact that they had experienced just three fatalities in 172,000 jumps, compared to 30 in 153,000 jumps at Ringway. However, the argument was not sufficient to sway the RAF.

For Agate and his fellow PJIs there was then a blessed respite of nearly two months, until the death of 22-year-old Private Arthur Dixon from Highgate on 12 October 1943. It was an event which would impact directly on Charles Agate and on his commanding officer. Arthur Dixon had volunteered for the airborne forces just a month before and was killed on the first aircraft jump of training course No. 86 after his parachute canopy became caught in a wheel spat of the Whitley and was torn. Maurice Newnham recounts what happened next: 'With Agate I jumped into my car, and we tore across to where the unfortunate man had fallen. I knew that there was nothing we could do for him. Agate rushed back to the control hut to stop all future jumps as the parachute had snagged on a broken piece of metal' (Newnham, 1946). Course No. 86 was notable for the high attrition rate. Out of the 227 trainees there were fifteen injured and nine who refused to jump. Most of the injuries were sustained as a result of rough weather conditions.

There would be two more deaths before the year was out. On 11 November Sergeant van Rees suffered twisted lines, and on 22

December, Lance Corporal McPhedran was unable to control his exit from the Whitley and fell to his death.

***

With USAAF personnel now at Ringway and Tatton, there were inevitably many direct comparisons between the virtues of British and American methods. Charles Agate recognized that the long-awaited Dakota was superior to the British Whitley. He told the BBC's Don Durbridge in 1974: 'They had the Dakotas with a side door, and you could jump 20 men out of the side door. Bom bom bom bom bom, one after the other . . . providing nobody got stuck in the door.'

It was immediately obvious that the Dakota's spacious fuselage made movement inside the aircraft far easier and allowed men to exit far faster than from the cramped Whitley. Because the men could exit faster this also had the benefit of bringing the men closer together on the ground. There were relatively comfortable seats for up to twenty-five men or more, plenty of space between the two rows of seats to allow them to move about the plane, smoking was permitted and there was even a toilet at the rear end for those whose nerves got the better of their stomachs. There were windows too along the whole length of the fuselage. The Dakota though was not without its detractors. The exit door was relatively low, and this meant that even the smallest men had to crouch down to get through it, increasing the danger of rolling out instead of jumping out of the aircraft.

There was another major problem. When dropping a stick of twenty-five men they ended up being spread out on the ground over 1,000 yards (914m). It was decided that although twenty-five parachutists could be carried, it was better to limit the stick to between fifteen and twenty.

In most other respects, Agate believed very strongly that British ways were superior. The British X-type parachute gave a much softer opening than the American T-5 because the static line was much shorter and was attached to the rigging lines, which were withdrawn simultaneously with the canopy. This meant that the soldier's body was moving at approximately the same speed as the parachute when it opened, which made for a much less abrupt brake to the descent. The British parachute also had the benefit of a harness with quick-release snaps for immediate shedding of the parachute on the ground.

To prepare the trainees for jumping from the Dakota, Agate oversaw the building of modified, larger cages with a side exit which were fitted under the Tatton Park balloons. Each paratrooper was required to jump with a heavy load of equipment, including submachine guns or folding carbines and even a length of rope to lower themselves in case they landed in a tree. Changes were made to the equipment issued to the trainees including a specialized jump suit with large pockets to carry extra rations, ammunition, or grenades. The paratrooper helmet was also modified with forked straps to secure the special chin cup.

***

The war was now entering a critical phase in which Agate would play a key role, not only as a parachute instructor but also as a participant in two of the defining actions of the conflict: Operation Neptune (D-Day) and Operation Market Garden (Arnhem).

Planning for Operation Neptune had begun as early as 1942, when General George Marshall visited airborne demonstrations by British forces on Salisbury Plain accompanied by Churchill. It was agreed that amphibious landings in Normandy would be preceded by an aerial and naval bombardment and an airborne assault which entailed the landing of around 7,000 British, 13,000 US and 4,000 Canadian paratroops. The American troops were to be trained in the USA but the British and some of the Canadians would be trained under the watchful eye of Charles Agate and the PJIs at RAF Ringway.

Agate knew little of the objective for which these men were being trained; only that there was a need to prepare thousands of troops for significant operations planned for the summer of 1944, and in the run up to D-Day, more than 10,000 parachute descents per month took place at Ringway.

Time was short, and there was so much pressure at Ringway to push trainees through that even in poor weather the instructors were told to 'make as many jumps as they could' to give confidence to the trainees. An instruction which suited Agate's growing obsession with jumping. However, on some days jumping really was impossible meaning that on rare occasions troops were sent off to fight not having completed the requisite number of practice jumps.

It was recognized that jumping in inclement weather was placing stress on many of the trainees, and Agate's smiling face and ready charm were not always enough to keep them calm. Bernard Winfield's brother Roland had procured Benzedrine in large quantities for Bomber Command from 1942 and had begun to issue two 5mg tablets per man for each bombing mission to be taken voluntarily.

So it was that over two days in April 1944 sixty parachute jump instructors were assembled at Tatton Park for medical experiments to test the effects of what was referred to in the Ringway Operations Log as 'dope' – Benzedrine, but also methamphetamine and other opiates – to help them withstand acute stress and anxiety and also to stave off tiredness. The man in charge of these experiments was Agate's friend Bernard Winfield.

In one particular experiment Flight Lieutenants Jimmy Blyth and Murphy made five descents in quick succession without using 'dope' followed by five having taken it. They reported feeling much less tired than they normally would after such intense activity. The Ringway Operations Log went on to note that:

'as far as records go, this is the first time that anyone has done so many descents consecutively in one day' (Air Ministry AIR 29/250, 1944). The recommended daily maximum under normal conditions was three.

This was like a red rag to a bull for the previous record holder: Flight Lieutenant Charles Agate. Newnham in *Prelude to Glory* describes Agate's response to having his record eclipsed by Blyth and Murphy: 'He couldn't bear the thought that anyone could have made more parachute jumps in a single day than he had so a week later he put the record up to sixteen: three in the morning and thirteen in the afternoon' (Newnham, 1946, p. 317).

***

Agate had no idea when D-Day would be or what it would entail, but he knew that action was imminent when the Ringway trainees were inspected by King George VI and Queen Elizabeth accompanied by 17-year-old Princess Elizabeth. The air of expectation was tangible. Laurence Olivier's epic technicolour film of Shakespeare's *Henry V* (which was partly funded by the British Government as a propaganda vehicle) was released on the eve of D-Day bearing the dedication to 'the Commandos and Airborne Troops of Great Britain the spirit of whose ancestors it has been humbly attempted to recapture'.

The film was leaden with patriotic symbolism and neatly omitted the less admirable parts of Shakespeare's portrait. For example, Henry's threat to unleash his troops to rape and pillage Harfleur if the city refused to surrender and the cutting of the throats of French prisoners during the battle at Agincourt, as well as his refusal to intervene to stop the hanging of his old friend Bardolph. The theatre and film critics of the British Press gave the film a lukewarm welcome, but it caught the public mood, and it went on to break all records during its 11-month run in London.

When D-Day finally arrived, Maurice Newnham presented Major General Richard Gale, who commanded the British 6th Airborne Division, with a doll made in the fashion of a PTS instructor, with uniform, cap and badges and named 'Percy from PTS'.

Louis Strange, who was now serving as Wing Commander at No. 46 Group and who had assisted in the planning for Operation Overlord, flew in Squadron Leader Dusty Miller's Dakota DC-3 acting, in his own words, as 'group observer, assistant despatcher, general cabin-boy and steward to the paratroopers'.

The PJIs were already used to accompanying SOE agents as despatchers on their flights over enemy territory. Both General Sir Richard Nelson 'Windy' Gale and Maurice Newnham were very much in favour of this, and a joint War Office/Air Ministry directive now paved the way for the instructors to accompany troops in the aircraft for the flight to the dropping sites on the big operations of 1944.

Agate travelled as a dispatcher and spotter on a Short Stirling with the task of dropping a group of path-finders three miles inland at the Orne River in Normandy at about 1 am, ahead of the seaborne forces who were to land at 6.30 am. The paratroops took off from several English airfields and the men were all in high spirits. They had been ordered to have their hair cut very short and some had got the barber to shave out a 'V for victory' sign on the back of their heads.

Anti-aircraft fire exploded around Agate's Stirling, causing the plane to shudder. The red light went on and each man had to check the man in front was properly hooked up to the static line. Finally, the green light came on and one after the other plunged through the hole in the floor of the plane. Agate was at hand to urge the men on, tap them on the shoulder and get them out as quickly as possible.

In June 1944, he was promoted to substantive Flight Lieutenant, his highest wartime rank and mentioned in despatches for a second time.

***

No sooner had Agate returned from the D-Day landings than he learned of the deaths of two of his fellow PJIs in a plane crash while on a perilous mission to occupied France. Sergent Phil Wilding and Pilot Officer Frank Copland, acting as dispatchers, were killed with most of the rest of the crew on 23 July 1944. Just a week later there would be yet another death in training at Tatton when Private Richard Wicks's lines twisted.

Agate was then plunged into preparing more paratroops for Operation Market Garden that was to be launched in September 1944. Work ramped up right across the Parachute Training School and Agate was also tasked with training conscientious objectors who would parachute into Arnhem with the other troops, to carry out bomb disposal or to work in Resuscitation Teams, giving care to badly wounded patients.

There were also refresher courses for those who had passed through RAF Ringway earlier in the war and the presence of so many familiar faces led to inter-unit sports matches. In April 1944 the RAF PTS rugby team parachuted onto the field for one of its games against the Army. In the following month, the Army team arrived for the return match by the same means.

Much has been written about Operation Market Garden, but it is enough here just briefly to summarise the action itself. The operation was intended to capitalise on the German defeat in Normandy by rapidly advancing on a narrow front into German-occupied Holland, before swinging east into northern Germany, thereby opening up the possibility of bringing the war to a conclusion by the end of 1944.

The ground advance by the Army would be preceded by a 60-mile airborne spearhead between Belgian-Dutch border and the town of Arnhem, the purpose of which was to seize and hold a series of vital river crossings. Three airborne divisions were assigned to the operation and Charles Agate was one of the twenty-five PJIs who served as despatchers on the pathfinder parachute drops, 'helping with equipment, tending those who were airsick, giving confidence by their presence' (Newnham, 1946, p. 306) – and then dispatching them. He was on the very first aircraft over Arnhem and assisted with the dropping of panniers, containers and other heavy equipment after the men had jumped.

The parachuting padres from Ringway whom Agate so admired also distinguished themselves in the operation at Arnhem. The Rev Robert Talbot-Watkins led groups of wounded to safety across the Rhine, returning under fire across the river. He was awarded the Military Cross for his unfailing courage and complete disregard for his own safety. At Arnhem Bridge, Father Egan spent much of his time at the Regimental Aid Post and continually visited the wounded who had been packed into the cellars of the houses around the small British perimeter. Medical supplies of all kinds were in short supply, but Father Egan brought what relief he could to those who had no option but to sit out the battle in pain.

Most of the PJIs returned to Ringway to listen for news of their charges. But the mission had not been a success at least partly because it was carried out in daylight, despite all the hazardous training and testing for nighttime parachutes the PJIs had carried out in the previous months. Of the 11,920 men delivered to Arnhem by parachute or glider 1,485 were killed, and 6,525 were taken prisoner. Overall, 3,999 of the Allied airborne troops involved in the D-Day landings were killed in action. The RAF lost 68 aircraft, along with 368 RAF aircrew and 79 despatchers.

Agate's daughter Lynette said that her father knew early in 1944 that the landings at Arnhem would not be the success the Allies hoped for, that thousands would die. Her father knew it, the other PJIs knew it, but they were not able to express their opinion. They had to get on with the job of training the troops for the big jump. However, one of his Ringway colleagues, Flight Sergeant Charles Bindon Carter,[69] did have a happier outcome. At Arnhem, he had to parachute out of his plane into enemy territory just before it crashed in flames. He was assisted by the Resistance to return to Ringway on 21 September 1944, just in time for his wedding.

There were bitter recriminations about where the faults with Operation Market Garden lay. The Army criticised the RAF for their selection of drop and landing zones irrespective of the views or needs of the troops they were delivering (in some cases troops were dropped seven miles away from their objectives in order to avoid the loss of too many aircraft). The RAF criticised the Army commanders for launching the assault in broad daylight. Although there may be something in this, but there is no doubt that the RAF's choice of landing zones for both operations removed the greatest attribute of airborne warfare, which is surprise. Regardless of where the blame should sit, the fact remains that many brave men died because of bad planning.

In May 1990, Anthony Deane-Drummond wrote to the *Journal of the Royal Signals Institution* in response to what he regarded as a well-researched article about the communications problems at Arnhem. 'Every single airborne operation undertaken before Operation Market Garden had emphasised that lightly equipped airborne troops must be landed either on or very close to the objective. This precept was not carried out at Arnhem and led directly to the fiasco.'

The strength, bravery and determination of the men involved is beyond question but the concentration of so many men in airborne warfare at D-Day and Arnhem demonstrated that large-scale airborne operations are invariably high-value, high-risk ventures.

It can be argued in the case of the D-Day operation that the invasion of Europe could not have gone ahead without an airborne force to secure the flanks of the invasion beachhead. In addition, an airborne force can be a force multiplier, in the sense that its mere existence obliges the enemy to divert resources into guarding against the possibility of airborne attack. However, one reason for the swift reaction at Arnhem was the fact that the German Army had been training extensively in anti-airborne operations.

Fortunately, lessons were learned from Market Garden and on the night of 23 March 1945, Operation Plunder was launched by the 21st Army Group under Field Marshal Bernard Montgomery. The operation included parachute and glider landings near Wesel with the aim of establishing a bridgehead across the Rhine. Within a week of the start of Operation Plunder, the Allies had taken 30,000 prisoners of war north of the Ruhr. With the Nazis now in retreat, the war was drawing to its final stages.

With operations at Ringway scaling down, for Charles Agate, like many of the other Ringway staff, the thought 'was it all worth it' must have crossed his mind, but if it did, he didn't appear to let it trouble him for long. When asked about this by Don Durbridge in 1974 he preferred to contrast his life, not with the men who fought, but rather with the teachers who stayed behind: 'I'd had a very, very glamorous war, whereas many of the other teachers, they'd been packed off down to the country with masses of children. I'm sure they had a much more difficult time and a harder time than ever I did parachuting and enjoying it so much.'

The true impact of Agate's 'glamourous' war would show itself later.

Chapter 19

The Real Impact

Charles Agate's job at Tatton was still not done. There was work to do for all the PJIs and testing and training carried on for what Newnham called 'all kinds of strange and unorthodox missions' (Newnham, 1946, p. 346).

Much had been learnt though in the preceding years and the injury rate had fallen to less than one in every 2,000 jumps. There were though still deaths at Ringway and between Arnhem and VE Day on 8 May 1945, there were eight more. Two of these – Privates Dupuis and Southall – were killed on the same day: 9 December 1944. M Dupuis was an 18-year-old member of the French SAS who made a normal backward landing jumping from a Dakota but died one hour later from a broken neck. H Southwell made his first jump from a Whitley just ten minutes after Dupuis but somersaulted and his lines got caught between his legs preventing the canopy from developing. He died at the same moment as Dupuis.

Just six days later, Polish Lance Corporal Jankowski died when making a night descent from a balloon. After the Christmas break, training resumed on 27 December. 19-year-old Private Jonathan Crabb from Coventry was the first of his stick to jump from a Whitley on training course 146. Pte Crabb's horrific death during on 27 December 1944 is recorded in the Ringway Operations Log as follows:

His parachute after leaving the bag wrapped itself round the tail wheel of the aircraft, and Pt Crabb was suspended in the slipstream of the aircraft. He made desperate but unsuccessful attempts to release himself. The aircraft flew round for 30 minutes until the pilot received instructions to land on the grass at the airfield. Private Crabb died a short while after the aircraft landed (Air Ministry AIR 29/250, 1944).

A similar incident had happened before on 10 December 1943, but two instructors, Sergeant P Benson and Sergeant T. Knowles, saved the man's life by managing to haul him back on board. The fortunate trainee was able to make a perfect jump and landing the very next day.

With the arrival of more Dakota aircraft, the use of the Whitley ceased on 1 January 1945. However, deaths continued. Two more Poles, Privates Jerzy Jan Stanisław Sukiennik and Dubiela Franciszek Zielinski, died on 21 February 1945 after making backwards landings from a Dakota. A Belgian, Private Nicholas Polys, died on 7 March, four days after he made a backwards landing and fractured his skull. The following day, on 8 March, Private J. B. Scudamore died while on a refresher course when his lines became twisted, and his parachute failed to develop.

Death stalked Tatton Park throughout the war and touched everyone. The anonymous 'Pegasus' writing in *Parachutist* in 1945 recounts this incident: 'A man I trained with very foolishly rushed over to the spot where a man had just crashed and found that it was a friend of his. I don't suppose he ever looked at jumping in the same light again' (Pegasus, 1944, p. 27).

Every man and woman, no matter how brave, had to face their very worst fears every time they put on a parachute and climbed aboard a balloon or aircraft; every time they went through the terrible strain of waiting: waiting for the weather to clear, waiting to board the plane, waiting in the rattling fuselage, and waiting for the green light. 'Pegasus' himself admits that on his first jump after an injury: 'I did what I had not done for 20 years . . . I wetted myself. The question should not be asked "how much nerve does it require?", but "what effect does it have on the nerve?"' (Pegasus, 1944, p. 28).

In Jack Dudley's book *The Face of Death* the author describes the psychological impact on the trainees even after successfully completing their first jumps: 'Some of us sang and laughed . . . we ate an enormous tea, our bodies relaxed, and the bow strung tautness of our minds slackened' (Dudley, 1958, p. 33) For one of their colleagues though, that tension would not go away:

> In the early hours of the morning I was awakened by a commotion from the room next door. It was Emile shouting, screaming at the top of his voice. He stared at us with wild, glazed eyes, the perspiration making his face look ghastly, and soaking his pyjamas. His teeth chattered. His bed rattled . . . Emile never did jump again (Dudley, 1958, pp. 33–4).

Superstitions helped many to cope, at least in the short term. One man refused to jump because he could not find the helmet he usually wore, and helmets bearing the number 13 were shunned as were those with twelve 'notches' chalked on them to indicate twelve jumps completed. Many trainees carried St Christophers or other lucky charms, some mass produced, some more personal items including 'coins, locks of hair, pieces of wood, coal, stone, chalk, brooches, pins, necklaces' (Pegasus, 1944, p. 58).

It is common in all armies to decorate vehicles and weapons with the name of girlfriends or with good-luck slogans and drawings but at RAF Ringway, this became an obsession. Crude drawings were artistically executed in chalks of every colour on parachute helmets. An order was issued to the effect that this practice should cease forthwith, but it did not, for if a man feels safer with 'I love Doris' written on his helmet nothing is going to make him jump without it.

Others carried out elaborate rituals before every jump, touching something or counting a set sequence of numbers again and again. One man always half-smoked a cigarette while waiting to board the plane, then stubbed it out and put it carefully in the right-hand pocket. It had to be the right-hand pocket. As soon as he landed safely, he got it out and smoked it.

There was also of course dark humour, often expressed in songs such as this, that were sung on the buses that took trainees to and from Tatton Park: 'Here's to the men dead already and here's to the next man to die' (Pegasus, 1944), or this, which is a British version of the American parachutists' apocryphal story of a packer, cheated in love, sabotaging her former lover's parachute:

> I'd like to find the Sergeant who forgot to hook me up, (Repeat three times)
> For I ain't gonna jump no more.
> I'd like to find the WAAF who tied a love knot in my line.
> For I ain't gonna jump no more.
> I'd like to find the pilot who forgot to throttle back.
> For I ain't gonna jump no more.
> I'd like to find the WAAF who put the blanket in my chute.
> For I ain't gonna jump no more.
> Oh, they wiped him off the tarmac like a pound of strawberry jam.
> For I ain't gonna jump no more.

Curiously, an alternative version is repeated in various Scout and Guide songbooks and is still sung regularly, and with gusto to the tune of *The Battle Hymn of the Republic* at Brownie camps across the UK!

> He jumped without a parachute from twenty thousand feet (repeat three times)
> And he ain't gonna jump no more.

Chorus
Glory what a hell of a way to die (repeat three times)
And he ain't gonna jump no more.

He landed on the pavement like a lump of strawberry jam
(repeat three times)
And he ain't gonna jump no more.

Chorus

They put him in a match box, and they sent him home to mum
(repeat three times)
And he ain't gonna jump no more.

Chorus

She put him on the mantel piece for everyone to see (repeat
three times)
And he ain't gonna jump no more.

Chorus

She put him on the table when the Vicar came to tea (repeat
three times)
And he ain't gonna jump no more.

Chorus

The Vicar spread him on some toast and said what lovely jam
(repeat three times)
And he ain't gonna jump no more.

Glory glory what a hell of a way to die.
Suspended by your braces when you don't know how to fly.
Glory glory what a hell of a way to die.
And he ain't gonna jump no more.

The constant exposure to horrific accidents raises the question of how the PJIs themselves dealt with it all. During his war service, Agate would have been under unprecedented levels of stress, and in constant fear for his life, a fact that no amount of pre-war motorbiking or scrapes with violent criminals could possibly have prepared him for. Like so many other servicemen, Agate dismissed the dangers with breathtaking nonchalance, telling Don Durbridge in his 1974 BBC interview: 'If the parachute doesn't open, well, of course you have no worries.'

It is a sentiment echoed by Air Chief Marshal Sir Henry Robert Moore Brooke-Popham reflecting in 1944: 'Airmen experience the full joy of a fearless heart; they exhibit a certain joyous carelessness of life, perhaps because they can feel with Peter Pan that "to die will be an awfully big adventure" – just a big adventure nothing more. This spirit is made evident in a special form of courage – the exhilaration of danger.'

It was a description that would have fitted Charles Agate well. Life was an awfully big adventure, so maybe for him death would be as well.

However, Edward Cartner acknowledges that parachuting must 'top the list of lonely and intensely personal activities' (Cartner, 2012, p. 121). Agate and his colleagues very largely had to deal with its impact themselves and although as 'Pegasus' suggests 'Psychiatrists had a field day when British parachuting was born' (Pegasus, 1944, p. 40) and there were psychiatrists at Ringway during the war, they were less concerned with aftercare than finding ways of relieving the tension of the recruits before a jump, organizing for example impromptu games of football on the runway before the men boarded the plane. Crucially, the recruits also had the comfort of the Ringway tea hut which had been opened by Mrs Smalley and her sister in 1942 and stayed open day and night for four years.

The services of the psychiatrists were of course available to the instructors as well, though there is a sense that many of the PJIs had little time for them, with Harry Ward being particularly dismissive: 'They even turned the headshrinkers loose on us. They wanted to investigate the "terrors and phobias associated with the seemingly unnatural act of leaping from aeroplanes". What a load of rubbish!' (Hearn, 1990, p. 167).

On one occasion a newly-appointed and very keen psychiatrist was interested in observing the impact on a stick of parachutists of one of them losing his nerve just before the jump. He went up in the plane and pretended to lose his nerve. The instructor promptly kicked him out of the hatch. One can perhaps conclude that this was Harry Ward. Agate at least seemed less dismissive, calling these highly trained doctors the 'neurosis specialists' when reflecting on his own post-war struggles.

A question which recurs with respect to the instructors is why anyone should volunteer for such a hazardous profession. Agate himself talks about a 'wonderful feeling of exhilaration' when the 'chute opens and Harry Ward perhaps typically says that 'beer would never have tasted so good; pound notes would never have felt so crisp; and girls would never have looked so pretty, were it not for the risks we daily ran' (Ward and Hearn, 2012, p. 93), which is in line with the findings of the psychiatrists he was so quick to deride: 'the psychologists discovered that the act of parachuting had an inspiring and beneficial effect on men and women' (Newnham, 1946, p. 125).

Agate's fellow motorbike enthusiast, T. E. Lawrence, was said to 'use his motorbike and its speed to block momentarily his thoughts and worries' (Yardley, 2000) and there is a real sense that for many at Ringway the act of parachuting allowed a blissful escape from their everyday cares, which in Agate's case must have included the precarious situation he had left behind at home. It offered a rare feeling of being alive in the present moment with Newnham talking about how 'the utter inevitability of not being able to change one's mind after leaving the aircraft appealed to me' and Ward describing, 'A great sense of freedom. I was responsible for nobody but myself' (Hearn, 1990, p. 43). Agate told Don Durbridge in his 1974 radio interview: 'If you've got a toothache, a headache or a hangover, there's no doubt about it, when your feet touch the ground, they're gone.' In *Parachutist* the anonymous author sums this up neatly:

> The notion of jumping into thin air is contrary to all human, earth-bound instinct, but even after so few as fifteen jumps, one becomes accustomed to it. Even the individual who is not reckless by nature and who perhaps cannot stand heights comes to regard it as nothing extraordinary. I would rather jump from a thousand feet with a parachute than jump into a swimming-pool from the thirty-foot board. (Pegasus, 1944)

But Agate's case is a special one, an extreme one even. He jumped hundreds of times more than any of the other PJIs, and in fact more than anyone else in wartime Britain. His record stood for decades. He volunteered again and again to test untried pieces of equipment, new forms of parachute, new ways of exiting the plane, new ways of landing. He jumped thirteen times in one day just to reclaim a record. He put his life at risk every time.

His words in the 1974 interview perhaps point to parachuting becoming for Agate something more than just a job. Referring to those toothaches, headaches and hangover he said: 'They come back in about a half an hour.' He calls this 'the drug effect', and is remarkably well informed on the subject: When interviewed by a *Surrey Mirror* reporter after he made his 926th jump he said: 'It is like a drug – just as other men crave for tobacco or beer, I crave once I am down, to get back into the air and fall again' (*Surrey Mirror & County Post*, 1945).

Twenty-nine years later he told Don Durbridge: 'Parachuting, in my opinion, does become a drug if you do a lot of it. It became a drug to me, a really vicious drug.'

It is an instructive comment: parachuting as a drug, an addiction even. It is not unknown. A quick Google search in 2023 for 'skydiving addiction' comes up with thousands of hits. Many of them are flippant, not really talking about addiction at all, but about the skydivers' abiding love of the sport. For £9.50, plus postage and packing, you can even get a t-shirt (choice of colours) emblazoned with the message: 'The world really does revolve around my skydiving addiction', but a few of them hint at a darker issue, with one blogger posting starkly: 'skydiving addiction: the struggle is real'. Again, Agate shows his grasp of his own situation:

> I know why it's a drug. Every time you do a parachute jump, if you stand at the door of an aircraft or you make a jump from the balloon or whatever type of jump you're going to do, you always get a slight nervous tension. You get a dryness of the lips, but eventually you pitch yourself out and the parachute opens. If the parachute doesn't open, well, of course you have no worries, but the parachute opens, and then your only worry is to make a nice landing . . .
>
> But this is the strange thing. Every time your feet touch the ground, you have a wonderful feeling of exhilaration. I think this is what happens: the nervous tension that you give out, or comes out from yourself, as you pitch yourself out, you're repaid by nature, as it were. When your feet touch the ground, you get this wonderful feeling of well-being and of exhilaration. That is the drug effect.

The addictive effects of extreme sports are now the subject of academic research. Writing about skydiving Giuseppe Musumeci asks: 'Why do so many athletes keep practicing extreme sports, even though they know the danger of risking their lives?' (Musumeci, 2021). His answer shows that in some ways Agate's own analysis of the addictive effect of repeated exposure to risk in parachuting was ahead of its time: 'The adrenaline rush increases the acceleration of blood flows to the muscles and brain, relaxes the muscles, and lastly helps with the conversion of glycogen into glucose in the liver . . . also the organism produces a large amount of dopamine which is known to elicit the sensation of pleasure similar to those experienced with alcohol and drugs.'

Professor Nora Volkov, director of the US National Institute of Drug Abuse, confirms this: 'It activates the dopamine reward system which imprints an unconscious memory that we describe as conditioning, and which becomes stronger and stronger with repeated use. We are led compulsively to repeat the behaviour' (Volkov, 2022). Volkov calls this a sort of 'shivering tolerance' forcing these thrill seekers to seek higher doses of emotion every time to reach the same sensation as before.

But not all risk-taking behaviours are necessarily harmful. Musumeci and others for instance acknowledge that there are other less dramatic factors in extreme sports which make them attractive or mildly addictive, and especially as they have 'the capacity to establish a strong bond between individuals, thanks to the dangerous elements of the activity that requires a high level of trust between people'.

If parachuting was a drug for Agate, it was one he certainly had the opportunity to indulge in repeatedly. Agate admitted in his 1974 BBC Radio Brighton interview that he usually did 'anything between seven and eight jumps every day. The most I ever did in a day was 16, and the most I ever did in a calendar month was 75.'

The image of Agate as an adrenalin junkie is a compelling one. We know that throughout his life he was intoxicated by speed, owning several motorbikes and in May 1940 he had been prosecuted at Epsom Petty Sessions and fined for speeding and failing to observe a traffic sign. He must also have experienced an adrenaline rush in 1932 when he leapt onto the running board of a speeding car to apprehend the suspected murderer Frederick Deats, but as the war drew towards its close in 1945 it does seem that Agate became more and more fixated on jumping for its own sake. What worries, what dark thoughts was he momentarily forgetting in the rush of adrenaline? Or was he simply jumping for the sheer pleasure of it?

We know that earlier in the war, Newnham had taken a kindly attitude to Agate's enthusiasms, describing him putting on a parachute as easily as a commuter puts on his bowler hat, but by 1945 even Newnham's attitude had hardened, wondering if parachuting had in fact become a 'mania' for Agate. Ward agreed: 'Agate developed an almost unhealthy enthusiasm for jumping from the balloon' (Newnham, 1946).

Rather than taking it easy as the war came to an end, he stepped up his relentless jumping and seems to have revelled in it. Newnham credited Agate with 1,400 drops up to VE Day on 8 May, still far short of the 1,601 he would achieve by the following summer. It seems that although the war was over, he just couldn't stop getting back up in the air and falling again.

Activity at Ringway really was coming to an end: a farewell dinner was held in September 1945 to mark the decision to move the No. 1 Parachute Training School to RAF Weston on the Green in Oxfordshire. Prime Minister Winston Churchill also paid one last visit to Ringway, but this time his mission was a more personal one. He wanted to shake the hand of Flight Lieutenant Charles Agate and the other parachute jump instructors to thank them for their dedication, and courage. Agate of course was still not finished.

Newnham left Ringway in October 1945, but a newspaper article shows Agate holding a cake at an Airborne Forces Security Fund Dance in Knutsford in December of the same year and boasting of 1,534 drops. The last training drops at Ringway were recorded on 28 January 1946, after a total of 429,000 live descents, but in another article a few weeks later in the *Surrey Mirror* he claimed 1,584 drops and reveals his ambition to reach 1,600, a total he reached on 4 June 1946.

***

For Newnham and others though, there was the very real frustration that not enough progress had been made during the war in parachute design simply because so many thousands of people had to be trained, and despite his constant battles for inquiry and research into twisted rigging lines, parachute design ended in 1945 more or less where it had started: 'the war ended three and a half years later with precisely the same design of parachuting equipment in use as had been evolved so hurriedly in the summer of 1941' (Newnham, 1946, p. 119).

The question that must also be asked is why it was necessary for the RAF to begin experimenting independently when Russian, Polish, German and even America techniques were already at such a high level that it seems almost perverse that Britain should consciously chose to ignore the lessons that it could readily have learned from others. The anonymous 'Pegasus' was infuriated: 'I cannot understand why it was necessary to start experimenting independently when Russian and German technique was already so well known about and the Americans had a film on the market showing how they did it' (Pegasus, 1944, p. 33).

The blame for this should not be laid at the door of the staff of RAF Ringway or the Air Ministry, but with the Prime Minister who had demanded an airborne capability, but who was not prepared to provide the equipment and the aircraft required. The fact that the men of Ringway were able to rise above these challenges is to their eternal credit. The notion that Churchill should be applauded for their determination, their constant endeavour and their human sacrifices is more questionable.

Deeper still was the niggling anxiety that perhaps, just perhaps, the entire war was unnecessary and all of it from the horrors of the London Blitz to the Holocaust could have been avoided. It would have been a brave man who asked this question in the immediate aftermath, but it was a thought that troubled many of those who had survived. If Britain had maintained a significant military deterrent capability after 1918 it might have been in a position to deter Hitler in his ambitions in the mid-1930s. It is certainly true that Hitler and his Wehrmacht were nervous about possible British and French reactions to the illegal occupation of the Rhineland in March 1936. In the event France and Britain did nothing, which fostered and encouraged Hitler's ambitions. The British government could not threaten the Germans with something it did not have.

British foreign policy was also focussed primarily on maintaining and policing the British Empire in which sufficient cracks were already appearing to suggest that if the sun was not yet setting, it was considerably lower in the sky than it was at the year of Agate's birth. In the years immediately after 1918 Britain hoped it had punished Germany to the extent that it would never be able to threaten peace in Europe and that Britain could now return to the days when its only security commitments were linked to defending the Empire. Britain simply was not prepared, militarily, politically or mentally, to go to war again in Europe. As a result, it had made no preparations for the possibility of a modern military campaign against a European country. Britain was living in a past that was being changed irradicably by the new breed of fascists who were busy overturning previously held notions of diplomacy and state behaviour.

Historians have tended to place most blame for Hitler's increasing boldness on Chamberlain's policy of appeasement, but in reality, Chamberlain had little choice than to strive for peace. The Great War and the slump that followed had left Britain significantly weakened economically. These problems were exacerbated by Government policy which favoured cuts in public spending and tax cuts over investment in public service and the Armed Forces.

British society remained totally dominated by the upper classes and their values and beliefs in the inherent superiority of British pluck, amateurism and individual heroics over well-trained, disciplined and properly-led foreign forces. The British Army had become intellectually moribund and dominated by men who lacked curiosity and interest in the novel or different. The RAF was run like a private aero club where the old guard of RFC air aces were lauded as gods and were allowed to define their own standards in terms of uniform, deportment and discipline. As a consequence, in both services the quality of military leadership was poor.

Of course, the ability of the British people to rise above these difficulties to withstand a German invasion and ultimately to beat the Axis forces cannot be dismissed as good fortune or the intervention of the Americans. There were times in 1940 where defeat seemed not only possible, but likely. The fact that Britain did not succumb was a source of justified pride and self-satisfaction to every British citizen. But still the doubt remained; did it have to be this way? The British people gave their verdict in the General Election of July 1945. Despite his apparent universal popularity and the nation's thankfulness, Winston Churchill not only lost the election, he was trounced. The Labour Party won a landslide victory, making a net gain of 239 seats, and securing 47.7 per cent of the popular vote. The swing was the largest since the Act of Union of 1800.

At RAF Ringway there was perhaps even more soul-searching. Most of those who trained there returned to civilian life and never parachuted again. The terror of those training jumps, or of the drop into Normandy or Arnhem, perhaps returning in the middle of a sleepless night, or being turned into stories for their grandchildren.

Their instructors though jumped hundreds, or in Agate's case, thousands of times. Agate was not only responsible for his own life, but also for the lives of the many hundreds of raw recruits who he trained and sent out of that hole in the bottom of the Whitley or that cage swinging from the balloon. Forty-two brave men died in training at Ringway during Agate's time. In a later BBC interview and in a subsequent newspaper interview he acknowledged that he had witnessed twenty-two of these deaths first hand, often being the first on the scene after a trainee hit the ground.

The Ringway Operational Log makes unsentimental and defensive references to these deaths often remarking about how few fatalities were being encountered. There is also a taste of victim-blaming where deaths are blamed on the parachutists for not following the advice they have been given.

However, Maurice Newnham himself was clearly troubled by doubts and concerns about failures in the parachute equipment and techniques and about the loss of Ringway despatchers on exercises late in the war such as the deaths of Sergeants Goodacre, Butler and Philpot – who failed to return from the attempt to establish a bridgehead across the Rhine at Remagen. At the end of *Prelude to Glory* he writes: 'We felt an overwhelming sense of grief and disappointment. It seemed to us that that our cherished weapon, which we had helped so much to create, had been misused. All the knowledge that had been gained from the study and experience of airborne assault during the past 4 years appeared to have been disregarded' (Newnham, 1946, p. 343).

Critics of the investment made in terms of men at Ringway have claimed that the airborne forces siphoned off high-quality Army manpower that would have been better spread around more conventional units. There have been others who have suggested that Ringway diverted scarce aircraft resources away from the RAF's primary role as a defensive force and a strategic bombing force. This view certainly seems to have been prevalent in the Air Ministry in 1940, but the small number of aircraft actually allocated to Ringway undermines this claim.

However, the question of whether the loss of life incurred in establishing an airborne force was worth it is more challenging. The original justification for establishing an airborne force back in mid-1940 was to provide a spearhead for an invasion of continental Europe. As we have seen, the 6th Airborne Division performed that role on the night of 5/6 June 1944. It could be argued that on that one operation the investment was repaid in full. However, the unnecessary loss of lives at Ringway, often due to reckless decision-making by men who were not suited to the roles they were given, inadequate equipment, training and leadership cannot be dismissed lightly. The report card must therefore remain somewhat mixed.

Since 1945, all of the world's major armies have retained a significant parachute element. The French made extensive use of parachute troops in the 1950s, the British Army used paratroops in the Falklands, the Balkans, Iraq and Afghanistan, and America used paratroops extensively in Vietnam, Panama, Haiti and Iraq. The reason for all this is simple. No one has yet come up with a better method of getting troops on the ground at short notice than by parachute. However, the question must be asked, could the loss of life at Ringway have been reduced had a more measured approach been taken and had an impatient and obstinate Prime Minister not made such an ill-considered and impractical demand in 1940?

***

When Newnham drove out of the gates of RAF Ringway for the last time on the morning of Monday 1 October 1945, it was almost five years to the day after his arrival. One of his final comments though hints at what he felt at the end of a such an intense period of highly-charged activity: 'I suddenly felt lonely and restless' (Newnham, 1946, p. 347). It was a feeling Agate would come to know all too well as he tried to settle back into family life at the home he had left so abruptly in 1939.

PART THREE

Coming Down to Earth

Chapter 20

A Hard Landing

Although there was a collective sense of relief that the war was over and that the country had stood strong against invasion, the war had been a catastrophe for Britain. Hundreds of thousands of British soldiers and citizens had been killed. Half a million houses had been destroyed and the country owed billions to the USA under the Lend-Lease programme. Almost a third of the entire wealth of the country had been wiped out.

Airborne forces had proved their worth, and according to Edward Cartner in *Jumping Beans* (2012) the Parachute Jump Instructors in particular were regarded as legends. As the war came to an end, there were very favourable terms on offer to a select few of the Ringway PJIs who were invited to stay on. They could, for instance, be awarded honorary aircrew status by virtue of their role as despatchers on airborne operations in the European and Far East theatres during the War. Some also chose to be transferred to the RAF's parachute training schools in India and in the Middle East. A few, including Agate, chose to stay on as instructors, but most returned to civilian life after the Royal Air Force Day event at RAF Ringway on Saturday 15 September 1945. Harry Ward, that self-confessed 'little cuss' who had felt 'socially unacceptable' at Ringway, set off around the world to run RAF officers' clubs. Robert Kronfeld, inventor of the Rotachute, was promoted to Squadron Leader.

Flight Lieutenant Charles Agate stayed on longer than most. In November 1945 it was announced that the majority of airmen and WAAF would be de-mobbed on 1 March 1946 and that only a few key members would be retained under the 'military necessary' proviso: primarily those engaged in the air transport arrangements for the repatriation of servicemen abroad (*Manchester Evening News*, 1945).

Charles Agate transferred with the school to Weston-on-the Green with a burning desire to achieve the world record for the number of jumps with a packed parachute; an ambition that he made no secret of and which he shared with a reporter on the *Manchester Evening News*.

The RAF, possibly seeing some public relations benefit in this, agreed that he could move to the PTS' new home at Weston-on-the Green in order to achieve his world record. However, Britain had more need of school-teachers than PJIs, no matter how experienced, and Agate was informed that he would need to achieve his record by May 1946 as that was the month ear-marked for him to be demobbed.

It is unclear whether Agate wanted to stay on at Weston still longer. He was evasive about this when pressed by the BBC's Don Durbridge in 1974, and there is a sense that it might have been out of his hands: 'I'd had my logbook closed – my last, my fourth, my fourth flying book – closed with 1600.' Perhaps he had developed a fear of going back to a routine that had begun to bore him before the war and the pressing need to restore his relationship with Marjorie.

In the closing months of the war there were frequent lectures at Ringway aimed at preparing for civilian life and it was clear that there was a widespread concern about the social problems that might arise from men returning to their wives and families after so long apart. Memories of the unemployment suffered by 'forgotten men' after the Great War were also comparatively fresh. However, as a 41-year-old qualified and experienced teacher he was exactly the sort of person that the Government wanted out of the services and back into employment in one of the new Secondary Modern schools established under the 1944 Education Act.

However, he was to have one last trick up his sleeve before finally returning to civilian life. It was a feat so original, even for Agate, that it would briefly bring him worldwide attention, being reported in newspapers around the world and would arguably be the one thing he would be remembered for, despite everything he had done in the war. The story is best told in Agate's own words:

> The night before the 1946 Derby, I had to go back up to the parachute training school at Manchester to hand back to the Navy the two motorboats that ran on my charge. They were boats we had been using on a very large deep lake where we had been training special agents to drop into the water.
>
> When I arrived back at Weston-on-the-Green, the new home of parachute training school, my Sergeant, Sergeant Humphreys, told me there was a horse called 'Airborne' running in the Epsom Derby on that day. I didn't even know this. I said, 'Well, is it a good horse?' He said, 'Well, it's about 66 to 1. You've been airborne for so long, why don't you put a pound on it?' He went on: 'You've got your gratuity to come, you're out of the Air Force in a short time why don't you put a fiver on it?'
>
> So, I gave him a fiver and Sergeant Humphreys went down to Oxford and he put the money on with a bookmaker.

To place the equivalent of about £250 in today's money on a rank outsider running in the Epsom Derby would be a risky strategy for most. Agate, of course, fell on his feet: 'I was very tired. I'd had no sleep, so I was trying to get a break in my caravan, but about 3.30 that afternoon there was a bashing on the door. My sergeant was there, and he told me "Airborne" had won the Derby.'

The race had attracted a huge crowd, estimated at up to 500,000, including the King and Queen as it was the first Epsom Derby to be run since the war. Airborne, the only grey in the race and wearing number thirteen, was an unconsidered outsider in a field of seventeen in a race run on soft ground. In the early stages, the horse was held up and was still well back turning into the straight. Gulf Stream took the lead in the last quarter-mile as his jockey Tommy Lowrey pulled Airborne wide to produce a sustained run down the centre of the course. He caught Gulf Stream inside the final furlong and won by a length. Agate explained what happened next: 'Well, I got paid out 50 to 1. I went in and saw the C.O at Upper Heyford and they allowed me to open my parachute book and do one more jump. I made that jump from a converted Halifax bomber at Weston-on-the-Green with all the bookmakers' money in my pocket.'

Over £300 in pound notes stuffed in his flying jacket would not have made the jump any easier. He goes on:

> I told all my lads on the ground: 'This is one more than I intended to do. If the parachute doesn't open, you can share the money.'
>
> I did it: my last jump and I didn't even fall over – a stand-up landing. I came out of the RAF with all this money, plus my gratuity. And in a way, I'm very sad to say this, with that money I bought my very first motorcar and gave up motorcycling.

Flight Lieutenant Agate's RAF career came to an end with that one last jump: his 1,601st, and with the equivalent of about £15,000 in his pockets, he must have felt very happy indeed.

For others who had served with him at Ringway, the end of the war was bittersweet and perhaps especially for the WAAF parachute packers. Joan Pearce who worked at Ringway records: 'I was demobbed on 16 August 1946. I wept a little weep for something intangible – the routine of life in the WAAF, the friends I made . . .' (Escott, *Our Wartime Days*, 1995, p. 191).

Winifred Smith, Ringway parachute packer, artist and impromptu wedding-dress designer, caught the mood as well: 'Although we were so young, we were so old and, shall I say, wise. We were old campaigners.

The laughter we all shared was the kind of laughter that never reached our eyes – we shared too many sorrows together' (Escott, *Our Wartime Days*, 1995, p. 192).

Like Agate, his friend Bernard Winfield left the RAF at the end of the war. He had been promoted to Squadron Leader, flown missions over occupied Europe and dropped into Arnhem. He had married in 1944 but the marriage did not last, and he married for a second time in 1948. Professionally though he was able to find more stability. He worked as a chest specialist at the Whittington Hospital in North London, a post he held for many years.

John Kilkenny, who had been promoted to Wing Commander in May 1944, returned to his pre-war work, this time as organizer of physical education for East Sussex, and went back to playing football at a semi-professional level. However, in 1947, after an injury ended his playing career, he re-enlisted back in the RAF as a parachute jump instructor and stayed on till 1958 when he reached the RAF compulsory retirement age.

The Polish, Czech, French, Russian and other nationalities who had trained at Ringway returned to the countries they had liberated. Though not all . . . At Cane Hill Psychiatric Hospital in Surrey, a special ward was created to house Polish airmen who had enlisted in the RAF. They had been traumatised in one way or another by their wartime experiences, had lost contact with or been rejected by their families back in Poland and had never returned. They seemed happy in this home away from home: chatting in their own language, singing, playing board games. Cane Hill Hospital was their home, and they were cared for and loved by the staff there. They stayed at Cane Hill till it closed in the 1990s and were sent out into the brave new world of care in the community.

But what of Flying Officer Charles Agate AFC? In the early decades of the twentieth century, he had in so many ways been like thousands of other men: tentatively building a career and a family. He was perhaps a little more reckless than most, but nevertheless was essentially an ordinary man. The Second World War put him in an extraordinary situation where again and again he did remarkable things and took exceptional risks. As the war ended would he retain what Cartner (2012) referred to as a 'large dollop of self-belief' (p. 121), and what Newnham (1947) called a 'sense of confidence and superiority' (p. 46)? What would happen to that self-belief, that feeling of inviolability, and was he really ready for a quiet respectable life?

There were early signs that when he did get back home, he wouldn't be able to steer clear of trouble. A newspaper report from January 1945 shows that he was taken to court again this time for having the wrong driving licence on his car when on leave in Surrey. Agate, using the type of ruse which had got him out of trouble before, said that it was his wife's car, though how he expected this to excuse the offence is unclear. The case, perhaps inevitably for this charmed man, was dismissed because it was his 'first offence' but as he left the court he shouted out: 'But it isn't my first offence!' The judge told him in no uncertain terms to shut up.

His love of horse-racing was undimmed and back in Epsom he had many connections in the racing world. One of these was the top jockey Charlie Smirke, who was very much a man after Charles' own heart: cheerful, self-confident and outspoken. Like Agate he had been prosecuted at Epsom Assizes for dangerous driving. Among Smirke's other misdemeanours, he had refused to have a vaccination before boarding a plane to fly to Maryland for a race, and in the account of his marriage given in the press, his new wife left the register office on her own in a taxi while Smirke and his two friends – the only witnesses to the wedding – left on foot in a different direction.

During the war Marjorie had found paid work driving jockeys up and down the country to races. It brought her a little income and kept her mind off what her husband might be getting up to in Cheshire. Agate took on some of this work too and used to run Smirke to race meetings in his beloved Jaguar XK120 sports car. One day Smirke was due to

ride the unfancied horse Fearless at Brighton Races. On the journey
down to Brighton, the jockey spoke admiringly of Agate's car, but also
moaned that the trip was a waste of time as he thought that Fearless had
no chance. Agate told him: 'Well, in that case, in the unlikely event of
your horse winning the race, I'll sell you this car at a knock-down price.'

It was one bet Agate wouldn't win. Fearless won the race and Charles
was compelled to sell his beloved car at a bargain price. He remarked
ruefully: 'Mrs. Smirke used that car for a long time afterwards' Mrs
Agate, once again, was not amused.

Nor had he lost his passion for parachuting. In a 1949 newspaper
article entitled 'Willing to pay £3 to risk his own life' it was reported
that he had spotted a parachute club preparing to jump on Epsom
Downs. He offered the RAF officer in charge of the group £3 to let him
go up with them. His request, bribe perhaps, was refused.

Agate never gave up his dream of just one more jump, as he
explained in 1974:

> Every year, the parachute training school has a reunion. And
> at the reunion, they always lay on a parachuting display by the
> present parachute instructors. Well, every reunion I have asked
> if I could parachute with the school because I could not bear
> to go and watch it. I think it's still so much of a drug that
> I want to do it and I know I can make the parachute jump and
> I think I could make a stand-up landing. And in order to do
> this, I've offered £100 to the RAF Benevolent Fund, or to the
> Parachute Training School's Comfort Fund, if they'll allow me
> to jump. I've been doing this since 1946. Call it stupid, but it's
> just something I want to do.

This was a man then for whom the 'drug' of the parachute drop was
still very real though back in civilian life it didn't have a ready outlet.
After the war, it seems that his addiction to parachuting became an

altogether darker and more insidious threat. It was, he said himself, 'a really vicious drug' and he admitted that after leaving the RAF, he began to struggle with his mental health. Interviewed in 2022, his daughter Lynette acknowledged that the post-war years were 'difficult'. There was, she said, 'friction at home' between her father and mother, and Agate was often angry. In particular, he didn't adapt well to being back at their comfortable bungalow, back at Norton, in unremarkable Burgh Heath after living in a sort of self-imposed five-year exile in a small caravan on the edge of Tatton Park with his beloved Alsatian Pat. Even Pat found it hard and became aggressive when she got home from the war, snapping at visitors and biting the postman.

Agate describes his condition like this:

> When I left the RAF, I was in an awful state. I nearly had to go back to the RAF neurosis specialists. I couldn't sleep at night. I used to bite my nails right down to the quicks and I just used to do all sorts of jobs at night to try and get over it . . . I was literally living and sleeping parachuting, and when it was suddenly taken away from me, the drug effect got into me, and I couldn't stop it.

Lynette remembers that he couldn't even sit down and eat with them for more than a few minutes: 'he would bolt down his food and then just jump up and be off'. In today's terms he seemed to be suffering from some kind of 'agitated depression', itself now understood to be often a symptom of post-traumatic stress disorder (PTSD). The problems he describes, insomnia, restlessness and anger, also seem to indicate what can only be described as withdrawal symptoms: a sort of cold turkey from jumping every day for five years out of a plane in an experimental or untested parachute, jumping with weights tied to his legs to test the effects of a hard landing, jumping into deep water to see if he could remove his parachute before he drowned.

He told Don Durbridge: 'I did eventually get over it', but how long was that grim 'eventually' before he did? Did he in fact ever get over it at all?

He suffered other setbacks as well. The Air Force Cross he had received from the King in January 1943 alongside his great friend Bernard Winfield, was stolen, and although the police eventually recovered the medal the thief had defaced it, turning the AFC into the arguably higher award of a scrawled 'DFC'. Then, in 1948, Robert Kronfeld, a man so admired by Agate that he always kept a photo of him, was killed testing a glider.

Agate began buying and selling second-hand cars again, and for a while even went back to a pre-war sideline as a cigarette machine salesman to pubs and clubs in South London. Slowly but surely though, he began to pick up the threads of his teaching career, though the educational landscape had changed dramatically with the 1944 'Butler' Education Act. The Act ended the traditional all-age (5–14) elementary sector which Agate had taught in before the Second World War and introduced a division between primary (5–11 years old) and secondary (11–15 years old) education. Agate though was able to work across both these sectors.

He went back on the Surrey County Council unattached staff list and worked in several schools between 1948 and 1952, starting as a teacher at Earlswood Secondary School and then standing in as head-teacher at four schools in quick succession in Charlwood, Leigh, Hook and North Holmwood, sometimes only staying for a few months. In a newspaper article published about him when he left Warlingham School in 1950 it was reported that he was 'hero worshipped by the pupils', but he had refused a leaving collection stating: 'I am always on the move, and I cannot have such a thing happening every time I leave a school.'

Restless as ever, he was even able to find time to run the Coulsdon Evening Institute. He succeeded in getting 500 students enrolled at the

Institute, nearly half of whom were adults. On 11 November 1949 he delivered a lecture about his parachuting career to the Coulsdon Boys Club. According to the reporter he thrilled the boys with his stories and his tales of his 150 experimental jumps (*Surrey Mirror & County Post*, 1949).

It took him years to settle down, and in fact, it could be said to be one of the most remarkable achievements of a remarkable life that he was able to pull himself together after the traumas of his wartime service to return to his previous career and to become such an inspirational figure to so many children. The opportunity finally to stay in one place came in 1952 when he spotted an advert for a headteacher at a village school in Merstham in Surrey.

Chapter 21

Building-up Again

In May 1952, at the age of 47, Charles Agate applied for the position of head of Merstham Primary School. He visited the school on 22 May 1952 and following a competitive interview process he was selected from a shortlist of three just five days later. As the *Surrey Mirror* reported: 'Odysseus returning to Ithaca could not have felt happier.' The former head teacher, Frank Shorter, retired after 40 years of service in the Borough of Reigate in July 1952 and Charles took over formally at 9am on 2 September 1952.

The social and political landscape in Merstham when Charles Agate took over was a minefield that he would have to negotiate carefully in the 18 years he was to stay at the school. His arrival was some seven years on from the national triumphs of VE and VJ Days, but Britain had not fully recovered from the war, and even the optimism surrounding the coronation of a new Queen was set against the backdrop of continuing austerity. In the early 1950s the Merstham school children had still been expected to spend part of the day learning about the importance of the British Empire, raising the Union flag and singing the national anthem. Pupils also took part in parades, dressed in patriotic costumes or military uniforms, but the enthusiasm for these practices and for the traditional Empire Day celebrations was beginning to wane.

It was not until July 1954 that food rationing finally came to an end, and the virtues of 'making do' had become ingrained in the British public. Parents advised their children to 'waste not, want not' and reminded them to use their pocket money to buy National Savings stamps for a rainy day while complaining that they did not know the value of money. Children wondered what their parents meant when they reminisced about eating oranges, pineapples and chocolate before the war.

Some of the Merstham children lived in homes that were poorly furnished and heated by burning coal or paraffin. Some bathed in a few inches of water, and wore cheap, threadbare clothes with 'Utility' labels. Although most homes had a cooker, vacuum cleaner and a plug-in radio, only the better-off had a washing machine so most people were still doing their washing by hand. Hardly anyone had a fridge and only one in ten had a telephone. For entertainment families listened to the radio or played gramophone records.

Most of the women with young children did not go out to work but stayed at home to look after the children. Many of the men of Merstham worked locally in traditional trades or local factories, but being on the main London-Brighton line, some worked in Croydon or in the City and it was a common sight to see the platforms of Merstham station packed with men wearing bowler hats and reading broadsheet newspapers.

Merstham in the 1950s was still a comparatively rural village. 'Top' Merstham with its ancient timbered houses based around the aptly-named Quality Street was separated by the railway line from South Merstham that was built very largely between the wars. There were some social tensions between Top and South Merstham and the men from South Merstham rarely ventured into pubs in Top Merstham.

People shopped locally. They had no need to go further afield. In Top Merstham, residents had the choice of two banks, three grocery shops, a ladies' and babies' outfitters, a butcher, newsagent, opticians, post office/stationers, estate agent and a boot repair shop. In South Merstham, there was no bank or estate agent, but a choice of eight grocery shops/general stores, three butchers, two fruit shops, two tobacconists and two hairdressers.

The post-war years were also a time of rebuilding and of new building. With much of London damaged by the Blitz there was a nationwide move to increase the amount of new social housing for rent in countryside locations that were accessible to major towns. Merstham, conveniently situated about 25 miles south of London and on the main railway line, was a prime target for development.

The first London County Council (LCC) planning application for new homes in Merstham was lodged in 1948 but was bitterly opposed by the Borough and County Council and numerous letters of objection were lodged. An example is the letter from a Mr F. G. Kerswell that was published in the *Surrey Mirror.* He wrote:

> It was a complete fallacy that the new population at Merstham could be absorbed in Redhill and Reigate. It would be just another dormitory area for London. That would be all right if there were not an acute position regarding transport, but they would have these people increasing the demands on a transport service which was already hopelessly inadequate. At the present time they were pressing the railway authorities for increased facilities, and were told that these could not be given, and now it was proposed to dump a population of 6,000 people into the area and aggravate the position.

Another reader wrote anonymously citing different objections:

> Sir, The scheme to build 2,000 houses in Merstham, of which a large number will have to be built on what was the village unfiltered sewage bed until comparatively recent years, has now been approved. I can hardly think Mr. Silkin and Mr. Bevan can have the health of the people foremost in their minds.
>
> I have lived in Merstham over 20 years and have seen cows in winter sink in up to their bellies in black slimy mud, the smell was terrible where the village sewage was soaking into the already winter water-logged ground. It would be interesting to

know whether the scheme has the approval or otherwise of the Metropolitan Water Board from the drainage and water supply standpoint. There is reason to believe that they consider the site most unsuitable.

This talk of 'these people' being 'dumped' in Merstham was a hint of the further social divisions to come.

Surrey County Council tried to get the land designated as a Green Belt Preservation area, but the LCC over-ruled these objections and obtained a compulsory purchase order in 1949. Planning consent was duly given by the Minister, subject to certain conditions, and building works commenced in 1950.

The houses of the new estate to the east of Top Merstham were planned in an attractive modern style. They all had bathrooms and small gardens, with children's recreation areas and green spaces. For some older Merstham residents, the building of the estate on what was previously open countryside was very unwelcome. Others resented what they saw as the lowering of the tone of the village. The estate brought in London people, unused to country ways who might not 'fit in'.

So, just as when some people in Top Merstham resented the newcomers in South Merstham, a distinct divide grew up between the residents of South Merstham and the occupants of the LCC Estate (or 'the Reservation' as the locals unkindly dubbed it). Two new schools were built: Albury Manor Secondary School and Furzefield Primary School, but here again social divisions were exacerbated when a zoning order was introduced to stop children from the LCC estate attending Merstham School, even though Merstham School itself was easily reached from the new housing by a footbridge over the railway at Merstham Station. The zoning order remained in place until the 1960s.

The 'Three Rs' dominated the Merstham school curriculum and maths lessons were confined to simple arithmetic. Times tables and weights and measures tables were learned off by heart with the whole class reciting them together first thing every morning. Reading and writing lessons took the form of handwriting practice, comprehension exercises, spelling tests, and writing compositions. Children were taught to learn proverbs and poems off by heart so that they could recite them at school assemblies. There was no 'gym kit' at Merstham School so the children just removed their outer clothes and did PE in their vests and bare feet or plimsolls, usually purchased from Woolworths.

The Schools Broadcasting Council had been set up in 1947 and wireless broadcasts became an integral part of teaching with programmes such as *Nature Study with Tony*, *Music and Movement* and *Sing Together*. Some of these programmes were very popular with the children though others found *Music and Movement* to be particularly excruciating, as a disembodied voice from a loudspeaker ordered them to 'sway like trees in the wind' or to 'buzz like a bee'.

The 11 Plus exam which had been implemented in 1947 was seen as the key to a 'better' education at one of the local grammar schools. In their final year of primary school, children at Merstham School, like those all over the country, had to sit this test which would decide where they would go for their secondary education. At Merstham School, Charles Agate – a proud Old Boy of Reigate Grammar School – made sure that the children got plenty of practice in the exercises that made up the 11 Plus exam, solving written problems, working out fractions and percentages and learning how to calculate simple and compound interest.

During Agate's time Merstham School become known as a hothouse for getting children through the 11 Plus but this didn't always make him (or the school) popular with other local schools with less resources or a less ambitious head. At an annual conference of local schools held at Furzefield School in 1968, Charles Agate addressed 200 parents to explain how the 11 Plus worked and why it was deemed important and necessary. Although this was probably well-intentioned, the reception was not entirely positive with one local man writing to the *Surrey Mirror* alleging that there was a quota system in place that favoured Merstham School over Furzefield School. Some local parents were so unhappy with the pressure they felt was being put on their children to do well in the 11 Plus exam that one wrote to the *Surrey Mirror* and signing the letter 'disillusioned parent'. Agate was quick to respond and the following week a letter from him appeared 'cordially inviting the disillusioned parent' to pay a visit to the school. 'Courtesy and good manners mean more than a high IQ', he wrote. In the same edition, another parent backed Agate and the school: 'The success of Merstham School comes from the secure happy atmosphere provided by staff who know their pupils as individuals.'

***

Charles, Marjorie and their daughter Lynette lived for his first few years at Merstham in the 'School House' at the end of the school drive. Lynette was 17 when they moved there and she had ambitions to become a fashion model, though her father would have preferred her to become an air hostess. 'He wanted me to see the world', she said later. Lynette was showing much of her father's energy and love of speed though, becoming a keen horse rider and motorcyclist, occasionally riding bikes in speedway races. She also built up a lucrative sideline in selling on the clothes she had worn for the photo shoots to major retailers and clothing suppliers. Bringing boyfriends home to meet her glamourous mother and charismatic father could sometimes be quite trying. She admitted to being jealous of her mother who used to flirt with her boyfriends. 'I fell out with one or two of them because of that' she said. Nor was it necessarily any easier introducing these young men to her father: 'He used to sit my boyfriends down at the table and tell them those long stories of his about the war. Of course, I'd be embarrassed.'

Charles and Marjorie's choice of holidays was perhaps surprising in the light of his passion for fast cars and his daredevil war service. 'He actually hated flying as a commercial passenger, and never wanted to go abroad', Lynette explained, 'holidays were always the same: driving the caravan down to Devon and Cornwall.'

It seemed also that the couple had not fully resolved their pre-war differences and that Marjorie still did not fully trust her husband. Lynette remembers 'tempestuous arguments . . . usually about other women, though they made up afterwards very quickly'. These issues would continue to beset their marriage during his time at the school.

A man as restless as Charles, of course, was never going to be just a headmaster. He continued to build up his sideline in renovating and selling second-hand cars and used the school playground as his workshop and sales yard, something which would land him in hot water with the Governors. His nephew Martin Thomas – the son of Agate's sister Ivy – recalls that 'Uncle Bertie' sold his father his first car.

1955 was the year that the first edition of *The Guinness Book of Records* was published, featuring a British Parachuting Record: 'set by Flt. Lt. Charles Agate A.F.C (born March 1905) of the RAF, who totalled 1,601 descents with packed parachute between 1940 and 1946'. Possibly emboldened by this newfound fame, Agate continued to petition the RAF to let him make one last jump.

The wider Agate family was changing. Agate's mother had died in the 1930s, but his father remarried a woman who came to be known as 'Aunty Nell' and was well liked by the family.

There was sadness though too for the Agate family. Charles' sister Norah died in January 1957 and her husband Stanley died just a year later in January 1958. Ivy Agate's son, Martin Thomas explained:

Norah was a nurse, and I believe she was unable to have children. Hence her two children, Susan and David were adopted. Unfortunately, Susan turned out to be unable to walk, although she had no mental impairment. My mother and Norah were very close, and I remember my mother being particularly upset by Norah's death. My understanding is that my parents were executors to Norah and Stanley's Will, and I do explicitly remember my parents to be rather taken aback by this meaning that they automatically became Trustees for the future care and wellbeing of the two children.

I don't think Charles had any similar obligations, but he seemed to take some interest in David's future. There might even have been talk of Charles adopting him, or at least bringing him up as his own son, but clearly that didn't happen.

David, who went on to become a successful solicitor in the West Country picks up the story and gives us another insight into the character of his unconventional uncle:

Charles Agate was my uncle and my hero for the short time that I knew him closely. I never got to call him Bert which would have been far too familiar for a boy on a push bike. His sisters Norah, Ivy and Mary used to refer to him as Bert when relating one of his life experiences.

I was very lucky to be adopted by Norah and her husband Stanley from birth in 1945. Charles was quite different from Norah, a nursing Sister, and the other two sisters who were both rather staid schoolteachers. Charles was not at all the same as any adult I had previously known!

Nora fell ill in the mid-1950s and Charles used to come over to see her – a round trip of some 50 miles – and he would take an interest in me then aged about eleven and sometimes slip me 5 shillings – a handsome addition to pocket money in 1956, and on one occasion 10 bob so I could buy some special handlebars for the bike which was my most valued possession and of course meant freedom.

He would take me to see football matches at Kingston and at Redhill and at first, I was somewhat alarmed when he would get into arguments with the opposing team fans in the crowd but later, I understood it was just good-natured badinage.

He was a great motorcycle enthusiast and took me to see Wimbledon Speedway and later to the World Championship speedway races at Wembley Stadium. Before then, I had no idea what speedway was, but I soon got the idea when he drove into the car park at Wimbledon, and we could hear a race in progress. Charles told me that his daughter Lynette had taken part in a ladies' race of some sort. I think he must have been a marvellous father.

When Norah and Stanley died I was taken on by Charles' sister Ivy, but they already had two younger children of their own and after a not very successful period Charles and his lovely wife Marjorie took me on in their school house home in Merstham. I think that was in about 1959.

Life became much more exciting, and I began to learn a little more about this interesting man and his family. He was a natural leader, heroic in the War and full of life. I did not know until that time that he had been a parachute jump instructor. He had been presented with a plaque which he kept on the mantelpiece recording the record number of jumps he had made, and which led to the award of the Air Force Cross medal.

Charles was a tough-looking man with an ever-present undercurrent of fun and was greatly respected. I remember being told that he had tried to arrange to make a parachute jump years after the war but was turned down on account of his age and I suppose insurance was not available. What an irony!

He had kept his original Irvin Flying jacket – the sort worn by Spitfire pilots – and I had hoped that it might one day come my way, but it was far too big for me at the time, and I think it went to benefit a charity.

Charles was a real sport. I can remember him sharing the ice-slides in the school playground with the children taking his turn in the queue with them and with me.

He introduced me to cars which subsequently became a lifelong passion of mine. He owned a 1950s Oldsmobile Rocket 88, light blue in colour which was unusual for cars in the post war years as they were mostly black. It seemed huge by comparison with English cars. He allowed me to steer it on the road whilst sitting in front of him in the driver's seat, and he taught me the controls of a car and I was allowed to drive around the school playground and playing-field on my own – out of school hours, of course.

He used to buy and sell cars as a side-line, mostly modest small saloons as there was petrol rationing of course and they were inexpensive to buy and to run. In those days I think he would buy for about £120 and sell for £150. Sometimes he would come home with some special car, and I remember setting my heart on a 1930s Singer Le Mans which was like a two-seater MG of the period.

Charles bought me an air-rifle and one evening long after the school children had gone home, we both went out into the playground in decreasing light, and he encouraged me to shoot at an exposed outside light which had come on. He stood right behind me, and I shot the pellet and hit the bulb which immediately burst into flames and shattered glass. Spontaneously we both ran away giggling with delight. Shameful of course, and him the school's head-teacher!

Marjorie was a strikingly good looking and kind woman. What else would you expect from Charles who seemed to me to have it all! I count myself as super-lucky to have been looked after by them for 2 years or so until it was time to move on and I became a full-time boarder at school. Then someone from my blood-family whom I had never met or even heard of magically appeared and I was moved away.

The explanation appears to have been that Ivy and her husband Albert were not entirely happy about Charles' influence on David. Martin Thomas recalls a heated argument between them: 'Charles asked me to leave the room, and then from outside I heard my father shouting "Now you listen to me!". I had never heard my father getting angry like that with anyone before.'

Charles and his sister Ivy were never reconciled. However, David's memories of Charles Agate remain warm:

We lost touch for a while but the last time I saw him in 1965 he was still at Merstham, and I wanted to show him my new Triumph motorcycle. He jumped at the chance to ride pillion up the road, so off we went – crash hats were not yet compulsory. He loved it and, in a way, things had gone full circle. He was a special man. It was a privilege to know him, and to have gained so many cherished memories of him.

Chapter 22

The Golden Age?

There was much to celebrate in the early years of the 1960s in music and fashion and by 1964 Beatlemania was in full flood. The film *Hard Day's Night* was playing to packed houses at the Majestic Cinema in Reigate and headteacher Charles Agate embraced the mood. He was captured in a photograph by a *Surrey Mirror* reporter wearing a Beatles' wig holding a toy guitar and leading the children in a rendition of Dora Bryan's hit song *All I Want for Christmas is a Beatle*. His pupils are looking up at him with smiles and some are clearly in awe of this unconventional headmaster. He had settled into his role and was thoroughly enjoying it.

Family life too for Charles was moving on. In 1960 his daughter Lynette married David Brett, and in 1962 Charles and Marjorie finally moved out of the school house in Merstham. For the princely sum of £1,050 they had bought Squirrel Cottage, a newly-built detached house in leafy Reigate. This would be their home for the next 10 years.

Charles had never given up the hope that he would be able to make just one more jump and although the RAF remained resolute, he seized an opportunity for the closest thing to it – a simulated descent from a static balloon under the canopy of Earls Court. The occasion was a Merstham School trip to the Royal Tournament on 14 June 1961. The Royal Tournament had been held every year (except the war years) since 1880 and was intended to provide the general public with insights into the skills and abilities of the armed forces.

The programme consisted of a display of physical training by the Royal Air Force, a cutlass and hornpipe display performed by the Royal

Navy, a simulated commando raid by the Royal Marines, a search and survival exercise by the RAF Flying Training Command and a drive by the King's Troop, Royal Horse Artillery. The headline item on the bill was a simulated airborne assault by the Parachute Regiment.

The next day, under the headline 'The Head Takes on Boy's Parachute Dare with an Ace up his Sleeve', the *Daily Mail* gave an account of what happened next:

> Form IVa watched the Red Devils through their parachute jump routine at the Royal Tournament yesterday, then ten-year-old Nicky Parsons leaned across to his headmaster and said:
>
> 'Bet you wouldn't dare do that, sir!'
>
> Which was how 55-year-old Charles Agate got in jump Number 1602 (indoor).
>
> He had a card up his sleeve when he took the dare. The boys and girls of Merstham County Primary School in Surrey knew he had been a parachute jumper – but not that he holds the world record with 1600 jumps in his six war years as an RAF instructor. His last jump though was 15 years ago – to celebrate Airborne's 1946 Derby win.
>
> But soon his rip cord finger tingled. And Nicky's dare was the last straw. His Head took off his coat, adjusted his parachute harness, and was hauled 90ft on a cable into the roof.
>
> Suddenly, he was on his way down to cheers from the children and from the Red Devils.
>
> How did it feel to be back in harness? Mr Agate had to confess:
>
> 'I didn't like going up – not used to it. But coming down? Ah, that brought back memories!'

Agate had landed on his feet at Merstham School at last and a mark of this was perhaps his attitude to corporal punishment. Prior to his arrival, Frank Shorter would regularly use corporal punishment for a broad range of minor misdemeanours. However, there are absolutely no entries in the Merstham School Punishment Book after Agate arrived.[70]

He was now clearly comfortable in his role and the way he dealt with parents reflected this. Lynette explained his soft touch to conflict resolution:

> Sometimes of course, parents used to come and see him because they were really angry about something to do with their child. When this happened, he used to take them for a tour of the school, then on a walk round the playing field all the time just chatting and being his usual charming self. By the time they all got back to his office, the parents had either calmed down enough to talk their issues through or completely forgotten what they were there for in the first place!

A few years later Agate would end up in court following a decision by Surrey County Council to re-position the school crossing to the top of School Hill by the War Memorial. Road safety had always been a concern for Agate and in previous years he had petitioned unsuccessfully for the authorities to put a zebra crossing lower down School Hill away from the main A23 London to Brighton Road which had become more and more busy and treacherous.

He disagreed vehemently with the positioning of the new crossing, and refused to use it, preferring to cross the road at the point where he thought the crossing should have been placed. On one morning, Agate and a fellow teacher were escorting a group of 130 pupils across School Hill. A lorry driven by a local farm manager drove up to the children without slowing down. Agate jumped in front of it and put his hand on the bonnet. Following an altercation with the lorry-driver the police were called and charges were brought against the driver. In the subsequent court hearing, the driver complained that the children were not on the recognized crossing and that Agate had 'banged his fist on my bonnet and told me with some heat that I had nearly run some children over'. The magistrate was not sympathetic, and the driver was found guilty and fined £3, plus costs of 17 shillings.

Later, a boy from the school was knocked over and killed outside the school. Will Fry, a pupil at the school at the time, still remembers 'the shock and pain of hearing Mr Agate announce this in school assembly'. Agate began a relentless and almost singlehanded campaign to force the local authority to build a footbridge over the road. It was finally opened in 1967 and has been renewed or replaced twice since, most recently in 2022.

Drawing on his wartime experience as a dispatcher and 'spotter' on D-Day and at Arnhem, Agate never failed to remind his pupils in assemblies that their eyes were precious, and they had to look after them. One weekend, ignoring Agate's advice, a boy's eye was punctured playing bows and arrows with raspberry canes at the bottom of his garden. After weeks of recovery in hospital and at home the boy returned to school wearing dark glasses. Agate brought him up on stage in front of the whole school, pointed to him and said:

'What have I been telling you all these years? You see what happens when you don't listen!'

It is also from the early 1960s that we begin to hear from former pupils of some of his more eccentric and endearing practices. The first few weeks of December 1962 had been changeable and stormy, but then on 22 December, there was an abrupt change in the weather as high pressure dragged bitterly cold winds across the country. Once this weather pattern had set in, it did not change much for the rest of the winter. On 24 December, a weather front moved south across the UK, turning to snow as it did so. This snow set the scene for the next two months, as much of England remained covered every day until early March 1963. Blizzards, snowdrifts and blocks of ice were commonplace, and temperatures dropped below -20°C. However, whereas in Victorian times, and again today, this would have affected school attendances, in 1963 most children were able to make their way to school on foot and make the most of the conditions when they got there with the full support of their headteacher. Agate would go into school particularly early and make ice-slides in the playground. He would then grant the children 'extra play' and would join them for snowball fights on the school field. Always ready to roll his own sleeves up, Agate also took on the toilet-cleaning duties for several weeks when the school was left without a caretaker. These then would appear to be what might be called golden years for Merstham School and for Mr Agate.

But the second half of the 1960s was a time of worldwide social and international upheavals with the Paris riots of May 1968, the worsening of the Vietnam War and the Troubles in Northern Ireland, Enoch Powell's inflammatory 'Rivers of Blood' speech and the assassinations of Bobby Kennedy and Martin Luther King. It was also a time of political change in England with years of Conservative Government finally giving way to Harold Wilson's Labour Party in 1964, though the Parliamentary constituency of Reigate in which Merstham sat remained a Conservative stronghold. However, the small but active group of Labour supporters in South Merstham were hopeful that the tide could be turned with the influx of working-class people into the Merstham LCC estate and so by the early 1960s the divisions between 'Old' and 'New' Merstham remained pronounced. Charles Agate was a firm supporter of the Conservatives and some of the parents of South Merstham children believed that he favoured the children of 'Old' Merstham and courted their parents, with one of these South Merstham pupils from the time commenting decades later: 'He didn't take much interest in me, but he really encouraged my cousin, but then she lived in Top Merstham.'

In 1966, the school's dancers became unwittingly involved in a minor political controversy when they performed at the Conservative Association Fête. A local resident wrote to the *Surrey Mirror* to protest about the involvement of the children in an event designed to raise funds for a political party. Charles Agate was forced to defend his decision, writing to the Local Education Authority that all the children performed with their parents' permission, a response that did not particularly endear him to those who questioned whether he would have allowed the children to perform at a Labour fundraising event.

Merstham School was not insulated from the changing political and social climate. In 1965 local education authorities had been asked to submit plans showing how they intended to reorganize on comprehensive lines. It was thought that there would be advantages if children did not transfer to secondary schools until they were 13. 'Middle schools' catering for children between the ages of 9 and 13 were suggested as one way forward and at the start of the new academic year, the Surrey Education Authority announced that there was a need for just one middle school in Merstham. Merstham County Primary School would be reduced to a 'First School' only. This led to the entire staff raising their objections with the School Governors. Further protests were raised with the Council by Agate, the teachers and parents.

Agate of course had never been someone to keep quiet in the face of injustice and was never afraid to challenge authority and as part of this campaign, he wrote to the *Surrey Mirror*:

> I don't want to see young families split at the age of 8 plus and forced to send their children to a school not of their own choice . . . I have no problem with the Plowden Report, providing first and middle schools are kept on the same site for the benefit of families. This will be appreciated this winter when young children will be going to school almost in darkness.

His outspoken approach led to conflict with the Governors and the Divisional Education Office in Kingston, which Agate always referred to disparagingly as 'The Office'. He was, according to daughter

Lynette, 'always at loggerheads with them' but one day a telegram of support, sent from Brighton, arrived on Agate's desk, apparently from an unexpected and very high-profile person: none other than Edward Heath, then leader of the Conservative opposition. The telegram read. 'Every success in your fight against dictatorial policies – Edward Heath'.

This seemed like an unusual and highly significant intervention in such a locally sensitive issue and Heath's staff moved quickly to deny all knowledge of the telegram, adding that Mr Heath was not even in Brighton when the telegram was sent. The telegram was declared a hoax, but the mystery of just who did send it was never solved, though one well-known local troublemaker could never be fully ruled out.

The chair of the Merstham School Governing Board in 1968 was Charles Garnsworthy, who had contested the Reigate constituency as a Labour candidate in six general elections and who had been made a Life Peer, as Baron Garnsworthy of Reigate in 1967. In February 1968, Agate was censured by Garnsworthy and told that he must not speak out publicly against education policy. Agate noted in the School Log that he accepted this injunction 'with reservations' (heavily underlined). A further Governors' meeting was held on 3 March with Baron Garnsworthy in the chair. Mr Agate had been ill and had to obtain his doctor's permission to attend, but his illness did not prevent him from making statements which clearly upset the chair.

By the start of the 1968/69 academic year feelings were running very high and on 15 October 1968 Agate addressed nearly 500 people at a public meeting in the school hall. When he turned up for a meeting at the Divisional Office a week later, he was barred from entering. He marks this ignominious exclusion with a pointed 'No comment!' in the School Log.

His protests were to no avail and just four days later at a second public meeting at Frenches School, Agate informed an even larger gathering that the decision had been made: Merstham School would be reduced to 'First School' status with the closure of the infants section.

So, by the end of the 1960s, with Charles Agate approaching the required retirement age for teachers of 65, Merstham School was itself perhaps showing signs of more unwelcome change. Isolated incidents of vandalism had affected the school since Victorian times, but random acts of hooliganism increased significantly during the late 1960s. However, an attack on 20 April 1970 was worse than anything previously encountered. The school was broken into, and the kitchen was sprayed with the fire extinguishers. Some of the other classrooms were damaged and books, windows and locks were destroyed. There were further attacks on the school shortly after and for a period, the local CID were regular visitors to the school and Agate clearly struggled to come to terms with these harsher new realities, as he told Don Durbridge in his 1974 BBC Radio Brighton interview:

> I don't think children have changed all that much. I think the worst thing about children today is the actual vandalism that they do. We all got up to tricks and fun in the old days, but I can't remember that we ever went out and deliberately broke things like they do today, and this is something I can't quite understand. I can't put my finger on it and say why they want to smash things up, especially when most of the things they smash up belong to their parents.

Despite, or possibly because of, these concerns, Charles Agate applied to the local education authority to extend his tenure as headmaster at Merstham School. Like Maurice Newnham 25 years before, it seems the authority had had enough of the man who perhaps had spoken his mind once too often, followed his own path a bit too much. Hs request was declined.

Charles Agate retired in July 1970. To mark the occasion, the children decorated their classrooms with sixteen model planes each dropping ten paper parachutists, plus one, to represent the record number of parachute drops their headmaster had made. A testimonial fund of just over £100 was presented to him and he duly handed over the entire amount to the Leukaemia Research Fund in memory of the two little girls who had died from this condition in the last six years.

In his final entry in the School Log, he records: 'I, Charles Agate, today retired from duty as teacher and headmaster of this School.'

It was the end of an era, for the school, and for Mr Agate himself.

Chapter 23

An Awfully Big Adventure

Retirement, and the 1970s, began well for Charles and Marjorie Agate. They spent a year or two in Squirrel Cottage but were then lured back to the South Coast and to Sussex. They moved to a large house overlooking the sea at Shoreham Beach. It was a nostalgic choice. Charles and Marjorie used to motorcycle down to Shoreham before the war, making a fire on the beach and sleeping under the stars.

Charles liked Shoreham Beach because it was what he called a 'nice mixed area with young families and a few – but not too many – retired people'. He even changed his sporting allegiance from Crystal Palace to Brighton & Hove Albion and enjoyed regular trips to the Goldstone Ground during one of the team's most successful periods in the first division, culminating in an appearance at the 1983 FA Cup Final.

He certainly wasn't ready to settle down, and according to daughter Lynette he would never do any of the other normal sedentary activities one expects – perhaps wrongly – of older people. His years-long obsession with that one last parachute jump did not end when he retired to the seaside either and he continued to ask the RAF to let him do a jump at the Parachute School reunion, just as he had been asking them every year since 1946. By 1974 though, he was finally beginning to realize that the RAF would never let him jump again, as he explained in his interview with the BBC's Don Durbridge:

So, this year is the last time I'm offering the £100 if I can do one more jump. I want to do this as my last link with the school which I helped form, because I was the only one who was parachuting right from the time the school was formed until six months after the end of the war. I was there the whole time and I feel that this is just something I want to do.

He clearly found it hard to accept the RAF's rejection and still showed the same self-belief and casual indifference to his own safety as he had throughout the years at Ringway and Tatton Park:

Of course, it would be risky if I'd become very big and heavy. If I was a 15 or 16 stone man, it would be different. I could break an ankle or something, but there'll be no worries as far as they were concerned, and if they want me to sign a document saying that I accept full responsibility, of course I would do so . . . but this is the last year that I'll try, because next year I will be 70.

Even when he did reach 70, this restless man was not going to sink into easy retirement. An ice-cream kiosk came up for rent on the beach, he took it on and ran it until shortly before his death. It was here where from time to time former pupils from Merstham School, now grown up and perhaps on a day out with their own young families, would spot him serving ice creams. He would, invariably, remember them, greet them warmly, offer them free ice creams, and then sit on the chairs outside his kiosk and chat, stopping occasionally to get up and serve another customer.

It was a time for reflection, though more about his teaching career than his time in the RAF, which he rarely talked about. Don Durbridge asked him how he would like to be remembered: as the parachute-jumping world record holder or as a lifelong teacher? He answered: 'Well, I naturally much prefer to be known as a teacher. And if I started my life again, I would still want to be a teacher, chiefly because I've had so much happiness from children.' He was concerned though about the state of the profession he had loved so much and in particular about the decrease in the real value of a teacher's salary:

> I can't imagine any young teacher today who could possibly buy a nice bungalow like we did when I started. That bungalow today would cost approximately £18,000 or £19,000. There has been a tremendous drop in the amount of money that a teacher takes home, so this must contribute to the shortage of teachers and the unsettledness of the teaching profession generally . . . The people I feel sorry for are the young teachers, aged 25 or 26, who've just got married, maybe having children. Well, I can assure you, they are very, very hard up indeed. We had some of these at Merstham, and I felt sorry for them.'

His words ring true today, as do his thoughts about the workload and selfless commitment required of a teacher:

> The trouble is that as a teacher you can put in thousands and thousands of hours over-time, and you never get a penny for the extra time that you put in. And of course, if you love children, you do put in a lot of extra time. There are a lot of teachers who give double their normal teaching time to helping children. And I wish in a way that some type of overtime could be paid to these teachers.
>
> I once worked out that one teacher I knew at Merstham put in thousands and thousands of hours extra time. I tried very hard to get her some sort of note of this. I was hoping she might get the MBE or something like this. I put a long letter up to the Education Authority, but nothing came of it.

This teacher who Agate tried so hard to get an honour for was Doris Cox, who, according to his daughter, Agate 'adored'. If anyone deserved an honour for her lifelong commitment to one school, it was surely her. A pupil at Merstham School in the 1930s, 'Miss Cox' returned to teach at the school just after the war, rising to become Deputy Head until her retirement in 1985 and then continuing as a Governor for many years.

In retirement, Agate remained the relative loner he had been in the war. He didn't keep in touch much with the people he had served with at Ringway and Tatton Park, and certainly not with the 'Yorkshire Birdman' Harry Ward who had put him through such an unnecessary and terrifying ordeal on his first day at the airfield. Ward ran a series of pubs in Yorkshire and wrote his memoirs. He died in the year 2000 at the age of 97. One of the padres Agate had so much admired at Ringway, Father Bernard Egan, also returned to teaching, at Donhead Prep School in Wimbledon where he became Headteacher and retired a year after Agate in 1971 when injuries he had received at Arnhem meant he could no longer walk. He died in 1988 aged 83.

Bernard 'The Doc' Winfield, Agate's only real friend at Ringway and frequent companion in his caravan at Tatton Park, did not slip into quiet retirement either. With his third wife Ann he bought an isolated cottage in the Derbyshire Dales where he created a spectacular garden that cascaded down the hillside and planted thousands of daffodils and snowdrops along the footpaths round his home. He took up the cello, which he played outdoors to an audience of cattle, learned dry-stone walling and applied his medical skills to the health not only of his farming neighbours but also their livestock. He died in 2007 and his nephew wrote this in his obituary which shows he was in so many ways remarkably similar to his friend Charles Agate:

In company, Bernard Winfield could be reticent to the point of silence. He would slip away to prune a shrub or upholster a chair. He hated parties. But one to one, adults felt impelled to unburden themselves to him. He was always supportive, providing advice and reassurance, a small cheque, a shoulder to cry on. To children, he was the magic man who created the biggest bonfire, the loudest fireworks, the scramble up the Cornish cliff to escape the incoming tide, the thrill of outdoor skating on thin ice. He would have had an uneasy relationship with today's health and safety officers.

Winifred Smith, Ringway parachute packer, art graduate and impromptu wedding dress designer, emigrated to Canada in 1947 where she lived with her Canadian husband. She continued to paint, work with ceramics, was a member of the Canadian Federation of Artists, and published several books of poems. She died on 10 March 2020 aged 100.

RAF Ringway, of course, has long since ceased to exist, and although Manchester Airport was popularly known as Ringway Airport into the 1980s it is now very proudly Manchester International Airport with three terminals and a poignant and well-tended garden with stone memorials to those who had served at Ringway during the war: the Polish forces, the WAAF, the parachute packers in particular, the SOE agents and other trainees, and, of course, the parachute jump instructors who trained them all.

Tatton Park was gifted to the National Trust when Lord Egerton died with no heir in 1958. The mansion is open to the public, there are walking trails, year-round activities for families, a café and a bookshop. The booklet *Tatton in the War* written in 1985 is currently out of print, but the staff are always willing to tell the story of wartime Tatton to visitors. The parkland is spectacularly beautiful: the old landing ground now the home to herds of deer, and Rostherne and Melchett Meres still frozen over in winter and glistening in the summer.

There is a stone memorial to the Parachute Training School on a rise, and in the distance you can clearly see the control tower at the airport. There are still traces of what went on in the war and the rangers are proud to show visitors the tank tracks, the gap in the trees where that Whitley crash-landed in 1943, unnoticed – apparently – by the lord of the manor, and the spot where an unexploded German bomb was found just a few years ago. There are also, if you know where to look, two concrete blocks in the ground with iron rings inset in them. These are the remains of the anchor points for 'Bessie', the site of so many of Agate's 1,601 jumps and the corner of the park where he lived in his caravan. A Tatton Park resident for five years.

By 1976, a year after his 70th birthday and two years after the radio interview which showed him at his happiest and most relaxed, Charles Agate seemed like he was finally settling down to a quiet life in Shoreham Beach. There were though still to be dark twists in the life of this remarkable man.

In 1977 his father Albert Agate, the man he had surely made so proud, died, aged 99, and just the year before Charles' beloved wife Marjorie was diagnosed with breast cancer. She underwent a mastectomy, but without perhaps the treatments and therapies she may have received today, the prognosis was bleak and after a short period of illness, she died, leaving Charles, in Lynette's words, 'absolutely devastated'.

He was undoubtedly not always an easy man to spend her life with and his recklessness and unpredictably had often infuriated Marjorie. He had also betrayed her in 1939, and rumours about affairs at Merstham School had dogged his 18 years there, but despite the rows she had forgiven him. They clearly adored each other, and she had been his one great love and constant presence, from the day he literally bowled her over outside a hairdresser shop in Purley, through the uncertain years of the war, the difficult period in the late 1940s and the challenges of leading a school for nearly two decades.

Charles moved from the large house he and Marjorie had bought together to a penthouse apartment which overlooked the refreshment kiosk he continued to run. He was high and dry again, and on his own, as he had been throughout the war years in his caravan at Tatton Park. It was perhaps no surprise to his family that in the years after Marjorie's death he had several girlfriends, and all much younger than him. There was Sylvia who was married throughout their affair, and Christine who was his partner in his last years.

With the passing of the years however, he didn't look after himself very well, always avoided going to the doctor, and as his daughter Lynette explained in an interview more than 35 years later, 'he ate a lot of fish and chips'. Perhaps it was not surprising then that eventually he developed diabetes, and the gangrene often associated with this condition brought him great pain, particularly in his legs. Reluctantly he agreed to a short stay in Brighton Hospital in the late autumn of 1986 where a nurse, clearly unaware of the stature and background of the man, said to him: 'if you don't look after yourself Mr Agate, we will have to cut your toes off.' It was a cruel and insensitive remark to a man who had always taken such pride in making a standing landing, and his daughter Lynette never forgot it. In 2022 she said: 'I hated that nurse for saying that.' But the nurse's comment caused much greater hurt and distress to Charles Agate himself, though he was not a man to express his feelings easily and no one was aware exactly how deep that hurt had been felt.

Lynette recalls that when she and her husband Jim were waiting for her father to be discharged, he spent a very long time in the hospital's pharmacy. 'I couldn't understand why', she said later. Charles though was still apparently quite well and active and a few days later he drove to a recently opened RAF retirement community in Storrington[71] near Pulborough. He wanted to see what it was like but on his return, he seemed shaken and told Lynette that it was 'awful'. He also said this: 'You know Lynette, there is no one else. You are the only one. I have left all my money to you.' A little taken aback, Lynette drove back to her home in Chichester.

The next day she had a phone call. It was Charles ringing from his flat. He was calling to tell Lynette that he had 'had enough of it all'. He was going to kill himself and had already taken the right pills to do the job. He was quite calm and determined and said it was fine and that it was the end, and he was OK with it.

Lynette and husband Jim immediately drove over to Shoreham Beach, but 21 December 1986 was an icy night, and the roads were difficult. When they got there, he was lying on the floor of his flat with his arms folded across his chest. He was wearing round his neck a gold medallion with '1601' on one side and 'CA 1941–1946' on the other. He had meticulously arranged his medals and other memorabilia from the war years all around the room and around himself on the carpet. The emergency services tried to revive him, but it was too late.

An inquest was held nearly two months later, and a death certificate issued on 18 February 1987. Under Cause of Death the registrar wrote: 'Overdose of Cyclizine associated with Diconal. Open Verdict.'

Lynette later said: 'I had no idea where he got the pills'.

Cyclizine is an antihistamine prescribed to stop nausea. It is possible that Agate had been prescribed this during his recent short stay in Brighton Hospital, and that these were the pills he was waiting for at the hospital pharmacy a few days earlier. With Christmas approaching he may have been able to persuade the pharmacist to give him an extra supply to tide him over the holiday period. But the presence of diconal, which also contains cyclizine, is more problematic. Diconal contains dipipanone hydrochloride which at the time was controlled as a Class A drug by the Misuse of Drugs Act 1971 and was subject to full restriction by the Drugs Regulations Act of 1973. Although it could be used by doctors in terminal cases of carcinoma or very severe pain, Agate was not known to be in either of these categories. It was however also prescribed to opiate addicts as a heroin substitute and at the time the combination of diconal and cyclizine was commonly favoured by young addicts and multiple drug users and was the subject of many thefts from pharmacies in the 1970s and 1980s. It had also been associated with several suicides.

The answer to Lynette's question can only ever of course be the subject of speculation. Her father had been one of the PJIs who took part in Bernard Winfield's trials with Benzedrine, methamphetamine and other opiates in April 1944 but these were controlled trials and there is no indication whatsoever that he continued to use drugs such as these over the next 40 years, years marked by his success as a head teacher. It is possible though that during these trials in 1944 and perhaps chatting with Winfield in his caravan he did become aware of the deadly potential of certain drugs, but that still doesn't answer the question: where did he get the Diconal from?

At 76 years old in 1986, living in glorious isolation in the Peak District nearly 250 miles from Shoreham and no longer a practicing GP, Bernard Winfield can surely be ruled out. There was though a growing dance and drugs scene in Brighton just along the coast which may have provided potential suppliers in Shoreham, but how this kindly 81-year-old headmaster with gangrene was able even to contemplate negotiating the complicated world of drug dealers is hardly imaginable. The question of how he got hold of the drugs which killed him will remain unanswered.

The question of why he took the decision to end his life can also only be guessed at. Although statistically it is relatively rare in 2024 for an 81-year-old man to kill himself, men in the 80–84 age range in 1986 came under the highest suicide rate, according to the Office for National Statistics (ONS), although that may at least in part be explained by the fact that there were fewer men in that age bracket 40 years ago.

His last phone call to his daughter suggests that he may have decided that he did not want to live as an invalid in constant pain, though he had faced such challenges before. Pain was clearly something he was used to. He also still had much to live for: chatting with customers and former pupils outside the ice cream kiosk, his daughter and two grandchildren, his partner Christine, a relaxed life beside the sea.

Perhaps though it was a simple decision to make. Because for this man who had jumped out of airplanes 1,601 times, often relying on experimental and untested parachutes, or with weights tied to his legs, a man who had jumped into deep dark water, and watched men he knew and had trained die, perhaps for this man, death really had lost its sting. 'If the parachute doesn't open, well, of course you have no worries' he had said, and on 21 December 1986 he simply decided that he had reached the end of a remarkable life and was ready to embark on another 'awfully big adventure'. He left no note.

Only immediate family attended the funeral, and a simple stone in a chapel in Worthing commemorates Charles and Marjorie Agate, but perhaps a more appropriate epitaph for this man who stared death in the face so many times, did so much to develop Britain's airborne force and brought the joy of learning to thousands of school children is to be found on the badge of the Parachute Training School itself:

Knowledge Dispels Fear

Epilogue

An elderly man stands nervously by the phone at his home in a small market town in Essex. He has a shock of white hair and despite the stiffness of age, holds himself remarkably upright. A military bearing – almost. His name is Derek, but he was born Keith Davies, and was adopted at birth. His birth mother was Eileen Queenie Davies, a domestic help at Stoughton School near Leatherhead in Surrey. His father was a teacher at the same school.

Derek is a practical man, an engineer with a lifelong love of motorbikes. His daughter has inherited this passion and runs a business renovating classic cars and motorbikes. His other daughter is the adventurous type. She lives in America and loves skiing, hiking and sports with a degree of risk.

Derek had always wondered about his natural father but had nothing to go on until his daughter had begun to investigate her father's family tree and had used a DNA database to identify her grandfather.

He picks up the phone and tentatively dials the number his daughter has given him. The phone is answered by Lynette, the 89-year-old daughter of Flight Lieutenant Albert Edward Charles Agate. She has been expecting this call.

'Hello, Lynette, I think I am your half-brother.'

It is the start of a new chapter in the remarkable life of the man who tested parachutes.

Appendix A: The Physics of Parachuting (and the Causes of Failure)

How Parachutes Work

When a parachutist makes a jump two elements act on the body and on the opened parachute. Firstly, gravity causes the parachutists speed to increase, but then the air exerts resistance slowing down the parachutist until a 'terminal velocity' or constant speed is achieved. The greater the surface area the parachutist presents, the greater the resistance, and therefore the lower the falling speed becomes. Weight and position of the body are also important factors that influence the terminal velocity.

Depending on body weight, size and shape, a parachutist reaches a terminal velocity of an average of 200km/h in free fall. The aim of the parachute is to create enough resistance to reduce the falling speed to 20km/h to enable a soft landing.

There are two modes of parachute activation: manual and automatic:

- Manual activation is sometimes referred to as the 'pull-off' method when the parachutist pulls a 'ripcord', which begins the process of extracting the parachute from the bag in which is located.
- Automatic activation is when the parachute bag is attached by a line to a fixed point in the aircraft or balloon and the parachute is extracted by gravity as soon as the parachutist falls.

Component Parts of a Parachute

- **Bag** is the place where the canopy is stored.
- **Canopy** is another name for the parachute itself, the piece of silk or nylon that reduces the vertical speed of the fall. This is the part that exerts the most resistance to air.
- **Container** is the backpack where all the equipment is connected to the harness.
- **D-ring** is a triangular-shaped buckle at one end of a static line and the strop that connects to a strong-point in the aircraft.
- **Harness** is the webbing that attaches the parachutist to the parachute, distributing their body weight evenly.
- **Lift Webs** or **Web Risers** are webbing bands that form part of the harness that runs the length of the parachutist's torso, attaching directly to the adjustable leg straps and chest strap. These straps are designed to hold the parachutist firmly and comfortably under the canopy.
- **Lines** (also known as **Suspension Lines** or **Rigging Lines**) are the ropes that connect the parachute to the harness. These are normally in groups of four called Risers.
- **Links** are the webbings that joins the Suspension Lines to the Risers.
- **Periphery** or **Skirt** is the reinforced hem of the canopy.
- **Ripcord** is the grip that the parachutist must pull to activate the parachute opening sequence manually.
- **Sliders** are used to help the parachute open symmetrically and in stages for a smooth and controlled opening.
- **Static Line** is the tape/webbing that is attached to a fixed point in the aircraft or balloon for automatic opening.
- **Straps** are the webbing components of a harness.
- **Strops** are lengths of webbing connected to a strongpoint in the aircraft by a triangular D-ring.

- **Vents** in the canopy act as a relief valve for the high internal pressure within the parachute at the instant of opening.

Specification of the X-type Parachute

The GQ X-type Parachute Mk 1 (15A/475) was adopted late in 1940 and continued in service with several modifications through till the end of the war. The X-type did not have a reserve parachute, but instead was provided with an internal deployment bag. The static line was stowed externally under two vertical pockets, and bungee loops for the suspension lines were hidden inside the bag. The harness was built with double layered Type VIII black dot webbing and sewn with heavy Irish linen seven-cord. The harness featured the fully-circular quick release box developed by Irvin.

It had square hip rings and chrome adjusters. Three web straps in a 'Y' shape held the harness to the pack. The canopy measured 714cm in diameter and was made of silk, cotton (ramex), and nylon. There were twenty-eight rigging lines, each 7.6m long with a minimum breaking strength of 181kg running from the edge of the canopy to four D rings attached to four web risers or lift webs. Descent speed was around 7m/s.

When wearing an X-type parachute, the wearer is not suspended by the shoulders, but is seated as in a swing. The harness coming up behind, and in front of the arms, coming together above the shoulders, where some adjustment was possible, a strap across the back, and in front, a strap from either side of the harness, one with a lock, the 'Box', the other with a metal plate attached which had a half-inch hole in it to be slotted into the 'Box', two longer straps hanging from the bottom of the harness, each with the same metal attachment, which were threaded in front of the thighs, round behind the side straps and brought forward to be slotted into the 'Box'. To unlock the box, the circular metal plate had to be turned clockwise and given a thump, after which it would fall apart.

Causes of Parachute Malfunction

- **Twisted rigging lines**: This is where the front and back sets of the four sets of rigging lines become interwoven above the lift webs in two strands like a thick rope. This slows the development of the canopy, so the rate of fall increases and control becomes impossible until the body revolves through 360° and the twists are eliminated.

- **Blown periphery** (or **Thrown lines**) is when part of the parachute canopy skirt hem passes under the shirt hem of another section and between the suspension lines causing the parachute to inflate inside out.

- A **Streamer** is when the canopy fails to develop until the last moment.

- A **Roman Candle** is a type of 'streamer' which fails to open at all.

Appendix B: Structure of the RAF 1941–1945

Squadrons
The basic building blocks were squadrons, which formed the operational units of the RAF. These squadrons were composed of aircraft and pilots available for missions. A typical squadron had twelve aircraft and pilots ready for operations.

Wings
Squadrons were grouped into wings. By May 1941, each Wing was under the tactical control of a Wing Leader, typically holding the rank of Wing Commander.

Stations
Wings were further organized into stations, which served as operational bases. Stations housed multiple squadrons and provided logistical support for their operations.

Groups
Stations were organized into Groups. These Groups coordinated the activities of multiple stations.

Commands
The RAF was divided into various commands, each responsible for specific functions. For instance, RAF Fighter Command oversaw fighter operations, while other commands handled bombers, coastal operations, and transport.

Appendix C: RAF Ranks 1941–1945

Commissioned RAF Ranks

Pilot Officer

This was the lowest-ranking commissioned officer. A Pilot Officer was in the early stages of their career. Responsibilities included undergoing initial training, gaining practical experience, and supporting more senior officers in various capacities.

Flying Officer

A Flying Officer was a junior commissioned officer responsible for demonstrating proficiency and leadership capabilities. They actively participated in operational activities, supporting the execution of missions and coordinating with team members. Flying Officers also served as liaisons between higher-ranking officers and enlisted personnel, ensuring smooth communication within the unit.

Flight Lieutenant

This was a mid-level officer who managed and led teams in specific roles. They played a key role in overseeing day-to-day operations, providing guidance to subordinates, and ensuring that mission objectives were met efficiently. Flight Lieutenants were also involved in the planning and execution of tactical missions.

Squadron Leader

With increased experience, a Squadron Leader took on a leadership role, overseeing entire squadrons. They were responsible for managing operational units, ensuring the readiness of personnel and equipment, and coordinating activities to achieve mission success.

Wing Commander

A Wing Commander was a senior officer responsible for managing multiple squadrons. They were involved in strategic planning, policy implementation, and overseeing the overall efficiency of operations. Wing Commanders contributed to the broader organizational goals, ensuring that their assigned units were well-prepared and aligned with RAF objectives.

Group Captain

As a high-ranking officer, a Group Captain was tasked with broader operational and administrative duties. They provided leadership at the group level, overseeing multiple squadrons and ensuring that organizational objectives are met. Group Captains played a pivotal role in shaping the direction of their assigned groups and contributing to RAF policy development.

Air Commodore

An Air Commodore held a senior leadership position, often involved in policy-making and overseeing large-scale operations. They provided strategic guidance, contribute to the development of RAF initiatives, and ensure that their assigned areas operate efficiently. Air Commodores were key decision-makers within the RAF's leadership structure.

Air Vice-Marshal

As a senior leader, an Air Vice-Marshal played a critical role in strategic planning and execution. They contributed to high-level decision-making, shaped policy, and provided guidance to subordinate officers. Air Vice-Marshals were integral to the effective functioning of the RAF, using their expertise to enhance overall operational capabilities.

Air Marshal

Air Marshals held senior leadership positions and were responsible for high-level command and control. They contributed to the formulation of major strategic decisions, ensuring that RAF operations aligned with broader defence objectives. Air Marshals played a crucial role in shaping the overall direction of the RAF.

Air Chief Marshal

As one of the highest-ranking officers in the RAF, an Air Chief Marshal served as a senior leader with responsibilities in command and control. They played a key role in shaping strategic objectives, providing guidance to subordinate commanders, and contributing to the overall effectiveness of the RAF.

Non-Commissioned RAF Ranks

Lance Corporal RAF Regiment

Within the RAF Regiment, a Lance Corporal held a non-commissioned leadership role. They were responsible for leading small teams, overseeing security operations, and ensuring the effective implementation of regimental tasks. Lance Corporals in the RAF Regiment played a critical role in maintaining the security and defence capabilities of the RAF.

Corporal

As a Corporal, non-commissioned officers took on additional responsibilities, including the supervision of teams and the coordination of operational tasks. They contributed to the overall effectiveness of the RAF through their leadership roles, ensuring that assigned duties were carried out with precision and efficiency.

Sergeant

Sergeants in the RAF held supervisory roles with responsibilities that include managing personnel, overseeing day-to-day operations, and contributing to the planning of tactical activities. They played a key part in ensuring the smooth functioning of their units, providing leadership and guidance to those under their command.

Flight Sergeant

A Flight Sergeant was a senior non-commissioned officer responsible for providing leadership and guidance to personnel within their unit. They played a critical role in overseeing operational activities, contributing to the planning of missions, and ensuring that their teams are well-prepared for assigned tasks.

Warrant Officer

As the highest-ranking non-commissioned officers, a Warrant Officer held significant leadership responsibilities. They provided guidance at the highest levels, contribute to strategic decision-making, and played a crucial role in maintaining discipline and morale within the RAF.

Members of the RAF typically advance through ranks based on the number of years they have served, but in wartime there were many examples of individuals advancing rapidly up the ranks as vacancies arose and circumstances demanded.

Notes

1. Killegar House is a fine eight-bay country house approached via a long drive through beautiful lakeland scenery, and the home of Lord and Lady Kilbracken.
2. The Wright brothers' claim to have flown was widely doubted until 1907. This was primarily because the brothers were advised by their patent attorney to keep details of their machine confidential.
3. In 1960, the UK Antarctic Place-Names Committee (UK-APC) named Mount Berry, a mountain in Antarctica, after Berry in recognition of his record.
4. The Empire Day idea was conceived by Reginald Brabazon, the seventh Earl of Meath. He was an ardent imperialist and tireless campaigner for the introduction of military values and discipline in public elementary schools.
5. Rugby School lost 21 per cent of their serving men, and Sevenoaks lost 10 per cent. At public schools with a military tradition the figures were even worse. Wellington had an average of 500 pupils before the War; 699 Old Boys were killed in action. At Haileybury one in three of the boys who entered the school between the 1890s and 1912 died in the War. A wall painting at St George's, Harpenden commemorates seven School Captains, six of whom held the post in succession.
6. Leatherhead Central School is now known as Thirfield School.
7. At Leatherhead Central School all corporal punishment took the form of strokes of the cane to the outstretched palm, administered in front of the class or, in the worst cases, the entire school.
8. On leaving school she studied to become a teacher at the London University. Here she met, and later married, Albert Thomas, a fellow schoolteacher, and they lived and worked together at St Martin's School in West Street, Dorking.

9. The USD-9 was a biplane that was the first aircraft to fly with a pressurized cockpit.

10. Captain Stanley Keith Muir (1892–1917) was an Australian soldier who fought at Gallipoli and in the Middle East during the Great War before transferring to the Royal Flying Corps. A very experienced pilot who had made the first solo flight from England to Sweden, he died in a flying accident in 1917.

11. John Tranum died on 7 March 1935 when he had a heart attack while broadcasting from an aeroplane five miles above Denmark. Harry Ward remarked: 'He was a frightened jumper. That is the time to quit' (Ward and Hearn, 2012, p. 91).

12. Henry Wilfred Ward (1903–2000) was born in Hackney, but moved with his family to Bradford when he was 6. He joined the RAF and trained as a carpenter-rigger. He later went to the parachute section at Northolt as a packer and became a parachutist himself when the commanding officer challenged him to jump with a parachute he had just packed. He made his first descent from the wing of a Vickers Vimy biplane bomber. When Corporal Arthur East was killed making a jump, Ward took his place in the RAF's demonstration team. Ward left the Service in 1929 and became a London bus driver, and when the bus company formed its own flying club, he became a member of the Royal Aero Club in 1932. He was soon earning more from display parachute jumping than from bus driving, so he left his job for the life of the travelling air circus where he appeared billed as 'the Yorkshire Birdman'. Ward worked briefly as a mechanic for Imperial Airways before becoming a civilian instructor at the RAF's apprentice school at Cosford. He was posted to Ringway in October 1940. He was awarded the Air Force Cross in 1942 and posted to the staff of the Army's 1st Airborne Division. He finished the war as a squadron leader at the headquarters of 38 Group at Netheravon. A civilian again in 1945, he managed officers' clubs in Greece and Germany. Returning to England in 1951, he ran a succession of hotels and pubs in Yorkshire. He lived to be 97.

13. Frederick William Deats (1887–1960) was born and lived all his life in Burgh Heath in a garage and tea rooms called 'the Nook' which was

swept away when the road was widened. He married Ellen in 1918 Banstead and they had one daughter, who was also called Ellen and a son Robert. Deats had had several run-ins with the law before he became a suspect in the murder of Agnes Kesson case, a young girl from Falkirk who had once worked in the tea-rooms. The police found her body in Horton Lane. Scotland Yard detectives interviewed Deats, took photographs of the house, garage and cellar and prised away the wooden tread of one of the stairs leading to the cellar. At the inquest a woman called Elsie Greenhalgh came forward and claimed that Deats had also 'waylaid' her and followed her down the road. On 18 July 1930 a crowd gathered outside the garage and Deats ordered them away, waving a tyre lever. He claimed that the bloodstains on the stairs were caused by the butcher who had previously occupied the premises. He told journalists 'I have nothing to conceal'.

14. The Junkers Ju 52 was first introduced during 1930 as a civilian airliner, and adapted into a military transport aircraft. The aircraft's design incorporated a corrugated duralumin metal skin as a strengthening measure, which was a material design pioneered by Junkers and used on many of their aircraft. Thousands of Ju 52s were procured as a staple military transport of the Luftwaffe.

15. Jock Colville, Churchill's private secretary, wrote that Ismay had the 'tact, patience, and skill in promoting compromise' needed to keep the war running smoothly. Ismay had the additional advantage of being admired by the Service Chiefs for his long and distinguished record as a soldier. He also gave Churchill advice on military matters, and often begged him to be reasonable when he contemplated foolish actions, believing that Churchill's greatest fault was his impetuous nature and impatience with opposition. Churchill later admitted that he owed more to Ismay than to anybody else, military or civilian, in the whole of the war.

16. The Avro Anson was a twin-engine multi-role aircraft developed during the mid-1930s from the earlier Avro 652 airliner in response to a request for tenders issued by the Air Ministry for a coastal maritime reconnaissance aircraft. The Anson was soon found to have become

obsolete. Large numbers were put to use as multi-engine aircrew trainers.

17. The Airspeed Oxford was a twin-engine monoplane developed in the 1930s in response to a requirement for a capable trainer aircraft that conformed with Air Ministry Specification T.23/36. It was used for training aircrews in navigation, radio-operating, bombing and gunnery roles.

18. The De Havilland DH.89 Dragon Rapide was a 1930s short-haul wooden biplane developed to carry six to eight passengers. Many of the civilian Rapides were pressed into service with the RAF and Royal Navy. Referred to in military service by the name de Havilland Dominie, the type was employed for radio and navigation training, passenger transport and communications missions.

19. The Vickers Wellington was a twin-engined long-range medium bomber designed started in response to Air Ministry Specification B.9/32 for a twin-engined day bomber capable of delivering higher performance than any previous design. A key feature of the aircraft was its geodetic airframe fuselage structure, which was designed by Barnes Wallis. The Wellington was used as a night bomber in the early years of the Second World War, performing as one of the principal aircraft used by Bomber Command. During 1943, it started to be superseded by the larger four-engined heavy bombers such as the Avro Lancaster.

20. The Bristol Blenheim was a light bomber originally designed as a civil airliner, after a challenge from the newspaper proprietor Lord Rothermere to produce the fastest commercial aircraft in Europe. The Type 142 model first flew in April 1935, and the Air Ministry ordered a modified design as the Type 142M for the RAF as a bomber. The Blenheim was one of the first British aircraft with an all-metal stressed-skin construction, retractable landing gear, flaps, a powered gun turret and variable-pitch propellers. The Blenheim was faster than most of the RAF's biplane fighters in the late 1930s but technological advances soon left it vulnerable if flown in daylight, though it proved successful as a night fighter. The Blenheim was effective as a bomber, but many were shot down.

21. Beaverbrook's appointment to the War Cabinet was based primarily on his willingness to support Churchill's personal opinions, reinforcing his prejudices as A.J.P. Taylor commented in his biography of Beaverbrook: 'In this new world of government Beaverbrook remained what he had always been. He did not run the ministry as a trained administrator, or a politician would have done. He ran it as he ran his private life. He ran it as a drama, working through individuals, not through committees, and ready to fight every level.'

22. RAF Henlow in Bedfordshire was used to assemble over 1,000 Hawker Hurricanes which had been built in Ontario, Canada. After test flying in Canada, they were disassembled and sent to Henlow in shipping containers and reassembled. Henlow was also used as a repair base under the direction of No. 13 Maintenance Unit.

23. No. 1 Commando had been formed at the same time by the order of Winston Churchill who had called for volunteers for a marine force that would 'develop a reign of terror down the enemy coast'.

24. Lieutenant Colonel John Frank Rock (1905–42) was the son of Frank Ernest and Alice Maud Fanny Rock, of Cranleigh, Surrey. He served with the Royal Engineers and was later attached to 1st Wing Glider Pilot Regiment. He died of wounds on 8 October 1942, aged 37 years old, as a result of an accident in a Hotspur glider trial on 27 September 1942. He is now buried at Tidworth Military Cemetery, Wiltshire. The Official War Office Record, Airborne Forces, compiled by Lieutenant Colonel T.S.H. Otway DSO says: 'The greater part of the credit, on the Army Side, for the success of the initial experiments and trials must go to Major Rock, whose unfailing courage and determination in the face of all difficulties was an inspiration to others.'

25. Colonel Peter Cleasby Thompson (1913–80) was commissioned in 1933 and served with the Lancashire Fusiliers before the war in India, Palestine and China. He fought in France and Belgium with a Territorial battalion and was fortunate in being one of the few survivors who were evacuated from Dunkirk. Soon after his return to the UK, and by now a Temporary Captain, he volunteered for the airborne forces at its formation in 1940, and took command of B Troop, No. 2 (Parachute)

Commando. His 'capture' of Crown Prince Olaf's car during the first major demonstration of British Airborne Forces in front of a select audience in 1940 was later celebrated in the *Illustrated London News*. Peter was awarded a Military Cross for his role in leading an ambush on a German armoured column while serving with the 1st Battalion in North Africa.

26. Louis Arbon Strange (1891–1966) was born in Tarrant Keyneston, Dorset where his family farmed 600 acres. He was educated at St Edward's School, Oxford, joining the school's contingent of the Dorset Yeomanry. He joined the Ewen School of flying at Hendon Aerodrome in July and gained his Royal Aero Club Aviators' Certificate. In 1913 he was commissioned as a second lieutenant (on probation) in the Royal Flying Corps (Special Reserve). Just after obtaining his licence, he won his first cross-country race. He served with distinction in the RFC during the Great War but retired from the service through ill health (sciatica) in 1921. He then bought a 1,300-acre farm in Dorset with his brother Jack. Too old for a regular commission, on 18 April 1940 Strange returned to military service as a 50-year-old pilot officer in the Royal Air Force Volunteer Reserve. He was posted to 24 Squadron. Strange arrived in Merville in northern France on 21 May 1940 and was tasked with saving what aircraft and equipment he could. Two fighters were patched up and flown back to England and all remaining Hurricanes were cannibalised, leaving just one in flying condition. Strange took off in the Hurricane, an aircraft type he had never flown before, unarmed, and with most of the instruments missing. Anti-aircraft fire forced Strange up to 8,000ft where he was then attacked by several Messerschmitt Bf 109s. He dived the Hurricane to treetop height and managed to escape. A month later he was awarded a bar to his Distinguished Flying Cross.

27. The full list of instructors was Terry Oakes, Paddy Gavin, Bill Pacey, Kim Campbell, Lofty Humphries, Frankie Chambers, Taff Roberts, Bill Walton, Paddy Wicklow and Harry Harwood. Warrant Officer Joe Sunderland was appointed to head the team of parachute packers.

28. William (Bill) Brereton (1900–63) was born in Liverpool. He was a 39-year-old married man, working as an aircraft engineer in Liverpool

when war broke out. He joined Ringway as a flight sergeant and became a leading instructor at Ringway.

29. Boris Romanoff (1914–42), the son of Russian-born Theodore and Evelyn Mary Romanoff, of West Ealing. He was commissioned in the Royal Air Force on 7 September 1936 as an acting pilot officer. In that year he won a gold medal in the RAF's Wakefield Boxing Championship. Romanoff served as a pilot with 138 Squadron, which undertook missions over occupied Europe in support of the Special Operations Executive. He died on 10 March 1942 when Armstrong Whitworth Whitley Z9125 crashed on take-off from RAF Stradishall. Four Czech crewmembers (Fornusek, Janek, Jelinek, and Politzer) died alongside him, while Flying Officer Vaverka was wounded. Romanoff, who was mentioned in despatches, was cremated at Hendon Cemetery and Crematorium.

30. David Iain McMonnies (1913–88) was a career RAF serviceman who was involved in a serious aircraft crash on 8 August 1938 when his Hawker Hart (K2455) took off from Hendon airfield at 09:30hrs. It was to be flown north to Abbotsinch Aerodrome, Glasgow with a number of refuelling stops en route. As the aircraft arrived in the Scarborough area the coastline was obscured by a sea fret which reduced visibility. It was thought the pilot saw the cliffs at the last moment and he put the aircraft into a steep climb. The crash happened just in front of the Granville Hotel and close to the Marina Hotel. Somehow both the occupants only had scratches. McMonnies rose to the rank of Wing Commander. He died on 26 February 1988 in Liss, Hampshire.

31. John Ellis Munro Williams (1919–65) worked as a stunt parachutist for Cobham's Flying Circus in the 1930s and found work as an actor in pantomime and stunt work in the film *The Mystery of the Marie Celeste*. On 24 September 1935 he was fined for fly-posting at Hunstanton in connection with the parachute jumps from Redgate Bridge. In 1936 his parachute got tangled with that of Bill Hire at a display at Ramsgate. They were saved by a gust of wind that separated them. He made a number of parachute descents in connection with the air service operated on Hunstanton south beach for several seasons with Miss Pauline Gower (the daughter of Sir Robert Gower MP for Gillingham).

He joined the RAF as a Flying Officer on probation. He was brought down while serving as an air gunner in Eric Barwell's Defiant of 264 Squadron in the fighting off Dunkirk. Barwell had no option but to ditch after losing all the glycol in his Defiant. He was attempting to ditch when he stalled from about 20ft. Williams was sat partially out of his turret and upon impact was catapulted completely out of the Defiant. Barwell, after getting clear of the aircraft, had spotted Williams unconscious and floating face down – he swam to him and turned him over, holding him up until they were rescued by a British destroyer. He was promoted to Wing Commander and was awarded the D.F.C.

32. Earl Bateman Fielden (1900–85) was a member of Alan Cobham's Flying Circus before the war.

33. The five Whitleys were:

Armstrong Whitley AW38 Mk II	K7220 (T)	Rear turret removed
Armstrong Whitley AW38 Mk II	K7230 (Y)	Rear turret removed. Driver Evans died jumping from this aircraft.
Armstrong Whitley AW38 Mk II	K7231 (R)	
Armstrong Whitley AW38 Mk II	K7252	Crashed on the ground with K9041 on 10 October 1942. Twelve pupils killed.
Armstrong Whitley AW38 Mk II	K7262	

34. Sir William Gore Sutherland Mitchell, (1888–1944) rose to be Air Chief Marshal and the first RAF officer to hold the post of Black Rod.

35. During the Second World War, remote locations in western Scotland were chosen to serve as training areas for Allied units engaged in irregular warfare. Several country houses and lodges in the Lochaber area were requisitioned in order to accommodate small teams of men and women selected to serve as SOE agents. The remote location and mountainous terrain was also found to be ideal for training commandos for operations

against the enemy-occupied coastline of Europe. Both organizations trained their personnel to be tough, self-reliant individuals, who could operate without support for extended periods. Achnacarry served as the main commando depot for candidates from the UK, USA, France, Norway, Poland, Czechoslovakia, the Netherlands and Belgium from 1942 to 1945. The commandos were formed on the orders of Winston Churchill to carry out raids on enemy-held facilities along the coastline of occupied Europe. Commando training involved prolonged exercises in the surrounding mountains, with troops carrying all of their weapons and equipment and operating away from base for days at a time. Troops were trained in the techniques of amphibious assault, demolition, unarmed combat and the operation of enemy weapons.

36. Quilter's new system was subsequently linked to an improved harness designed by Irvin, which incorporated a patent quick release box.

37. The Bristol Bombay was designed in 1932 for service in Africa, India and the Middle East as a troop carrier, but it took six years from specification to first flight because of the complex construction of the aircraft and the fact that production at the Bristol factory was shifted to the Blenheim, one of the five priority types specified by Beaverbrook. Only fifty Bombays were built, and these were all required for their original purpose.

38. The Avro 504 was a Great War biplane that was made in large numbers between 1913 and 1932.

39. Robert Kronfeld was also passionate about another revolutionary project, but this one would not make it to the battlefield. He called it the 'rotachute' and it was, in part, a response to intelligence received that the Germans were working on a kind of backpack helicopter as well as on the development of parachutes which could hover above the ground and then deposit agents and saboteurs more accurately. Having fallen behind the Germans in the development of airborne forces at the outset of the war, the Allies were keen to outdo the technology used by the Germans in any way they could, and Kronfeld and fellow Austrian Raoul Hafner set out to solve the problem of producing a more controllable alternative to the parachute. Essentially a self-propelled rotor blade on

a self-supporting structure around and above the soldier complete with small tailplane, it could be said to be like a large, manned version of the modern-day drone. The rotachute went through various forms following its first test flight at Ringway on 14 March 1941 and grew from the initial idea of a small strap-on parachute alternative, worn by the parachutist into a substantial gyroglider flown by a pilot. Kronfeld was the pilot on this first test flight with photographs taken by Corporal Mundy in a Hector aeroplane. Tests at Ringway continued with dummy loads towed behind vehicles or dropped from aircraft, proved impractical and only about eight functioning rotachutes were ever manufactured before their development was abandoned in 1943.

40. Francis Wogan Festing (1902–76) was air liaison officer for the expedition to Norway of 1940, then, having been promoted to acting lieutenant colonel in April 1940, as a staff officer in the Operations Directorate at the War Office from May 1940. In September 1940 he became Commanding Officer of the 2nd Battalion East Lancashire Regiment and then in April 1942 he became Commander of 29th Independent Infantry Brigade Group which was the landing force of Force 121 for Operation Ironclad, the seizure of Vichy French ports and airfields in the Indian Ocean. In November 1942 Festing took command of the 36th Indian Division and at the beginning of 1944 in the Burma campaign.

41. Arthur John Capel, (1894–1979) served in the Army during the First World War in the Somerset Light Infantry and then Royal Flying Corps, He joined the RAF on its creation in 1918. He was involved in Pink's War, the RAF's first independent operation that was an air-to-ground campaign in Waziristan, and for which he was awarded the Distinguished Service Order. He rose up the ranks and served as Commandant of the School of Army Co-operation (1936–8), Air Officer Commanding (AOC) No. 22 (Army Co-operation) Group (1940), and AOC No. 20 (Training) Group (1941).

42. Stanley Watts is buried at North Sheen Cemetery in Surrey.

43. Sir Leslie Gordon Harvey (1896–1972) served as Air Officer Commanding-in-Chief Maintenance Command from 1952 until his retirement in 1956. He joined Royal Warwickshire Regiment in June 1917,

then transferred to the Royal Flying Corps. He was promoted to Flight Lieutenant in 1924 and served in the Second World War as Assistant Director of Repair and Servicing and then as Chief Engineer Officer at Headquarters No. 45 Group before becoming Deputy Air Officer Administration (Maintenance) at Headquarters Transport Command. In retirement he became a Director of GQ Parachute Company.

44. William George Hire (1907–84) was born in Folkestone and had been a member of Alan Cobham's Flying Circus in the 1930s and had managed nightclubs. He was appointed as Pilot Officer in 1940.

45. Cicely Paget-Bowman (1907–2005) embarked on an acting career in the 1920s and played opposite Rex Harrison in *Charley's Aunt*. In the 1930s she also had a number of small film parts in addition to her repertory work. With the outbreak of the Second World War she joined the First Aid Nursing Yeomanry (FANY) and was posted to the Central Landing School where she assisted the Medical Officer Captain Brian Courtney (RAMC) as ambulance driver and nurse. She spent most of her time on the drop zone at Tatton Park with her 'blood tub' (ambulance) and became very popular with the men of No. 2 Commando. After the war she resumed her stage career and appeared in a number of films most notably as Lady Queensbury in *The Trials of Oscar Wilde* (1960), appearing alongside Peter Finch and James Mason. During the 1960s she moved into television and had parts in *Z Cars*, *Dixon of Dock Green*, *Danger Man*, *The Troubleshooters*, *Father Dear Father*, *Hadleigh* and *The Forsyte Saga*.

46. John Greer Dill (1881–1944) was a senior British Army officer with service in both the First World War and the Second World War. From May 1940 to December 1941, he was the Chief of the Imperial General Staff, the professional head of the Army. However, Churchill disliked him, and he was posted to Washington, D.C., as Chief of the British Joint Staff Mission and then Senior British Representative on the Combined Chiefs of Staff. He was very highly regarded by the Americans and was particularly friendly with General George Marshall. Together, they exercised a great deal of influence on President Roosevelt who described Dill as 'the most important figure in the remarkable accord which has been developed in the combined operations of our two countries'.

47. William Dennis is buried in Manchester Southern Cemetery and commemorated on Panel 2 of the cemetery's Screen Wall.

48. The Short S.25 Sunderland was designed to conform to the requirements of Air Ministry Specification R.2/33 for a long-range patrol/reconnaissance flying boat. Sunderlands played a major role in the Mediterranean, performing maritime reconnaissance flights and logistical support missions.

49. Whitley T4165 crashed and was destroyed on 11 April 1941 at RAF Tangmere while on a mission to drop six Polish Army saboteurs to destroy the Pessac power plant in Bordeaux. The operation was aborted when the weapons container fell from the aircraft while over the Loire. An electrical fault is suspected. Two men died.

50. Whitley P5015 crashed at Ballater aerodrome, Aberdeenshire on 16 November 1942 killing two of the crew.

51. Rev Bernard Egan (1905–88) volunteered to be a chaplain to the forces soon after the outbreak of the war. He was the first chaplain to obtain wings, attending Parachute Course No. 5 at RAF Ringway in December 1941. He was accompanied on this course by another padre, the Reverend R. Talbot-Watkins. When asked about the point of undertaking the rigorous training, he replied that he considered it important to set an example to the men with whom he would be going into combat, and he had no right to judge them or to discuss their dangerous duties if he had not emptied the same cup to the last drop. He served in North Africa, Sicily, Italy and Arnhem. Bernard received a Military Cross for his actions at the Primosole Bridge in Sicily during July 1943. He was seriously wounded at Arnhem and taken prisoner. Liberated in 1945, the Rev Egan left the services due to his injuries and returned to teaching.

52. Bernard James Oliver Winfield was born on 3 May 1913, the son of a Cambridge law professor. He was educated at Shrewsbury school, and studied medicine at St John's College, Cambridge, where he also learned to fly. He graduated in 1932 and when war broke out, he was working as a GP in the East End of London amidst the ravages of poverty and tuberculosis until he received a commission as a Flying Officer

on 1 October 1940 and was appointed as the Medical Officer at RAF Ringway. He died on 26 January 2007.

53. William Averell Harriman (1891–1986) was an American Democratic politician, businessman, and diplomat who founded Brown Brothers Harriman & Co. He was a key foreign policy advisor to Democratic presidents, helping to coordinate the Lend-Lease programme and the implementation of the Marshall Plan.

54. Squadron Leader Jack Banham was killed over Europe a few months later when his Whitley ditched into the English Channel while returning from a special operation over Belgium on 29 January 1942.

55. Earl Fielden and David MacMonnies were transferred to No.38 Group.

56. The Short Stirling was the first four-engined bomber to be introduced into service with the RAF. It was designed during the late 1930s by Short Brothers to conform with the requirements laid out in Air Ministry Specification B.12/36. The Stirling entered service in 1941 but was relegated to second-line duties from late 1943, due to the increasing availability of the more capable Handley Page Halifax and Avro Lancaster.

57. The Avro Manchester was a twin-engined heavy bomber designed to conform with the requirements laid out in Air Ministry Specification P.13/36, which sought a capable medium bomber to replace aircraft such as the Armstrong Whitworth Whitley, Handley Page Hampden and Vickers Wellington. It made its maiden flight on 25 July 1939 and entered service in November 1940. It came to be regarded as a failure, as a result of its Rolls-Royce Vulture engines, which were underpowered and unreliable, and production was terminated in 1941.

58. The Avro Lancaster was a development of the Avro Manchester. It was designed by Roy Chadwick, the Chief Designer of A.V Roe & Company Limited and was powered by four Rolls-Royce Merlins. The aircraft was originally designated Type 683 Manchester III but was renamed Avro Lancaster after the first flight at RAF Ringway on 9 January 1941. The Avro test pilot was Captain Harry 'Sam' Brown. The prototype Lancaster was registered BT308.

59. The Handley Page Halifax was a four-engined heavy bomber developed to the same specification as the Avro Manchester. Both aircraft were

designed to use the Rolls-Royce Vulture engine, but the Handley Page design was altered to use four Rolls-Royce Merlin engines. The maiden flight took place on 25 October 1939, and it entered service in November 1940. Although regarded as inferior to the Lancaster it was a major component of Bomber Command and production of the Halifax continued until April 1945.

60. The Armstrong Whitworth Albemarle was a twin-engined transport aircraft developed that had been originally designed as a medium bomber to fulfil Specification B.9/38 for an aircraft that could be built of wood and metal without using any light alloys; It was subsequently re-designed as an aerial reconnaissance and transport aircraft. Plans for using the Albemarle as a bomber were abandoned. The Albemarle was used for special transport duties, paratroop transport and glider towing in the Normandy landings and Market Garden.

61. The Lockheed Hudson was an American light bomber and coastal reconnaissance aircraft. It was also used for dropping agents into occupied France.

62. Prepacked canisters were allocated code numbers according to their load; a unit requiring resupply simply had to communicate the code and the number of canisters required. The type of load was indicated by the colour of the parachute, so the contents could be identified without opening the container. The colours used were periodically changed to confuse the enemy. During Operation Market Garden, for example, the colours used were red for ammunition, green for rations, white for medical supplies, blue for fuel and yellow for communication equipment.

63. 8,314 Polish troops trained at Largo and at RAF Ringway, but only 364 were actually dropped into occupied Poland for the Warsaw Uprising.

64. Twardawa is buried in the Second World War plot at Manchester Southern Cemetery and commemorated on the memorial to the seventeen Polish casualties buried there. None are commemorated by individual headstones.

65. The second front referred to the potential creation of a new military front in Europe, separate from the one in North Africa. Britain and France sought to persuade the Americans that a second front was necessary in

order to alleviate the pressure on the Soviet Union, which was bearing the brunt of the war against Germany on the Eastern Front. It would also have freed up ports and industrial centres in occupied northern Europe.

66. Gerald McDonough from Beacon Hill, Hindhead, had attended the Imperial Service College and was granted a commission on 29 May 1929 and initially served with the Royal Tank Corps, before transferring to the South Lancashire Regiment. He was promoted to Lieutenant in January 1934 and Captain exactly five years later when he volunteered for the airborne forces, shortly after the formation of No 1 Parachute Brigade.

67. RAF Polebrook was the home of 90 Squadron RAF, which was equipped with the B-17 'Fortress I'. They were used for very high-altitude attacks in daylight, Unfortunately, the planes were not able to hit anything from such extreme altitudes. In addition, their crews found that the temperatures at this altitude were so cold that their defensive machine guns froze up when they tried to fire them. From 12 December 1943 to 12 June 1945, Polebrook was used by the USAAF.

68. Sir Colin McVean Gubbins (1896–1976) was given the responsibility for setting up the Special Operations Executive (SOE) and the secret Auxiliary Units, a commando force based around the Home Guard, to operate on the flanks and to the rear of German lines if England was invaded during Operation Sea Lion.

69. Sergeant Charles Binden Carter was the wireless operator/air gunner of an aircraft in July 1942 detailed to attack a target near Lille. During the run-up, Sergeant Carter's aircraft was repeatedly hit by light anti-aircraft fire. A cannon shell entered the gunner's cockpit, wounded him in the right hand and arm, exploded a flare-gun cartridge and set some ammunition on fire. Despite his wounds. Sergeant Carter continued to engage the enemy, delivering effective fire at the enemy's gun positions. When the aircraft flew clear of the fire zone, Sergeant Carter extinguished the fire in the well of the aircraft and continued to man his guns (*London Gazette* No. 35667, Dated 1942-08-14).

70. Agate's approach became the norm after the 1967 Plowden report recommended abolishing the cane and other forms of corporal punishment in primary schools.
71. The retirement housing at Washington Road, Storrington, Pulborough consisted of thirty-two self-contained retirement flats for ex-RAF personnel or their dependents.

Bibliography

Air Ministry AIR 2/7470 ARMY (Code B, 88): Airborne forces: Chiefs of Staffs memoranda, File Minute Sheet, Note 25.

Air Ministry AIR 29/250, 1944. AIR 29 250. Ringway: Air Ministry.

Air Ministry AIR 29/512, 1940. AIR 29/512. Manchester: None.

Air Ministry, 1942. AIR 81/16355. London: Air Ministry.

Arthur, M., 1992. *Men of the Red Beret*. London: Hutchinson.

Barker, R., 2002. *The Royal Flying Corps in World War I*. London: Robinson.

Brabazon, R., 1905. *The 'Empire Day' Movement*. London: Burt & Sons, Printers.

Buckingham, W. F., 2001. *The Establishment and Initial Development of a British Airborne Force June 1940–January 1942*. London: University of Glasgow.

Carew, T., 1954. *All This and a Medal Too*. London: Constable & Co Ltd.

Carson, A., 1986. *Flight Fantastic: The Illustrated History of Aerobatics*. London: Foulis/Haynes.

Cartner, E., 2012. *Jumping Beans: Personal reminiscences of an 'oddball' Royal Air Force Unit – No. 1 Parachute Training School*. s.l.:s.n.

Cheshire Archives and Local Studies, 1228-1961. *Egerton of Tatton Papers*. Chester: s.n.

Daily Record, 1917. 'Life-saving Parachute', 15 August.

David Gunnell, K. T., 2010. 'Suicide in England & Wales 1861-2007: a time trend analysis', *International Journey of Epidemiology*, 39(6), pp. 1464–75.

Dorking & Leatherhead Advertiser, 1905. 'The New School in Frenches', 28 October.

Dorking & Leatherhead Advertiser, 1905. 'Interesting Ceremony', 28 October.

Dudley, J., 1958. *The Face of Death*. London: Evans.

Escott, B. E., 1989. *Women in Air Force Blue: the story of women in the Royal Air Force from 1918*. London: Better World Books.

Escott, B. E., 1995. *Our Wartime Days: the WAAF in World War II*. London: Stroud.

Foot, M. R. D., 1984. *SOE: The Special Operations Executive, 1940-1946*. 1st ed. London: Pimlico.

Francis, M., 2008. *The Flyer: British Culture and the Royal Air Force 1939 – 1945*. Oxford: Oxford University Press.

Hampshire Telegraph & Post, 1936. 'Hitler's Peace Plan', 3 April.

Hearn, P., 1990. *Yorkshire Birdman: Memoirs of a Pioneer Parachutist*. London: Robert Hale Ltd.

Hearn, P., 1994. *Flying Rebel: the story of Louis Strange*. London: Stationery Office Books.

Hearn, P., 1997. *The Sky People: a history of parachuting*. London: Airlife.

Hoggart, R., 1957. *The Uses of Literacy: Aspects of Working-class Life, with Special References to Publications and Entertainments*. London: Chatto and Windus.

Hollander, N., 2013. *Elusive Dove: the search for peace during World War I*. ed. Jefferson, North Carolina: McFarland & Co. Inc.

Hunter, A. B. D. M., 1991. *The Gentlemen of Merstham & Gatton*. London: Book Guild Publishing Ltd.

Illustrated London News, 1940. 'The British Army in field exercises "somewhere in England"', Saturday 14 December 1940.

Illustrated Police News,1904. 'The Brutal Attack on a Lady at Redhill', 13 January.

Immigration & Nationality Department, Home Office, 1942. TNA HS 4/344. Home Office Personal Files, October.

Keegan, J., 2002. *Winston Churchill: A Life*. London: Penguin.

Kingsley, C., 1875. *Health and Education*. London: Daldy, Isbister and Co.

Lee, A. S. G., 1968. *No Parachute: a fighter pilot in World War 1*. London: Jarrolds.

Leicester Evening Mail, 1925. 'Goldsmths' College Rag', 17 June.

Lewis, G., 1994. *Wings Over the Somme*. London: Bridge Books.

Lewis, J. H., 1917. *Juvenile education in relation to employment after the war Report of the Departmental Committee*. London: HMSO.

Liverpool Daily Post, 1939. 'Answer to the Heinkels', 9 December.

Lucas, J., 1997. *The Silken Canopy*. London: Airlife Publishing Ltd.

Manchester Evening News, 1945. '1512 Parachute Jumps – World Record', 22 November.

Marshall, D., 2003. *Wild About Flying: Dreamers, Doers and Dare-devils*. Buffalo, New York: Firefly Books.

McCulloch, G., 2007. *Cyril Norwood and the Ideal of Secondary Education*. Basingstoke: Palgrave Macmillan.

MoD Air Historical Branch, 1953. *The Women's Auxiliary Air Force*. London: Air Ministry (AHB).

Muir, F., 1997. *A Kentish Lad*. London: Bantam Press.

Musumeci, G., 2021. *Progress of Journal of Functional Morphology and Kinesiology*. [Online] Available at: https://pubmed.ncbi.nlm.nih.gov/35323607/

National Army Museum, n.d. *Major John Carter*. [Online] Available at: https://ww1.nam.ac.uk/stories/major-john-carter/#.YZPD8dDP200

Newnham, M., 1946. *Prelude to Glory*. London: Sampson.

Nottingham Evening Post, 1918. 'Saved by Parachute', 5 December.

O'Connor, B., 2011. *Women of RAF Tempsford : Churchill's agents of wartime resistance*. London: Chalford : Amberley Publishing.

Pall Mall Gazette, 1919. 'Parachutes for Airmen', 9 May.

Pegasus, 1944. *Parachutist*. London: Jarrolds.

Portsmouth Evening News, 1916. 'Escape in a Parachute', 9 September.

Rees, J., 2020. *A Schoolmaster's War*. Yale: Yale University Press.

Reichhardt, T., 2012. *Berry's Leap*. [Online] Available at: https://www.smithsonianmag.com/air-space-magazine/berrys-leap-111412656/

Saunders, H. S. G., 1949. *The Red Beret*. London: Michael Joseph.

Shaw, K., 2014. *The Mammoth Book of Losers*. New York: Constable & Robinson.

Sheffield Daily Telegraph, 1917. 'Eyes of the Army', 22 December.

Silver, L. & Dawson, J., 1973. *A Social History of Education in England*. London: Methuen & Co Ltd.

Simon, B., 1965. *Education and the Labour Movement 1870-1920*. London: Lawrence & Wishart.

Simon, J., 1977. 'The Shaping of the Spens Report on Secondary Education 1933-38: An Inside View: Part I'. *British Journal of Education Studies*, 25(1).

Smith, J., 2006. *Empire Day in Britain 1904-1958*. Cambridge: Cambridge University Press.

Sunderland Daily Echo & Shipping Gazette, 1939. 'Mr Churchill Speaks', 3 September.

Surrey Mirror, 1905. 'Reigate Council report', 10 November.

Surrey Mirror, 1905. 'Frenches Road Board School', 5 May.

Surrey Mirror, 1909. 'Notes and Reflections', 21 May.

Surrey Mirror, 1917. 'Scholarships and Free Studentships', 29 June.

Surrey Mirror, 1919. 'Reigate Grammar School Sports' Day', 25 July.

Surrey Mirror, 1919. 'Reigate Grammar Service Memorial Service', 20 June.

Surrey Mirror, 1933. 'Alleged Assault at Burgh Heath', 20 January.

Surrey Mirror & County Post, 1945. 'Reigate Grammar School's Headmaster's Notes', 26 January.

Surrey Mirror & County Post, 1949. Holdsworld record, 17 November.

Tawney, R. H., 1922. *Secondary Education for All London*. London: The Labour Party.

Taylor, E., 1991. *Women Who Went to War: 1938-46*. Leicester: Ulverscroft.

The Times, 1920. 'A School Girl's Caning', 25 June.

Volkov, N., 2022. *The Science of Addiction*. [Online] Available at: https://addictioneducationsociety.org/dr-nora-volkow-explains-the-science-of-addiction/

Weekly Dispatch, 1910. 'Empire Day', 8 May.

West Sussex Gazette, 1931. 'Capt. Barnard's Air Circus', 16 July.

Wilson, A. N., 2003. *The Victorians*. London: W.W. Norton.

Yardley, M., 2000. *T E Lawrence*. New York: Cooper Square Publishers Inc., U.S.

Young, E. H., 1920. *Report of the Departmental Committee on Scholarships and Free Places*. London: HMSO.

Index